ORSON WELLES
IN FOCUS

ORSON WELLES
IN FOCUS

Texts and Contexts

EDITED BY

James N. Gilmore and
Sidney Gottlieb

FOREWORD BY

James Naremore

INDIANA UNIVERSITY PRESS

This book is a publication of

Indiana University Press
Office of Scholarly Publishing
Herman B Wells Library 350
1320 East 10th Street
Bloomington, Indiana 47405 USA

iupress.indiana.edu

Library of Congress Cataloging-in-Publication Data

Names: Gilmore, James, 1989- editor. | Gottlieb, Sidney editor.
Title: Orson Welles in focus : texts and contexts / edited by James N. Gilmore
     and Sidney Gottlieb ; foreword by James Naremore.
Description: Bloomington : Indiana University Press, 2018. | Includes
     bibliographical references and index.
Identifiers: LCCN 2017039080 (print) | LCCN 2017043173 (ebook) | ISBN
     9780253032966 (e-book) | ISBN 9780253032942 (cloth : alk. paper) | ISBN
     9780253032959 (pbk. : alk. paper)
Subjects: LCSH: Welles, Orson, 1915-1985—Criticism and interpretation.
Classification: LCC PN1998.3.W45 (ebook) | LCC PN1998.3.W45 O77 2018 (print)
     | DDC 791.4302/33092—dc23
LC record available at https://lccn.loc.gov/2017039080

1 2 3 4 5 23 22 21 20 19 18

CONTENTS

Foreword / *James Naremore*   vii

Acknowledgments   xi

Introduction: The Totality of Orson Welles /
Sidney Gottlieb and James N. Gilmore   1

1   The Death of the *Auteur*: Orson Welles, Asadata Dafora,
and the 1936 *Macbeth* / *Marguerite Rippy*   11

2   Revisiting "War of the Worlds": First-Person Narration in
Golden Age Radio Drama / *Shawn VanCour*   34

3   Old-Time Movies: Welles and Silent Pictures /
Matthew Solomon   52

4   Orson Welles's Itineraries in *It's All True*: From "Lived
Topography" to Pan-American Transculturation /
Catherine L. Benamou   80

5   Orson Welles as Journalist: The *New York Post* Columns /
Sidney Gottlieb   111

6   Progressivism and the Struggles against Racism and
Antisemitism: Welles's Correspondences in 1946 /
James N. Gilmore   131

7 Multimedia Magic in *Around the World*: Orson Welles's
   Film-and-Theater Hybrid / *Vincent Longo*   150

8 "The Worst Possible Partners for Movie Production":
   Orson Welles, Louis Dolivet, and the Filmorsa
   Years (1953–56) / *François Thomas*   176

9 Presenting Orson Welles: An Exhibition Challenge /
   Craig S. Simpson   201

   Index   223

FOREWORD

JAMES NAREMORE

Except for Alfred Hitchcock, more has been written about Orson Welles than about any other US filmmaker. This is perhaps not surprising, because the two men were at least arguably the most significant Hollywood directors of the 1940s, the peak decade of the classic studio era, and they have interesting things in common: the burning "R" at the end of *Rebecca* and the burning "Rosebud" at the end of *Citizen Kane*; the madmen at the family dinner tables in *Shadow of a Doubt* and *The Stranger*; the crazed clerks who rent motel rooms to Janet Leigh in *Touch of Evil* and *Psycho*. They also make fascinating contrasts with one another: Welles the exhibitionist versus Hitchcock the voyeur, Welles the baroque stylist versus Hitchcock the lucid exponent of suspense, Welles the critic of plutocracy versus Hitchcock the artist of anxiety, Welles the Midwesterner who became "un-bankable" in Hollywood versus Hitchcock the British expatriate who was one of Hollywood's most successful figures. The comparisons resurfaced in 2012, when the international *Sight and Sound* poll of filmmakers and critics announced that *Citizen Kane*, which for sixty years had been considered the best film ever made, had fallen to second place, just below *Vertigo*.

But Welles was a man of more varied talents than Hitchcock, and because his career had so many aspects, the literature on him continues to grow, to the point where it may soon outdistance any of his possible competitors. He was not only an innovative director of theater, radio, film, and television but also an actor, magician, painter, cartoonist, musician, costume designer, writer, journalist, educator, political activist, orator, and raconteur. He was chiefly responsible for "War of the Worlds,"

the most socially significant radio broadcast of all time, and he created
some of the most legendary radio dramas and theatrical productions of
US, British, and European history.

One of the twentieth-century's leading exponents of Shakespeare,
Welles gave us three remarkable Shakespeare films, each in a different
style, and a fourth (a color version of *The Merchant of Venice*) that has yet
to be restored and distributed. Because of his unusual education at the
Todd School for Boys in Illinois, he became not only a famous Bardolator
but also a lifelong pedagogue. In 1934, at age nineteen, he and his tutor
Roger Hill collaborated on *Everybody's Shakespeare*, a series of abridged
"acting texts" of Shakespeare plays with suggestions for how high school
students might stage them; and these charming, unpretentious class-
room books still have educational value. In 1939, following the huge success of his modern-dress, antifascist *Julius Caesar* in New York, Welles
supervised the Mercury Text Records, the first full-length recordings
of Shakespeare performances ever produced; with Roger Hill, he wrote
an article about the recordings for the National Council of Teachers of
English, and they were recommended as teaching aids in the first issue of
College English. In 1947, when movies were beginning to be widely used
in classrooms, Welles made ambitious plans for producing and directing 16mm educational films, but unfortunately, his American career was
nearing an end and nothing came of the project.

At the outset of World War II, Welles produced and, through no fault
of his own, tragically lost one of cinema's most ambitious educational
experiments—a film about Latin America combining documentary and
fiction, playfully entitled *It's All True*, about which we're given new information in this volume. One reason his producers scuttled the film was
political. Throughout the 1930s, Welles was deeply involved in Popular
Front activities, and after the war, he became increasingly outspoken,
publishing his views on American racism and renascent fascism in a
syndicated newspaper column and in other venues—matters discussed
in full by two essayists in this book. He had become the target of an FBI
investigation that was begun at the time of *Citizen Kane*, almost certainly prompted by J. Edgar Hoover's friend William Randolph Hearst,
and had he remained in the United States after 1947, when a congressional witch hunt for "un-American" filmmakers began, he would no

doubt have fallen victim to the blacklist. Instead he went to Europe for a decade, where he directed theater and transformed himself into a pioneer of the international art film—this last in a period before a strong distribution network for such things existed. New details about one of his most complex ventures in Europe, *Mr. Arkadin*, is found in another essay collected here.

In late life, Welles also pioneered what came to be known as the *essay film* and made original experiments with found footage and voice-over. No wonder that writings and films about him keep increasing in number. Interesting data about his prodigious career keeps surfacing, largely because repositories such as the one at Indiana University's Lilly Library have given a home to his vast archive. As another contributor to this volume points out, Welles presents both a challenge and an exciting opportunity for librarians and archivists. Because of their work, and because of continuing curiosity about Welles's career, the scholars represented in this collection have made new discoveries about such things as Welles's interest in the history of silent film, his legendary WPA production of the "Voodoo" *Macbeth*, and his elaborate stage extravaganza *Around the World*, which Bertolt Brecht regarded as a landmark of American theater.

George Orson Welles died in Los Angeles in 1985 with his typewriter in his lap, working, as always, on a new project. In 2015, the centennial year of his birth, important books, journalistic tributes, and an excellent documentary appeared.[1] There were also film retrospectives and public tributes across the United States and around the world. One of the largest, perhaps *the* largest, was at Indiana University, where Welles was the subject of an academic conference, a museum exhibit, and a comprehensive showing of his films.[2] Scholars, filmmakers, and visitors from the United States and seven foreign counties attended and participated in a discussion of Welles's last, unfinished film, *The Other Side of the Wind*, which at this writing is being edited posthumously for release. Because of those events, critics and researchers went to work on the essays you find here, all of them previously unpublished, and all dedicated to the idea that Welles was a multimedia artist.

Is there anything else to say about Welles? Yes, and the proof is in these pages. All great artists are sources of reinterpretation and new critical approaches, and many of the items Welles left behind—especially his journalistic writings, his unfilmed screenplays, his prolific radio broadcasts, and some of his more complex stage productions—remain incompletely explored. Anyone interested in him should welcome the information and insights in this book. Some may think the emphasis is on the margins rather than the center. Welles is best known as a "Sacred Beast" of cinema, but this book shows that his energy was boundless and everything he did was related. One hundred years from now, assuming the world still turns and humane democracy survives, people will still be writing about him.

JAMES NAREMORE is Chancellors' Professor Emeritus at Indiana University. He is author of several books on film, among them *The Magic World of Orson Welles*.

NOTES

1. Besides Chuck Workman's cogent documentary *Magician: The Astonishing Life and Work of Orson Welles* (2014), there were essays in *The New Yorker* and *The New York Review of Books*. Among the books were Simon Callow's *Orson Welles, Vol. 3: One Man Band* (New York: Viking, 2016), the third of a projected four-volume biography; Patrick McGilligan's *Young Orson: The Years of Luck and Genius on the Path to Citizen Kane* (New York: HarperCollins, 2015); Todd Tarbox's *Orson Welles and Roger Hill: A Friendship in Three Acts*; Josh Karps's *Orson Welles's Last Movie: The Making of* The Other Side of the Wind (New York: St. Martin's Press, 2015); A. Brad Schwartz's *Broadcast Hysteria: Orson Welles's* War of the Worlds *and the Art of Fake News* (New York: Hill & Wang, 2015); Esteve Riambau's *Las Cosas Que Hemos Vista: Welles y Falstaff* (The Things that We Have Seen: Welles and Falstaff) (Catalunya, Spain: Kadmos, 1915); F. X. Feeny's *Orson Welles: Power, Heart, and Soul* (Dresher, PA: Critical Press, 2015); and Matthew Asprey Gear's *At the End of the Street in the Shadow: Orson Welles and the City* (New York: Wallflower Press, 2016).

2. Local contributors were Jon Vickers, director of the University Cinema and Rachel Stoeltje, head of the Moving Image Archive. Also contributing were the University's president's office; the Media School; the library school; the Black Film Center Archive; and the Department of Spanish and Portuguese.

ACKNOWLEDGMENTS

The editors are grateful to the organizers of the Orson Welles Centennial Celebration, Symposium, and Exhibition, especially Jon Vickers, the director of the Indiana University Cinema, and all the presenters and participants at the symposium. This volume contains a selection of papers presented there, but unquestionably, the revised versions have also benefited from taking into account the totality of what went on there. We want to thank all the contributors to the volume for their energy, patience, and collegiality during the strenuous process of turning relatively brief conference papers into the more fully elaborated essays printed herein. Much in the final round of revisions was guided by detailed comments, corrections, and suggestions provided by two anonymous readers of our manuscript for the press, and we are grateful for their thorough critical attention, one of the highest compliments and services scholars can offer to one another. Finally, we want to thank James Naremore in particular: for support and encouragement through all the stages of assembling the book; for contributing a foreword that places our endeavor in the context of the Welles Centennial; for necessary advice and help on several occasions when the project seemed to be stalling; and for serving as the model for the kind of Welles scholarship to which this book aspires.

Sid Gottlieb wants to thank James Gilmore for welcoming him into the project as a coeditor long after the work had been initiated, and for being such an exemplary collaborator—generous, tireless, tactful, and fully geared up to bringing out the best in everyone involved. We worked long and hard but also efficiently and harmoniously on a volume that in fact often focused on the joys and pains, but mostly the benefits, of Welles's own collaborations, and I am extremely grateful to be part of a collaboration—and that of course includes working with the other contributors as well—that was so productive and enjoyable.

James Gilmore wishes to thank Sidney Gottlieb for lending an exceptional editorial eye to this book's development. Each chapter is the better for his precision, and I am the better for having watched him work. I also wish to thank Greg Waller, for helping initiate conversations with Indiana University Press; Craig Simpson and Barbara Klinger, for their help on planning the initial book proposal; and James Naremore, for working intimately on crafting the book proposal and offering assistance at key moments of the book's development.

ORSON WELLES

IN FOCUS

INTRODUCTION
The Totality of Orson Welles

SIDNEY GOTTLIEB AND JAMES N. GILMORE

While reflecting recently on directions for further research on the life and work of Orson Welles, Joseph McBride encouraged the effort to fathom "the totality of Orson Welles" by fully taking into account what may seem to be minor moments in Welles's career as a director (of theater and cinema), actor, writer, journalist, broadcaster, activist, and magician; and events, activities, and issues that might be classified as ephemeral.[1] The challenge that McBride offers is for Welles scholars and enthusiasts to pay particular attention to what has been avoided, overlooked, underappreciated, or misunderstood despite decades of previous research. *Orson Welles in Focus: Texts and Contexts* engages with that challenge, and as our title suggests, aims to bring him into focus in ways that are both deep and sharp. Our goal is to contribute to a full view of Welles's activities during a critical period in his life—roughly 1936–56, though there are references to works outside that time—by calling attention to important but previously neglected and in some cases, literally unknown elements of and contexts for his work. As McBride noted, these elements must be studied if we are to fully understand and appreciate Welles's ambitions, intentions, and achievements. Deep focus in scholarship, as in cinema, aims to not only show the various parts of a scene or subject but also to allow for an examination of how those parts interrelate, sometimes

harmonizing, other times clashing, and in Welles's case, often dynami-
cally energizing one another. Such an approach also displays these parts
not only in relationship to each other but situated in broader settings:
personal, aesthetic, industrial, social, historical, and political. Like
Welles, we are nothing if not ambitious. The essays collected in this volume use some old material in new configurations and much new material
from archives, plus fugitive, and sometimes newly discovered sources to
make the full range of Welles's activities as an artist, thinker, and activist
more visible. Welles, like Charles Foster Kane, requires a multiperspec-
tival prismatic approach, which reveals richness, complexity, diversity,
and even contradictions, but also continuity and an identifiable core.
What emerges is a portrait of what to many will be an unfamiliar Welles,
one that foregrounds his ongoing experimentation with numerous forms
of media and artistic production, and his dedication to the goal of making American society and the world at large more fair, just, and safe.

This is not, then, a book that starts and stops with the usual subjects.
Many of the acknowledged landmarks in Welles's career—*Citizen Kane*
(1941), *Touch of Evil* (1958), and *Chimes at Midnight* (1966), for example—
are barely mentioned herein. This should not be taken as an intimation,
implicit or otherwise, that they are anything but the masterworks they
have traditionally been judged to be, or that they should no longer com-
mand our attention as spectators, critics, and researchers. Rather, we envision this volume as a part of the movement that began during Welles's
centenary year in online discussions, cinema retrospectives, worldwide
conferences, and major publishing events, not to leave the masterworks
behind but to intensify the effort to plug holes in our knowledge of all
facets of Welles's life and work, expand horizons, shed light on dark corners, and broaden certain lines of inquiry. There are passing references
to the high canonical works of Welles in the following pages, but the emphasis is far more on previously less-investigated topics, such as changing
trends in radio aesthetics, put forth by Shawn VanCour as a necessary
context for a revised understanding of Welles's much-heralded "innovations" in his radio work; his work with humanitarian organizations
mobilizing against antisemitism as well as racism, activities that James
N. Gilmore describes extensively to help expand our knowledge of what
Welles did in the late 1940s; a history of the Filmorsa organization that

was his home base during the making of *Mr. Arkadin* (1955), a shadowy time of Welles's life made much more comprehensible as a result of extensive archival work by François Thomas; a consideration of the African performers who shaped the legendary "Voodoo" *Macbeth* (1936) far more than previously acknowledged, as Marguerite Rippy demonstrates; and a detailed analysis and recapitulation by Vincent Longo of the intricately interrelated and constantly evolving components that made up Welles's staging of *Around the World* (1946), a failure in some ways and a remarkable landmark in others. Other chapters follow up on areas of Welles's life and work that have already received significant attention, such as *It's All True*, but, as Catherine Benamou argues in her essay, still need to be further recognized as central in his oeuvre and of far-ranging impact and influence internationally. All the essays avoid the temptation to let enthusiasm for revealing a previously unknown part of Welles lead to uncritically trumpeting it as a newly discovered masterpiece. But the cumulative effect of recovering more of the totality of Welles is stunning: We have long known that Welles would be considered a major figure if he did nothing else but *Citizen Kane*. What we are now coming to realize is that he would—or at least should—be considered a major figure even if he had never made *Citizen Kane*.

Welles became famous for his theatrical work throughout the 1930s, and it is perhaps useful as well as apt to adopt theatrical metaphors to further explain what we are up to in this volume, perhaps beginning with the observation that while the deep focus we adopt in our approach here is often thought of primarily as a cinematic device, it is also a foundational element of the structure, practice, and experience of theater. Welles is most commonly talked about as a figure who occupies the central stage, basking in the glow of the spotlight, a position he relished and frequently demanded. The celebratory praise that still surrounds *Citizen Kane*—which was only recently "dethroned" from its number one spot on the British Film Institute's list of greatest films ever made, perhaps as much the result of a kind of *Citizen Kane* "fatigue" as of any thorough critical reevaluation—and the emphasis on Welles's rapid ascendency as a "boy wonder" have often been understood as a foil to his later years, where he worked to raise money independently to finance a number of projects that, for one reason or another, were never finished.[2]

In the various roles Welles played in the spotlight—as magician, as film director, as newspaper columnist, as radio broadcaster, as theatrical director, and as a public intellectual and celebrity—the focus has often been on Welles *himself* and his individual performances, temperament, and actions.

However, as much as a spotlight can illuminate a subject, it also creates a very narrow cone of light, casting much else into darkness. The other metaphor often used to describe Welles, a theatrical as well as musical one, is that of the orchestra leader, the conductor of a vast network of players and parts, illustrated memorably in well-known images of Welles in the radio studio collaborating on the "War of the Worlds" (1938) broadcast, or working with cinematographer Gregg Toland on the set of *Citizen Kane*. As much as Welles has been figured in popular memory as a singular figure of creative vision, many of the essays in our volume follow up on previous studies of his work that have also been carefully attuned to the others in the ensemble that is Orson Welles, including the actors in the scenes; the creative artists, musicians, and technicians behind the scenes; and the writers, producers, choreographers, dramaturges, and other kinds of consultants who helped envision and construct the scenes. The orchestra of Welles's life has also been full of those who played "out of tune," such as the RKO administration that ousted him and his Mercury Productions while he was in Brazil working on *It's All True*, or those with whom harmony was elusive, like the European producer Louis Dolivet, whose complex relationship with Welles in the 1950s is examined at length in François Thomas's contribution to this collection.

Our volume situates Welles in broad contexts of history, culture, and collaboration that often go unnoticed when one focuses on the spotlight and orchestra pit, and we believe that our expanded metaphor of the theater can help develop and articulate a complementary critical approach to those that foreground Welles's individual talents and contributions. We focus in particular on the backstage area of the theater—where important but somewhat overlooked rather than overheard conversations and collaborations occur—and the entirety of the theater itself: the space of the audience (reminding us of Welles's concern for the overriding necessity of connecting with that audience in a variety of ways) and the place of the theater situated in the real world (reinforcing our awareness of Welles's deeply held belief in the vital interrelation of art and society). In order to arrive at a full, deep, and sharp picture of Welles, we attempt to take into account not only everything Welles did inside this metaphorical theater, with the numerous performers, players, and partners who helped him do these things, but also, and perhaps equally important, how the conditions of the metaphorical (and sometimes literal) theater, including its embeddedness in a world much in need of change, encouraged certain forms of work.

Every essay in the volume examines Welles in one way or another in a broad combination of contexts that we conceptualize using the metaphor of the theater, including Sidney Gottlieb's examination of Welles's work as a *New York Post* columnist, which had an extensive run—more than six months—on a large stage in front of a very substantial audience; Vincent Longo's analysis of the mixed media aesthetics of Welles's production of *Around the World*, in which the fusion of theater and film releases often startling moments of dramatic and intellectual power; and James N. Gilmore's look at Welles's political work with humanitarian organizations in the 1940s, work that is thoughtful, passionate, compassionate, and, using the term broadly, Shakespearean—infused with a theatrical rhetoric and cultural resonance that is moving and persuasive. For example, *King Lear* and *The Merchant of Venice* are mobilized by Welles to aid in the efforts to protest the brutal police assault on the recently demobilized African American soldier Isaac Woodard and to combat various forms and instances of antisemitism.

Orson Welles is the subject of this book, but the individual essays rely heavily on recent trends in media and film history that have encouraged decentering, a wider view of contexts, a generous and rigorous deployment of archives, and a move away from textual analysis and individual biography. For example, Shawn VanCour's essay on the much-neglected second half of the "War of the Worlds" broadcast offers more an industrial history of a style than an analysis of Welles's individual contribution to the production; and, focusing particularly on interpersonal collaboration set in the midst of broader institutional and cultural practices and pressures, Marguerite Rippy's essay emphasizes the critical role that the African dancers Asadata Dafora and Abdul Assen played in

Welles's stage production of *Macbeth*, a role that is routinely effaced, for reasons that Rippy exposes and rightly contests. The goal in our volume is not so much to tell the history of Orson Welles, but rather to place him in multiple different histories.

The Welles uncovered in this volume is still very much the artist engaged with his art. We see this particularly clearly in Matthew Solomon's exploration of the largely unnoticed extent to which Welles's works look back to a particular era in silent cinema, elements of which he embeds in his films and dramatic productions to energize them, evoke powerful feelings of nostalgia and loss, and prompt reflexive analysis of the promises and perils of cinema. But the Welles that is reassembled throughout the essays gathered here is a figure who is also very much the artist and citizen engaged with others, in mutual, not merely one-directional ways: an auteur in good company. Acknowledging, even emphasizing, that Welles did not create alone does not—despite his own fears and the intentions of some of his critics—diminish or insult him.

Our emphasis throughout this volume on calling attention to important but perhaps previously unnoticed or insufficiently explored and appreciated areas of interest and activity that Welles contributed to and that, for lack of a better term, contributed to him is exemplified by the exhibition mounted during the first half of 2015 by Indiana University's Lilly Library, titled *100 Years of Orson Welles: Master of Stage, Sound, and Screen*. This exhibition was both the backdrop for and an essential part of the centennial conference that was the original impetus for this volume, and is described in detail by Craig Simpson, the curator of this exhibit, in his essay in this collection. Simpson shows how the carefully arranged display cases, packed with an abundance of material that is only a tiny sampling of what the Welles archives at the Lilly Library contain, allow us numerous paths to survey Welles's activities in his three main—and conveniently alliterative—arenas: stage, sound, and screen. There is in fact a fourth unmentioned "s" present in the comprehensive mapping and exploration of Welles attempted by both the exhibition and our volume: society. As we move through the texts and artifacts in the exhibition display cases and through the essays in this volume, many of which are scholarly display cases of archival material, we become increasingly aware of the depth, centrality, and sincerity of Welles's social and political engagement, visible not only in his day-to-day activities but also in his commitment to art (and mass media in general) and his celebrity status, all serving as vehicles of social and political progress. Thinking of Welles in terms of these four categories, especially the last one, paves the way for a critical adjustment in our overall conception of an artist and person often caricatured by a distorting focus on another "s" word: self. It would be misguided to overlook Welles's self-indulgences, self-aggrandizement, and other related instances and habits of self-concern and selfishness. But a deep and full look at Welles reveals much more about him that we should be not only taking into account but concentrating on.

The literature on Welles is often filled with special pleading, sometimes for, sometimes against him. But the animating force in more recent Welles scholarship is a triple injunction to take us beyond the limits of special pleading: to look at Welles again; to see, as much as possible, the whole Welles; and then to celebrate accordingly, truly with eyes wide open as we appreciate and as we criticize. That is the animating force behind our volume as well, and the essays herein revolve around addressing fundamental questions that are perennial, not just centennial: What do we expect to learn by doing more research on Welles? What lies between the frequently acknowledged peaks of Welles's achievements? What lies beneath and behind the Welles we think we know? What else is left to uncover, discover, and recover, and what might such evolving research teach us not only about the man himself and his texts but also about the various contexts—industrial, cultural, personal, and collaborative—of his life and work?

Taken together, the essays in our volume offer some provisional answers to these questions. We see a Welles who is remarkably kinetic. There may have been peaks and valleys in his achievements—although a lot, of course, depends on how we define achievement, which the contributors here propose can be attained without popularity, commercial success, formal perfection, and even completion—but rarely were there any lapses in his energy and effort in a wide range of activities and areas still not completely surveyed. One of these areas is media. While it has always been recognized that Welles worked extensively and skillfully in several different media, the essays in this volume expand our awareness of his ongoing experiments in multimedia and intermedia, overlapping terms describing not just the additive use of different media alongside one another but explorations of the dynamism of media juxtapositions and collisions that can produce more than the sum of their parts. And Welles was not only a practitioner but also a serious media analyst and critic, deeply concerned about the role of media in society, a subject examined in his newspaper columns, essays, and interviews, and also thematized in his theater productions and films.

The Welles who emerges throughout the volume is international, not only in terms of his literal travel experiences (which include some as an expatriate, discussed in the essay by François Thomas) but also in terms of the subject matter of his works and his overall artistic and political mentality. He was a proud but not a provincial American, and frequently took great pains to point out specifically and emphatically that the term "America" properly describes a large multicultural hemisphere, not a single country in the north. One of the messages that comes through nearly all Welles's activities discussed in this volume—for example, newspaper columns that report on a war that made attention to international news inescapable; theater pieces that traverse the globe or construct a powerful tragedy out of cross-national elements; a film about the "other" America sponsored but ultimately undermined in part by the North American government; and humanitarian efforts to counter worldwide racism and antisemitism—is that a true citizen (and artist) must embody extensive "Around the World" experience of one kind or another and must know and care about people throughout the world.

Engaging with others might well be identified as the key subtext of the entire volume. On a micro or personal level, we see this in the numerous studies in collaboration contained herein. Welles's "genius" is on full display throughout the essays, but it is a complex compound of individual talent and energy, including a kind of entrepreneurial ability that needs to be labeled as such and closely examined in any study of an auteur, and multidimensional partnerships with numerous people— partnerships that may be fragile, unstable, unequal, and troublesome, but may also be, as our contributors repeatedly demonstrate, essential and creative.

And the macro, social level of Welles's engagement with others is illustrated by the abundance of evidence confirming how progressive political activities, concerns, and subjects infuse and energize his life and work. Even a brief *News on the March* type of overview of Welles illustrates all this. He grew up in a privileged household, but in the presence of a mother who was both a determined creative artist and an energetic political activist, and he followed suit. He came of age in a culture of not only radical experimentation but of art for society's sake, and the early triumphs he was deeply involved with (especially *Macbeth*, *The Cradle Will Rock* [1937], *Caesar* [1937], and "War of the Worlds") were dramatizations, analyses, and powerful mobilizations against powers (corporate and governmental primarily, but also sometimes cosmic, with the latter arguably at least in part standing in for the former) threatening to overwhelm and crush humankind and democracy. The person famous for *Citizen Kane* was less well known but indefatigable as an adviser to and confidant of President Roosevelt, lecturer on the nature and dangers of and antidotes to fascism, advocate and practitioner of multiculturalism, progressive journalist, and committed chronicler of and battler against racism. And even in his later days, normally associated with increasingly reflexive projects (such as *F for Fake* [1973] and *The Other Side of the Wind*) and images of him sitting by himself in front of a moviola or using the voice he once used to roar against the unjust treatment of Isaac Woodard in wine commercials, he still nurtured and cherished a lively and forceful progressivism, as we see in his frequent reminiscences (in interviews and in his screenplay *The Cradle Will Rock*), topical comments on contemporary conservatism, and stinging political fable *The Big Brass Ring*. All this and more needs to be chronicled in detail—as the latest biographies of Welles are doing—but also routinely integrated into critical studies of Welles's works and our understanding of his ongoing ambition, appeal, and influence, which this volume takes as one of its prime goals.[3] Such an effort includes examining not how Welles's life and work was invigorated by his political engagement and concern, but also how it was circumscribed: we need to be more alert to how political forces (among others) affected the shape of his works (*It's All True*, portrayed by Catherine Benamou as a site of struggle between public interest and conventional privilege and power, is the classic but not unique example in Welles's career), his opportunities found and lost, and his path of diminishing returns and resources.

We commented earlier in this introduction about the advantages of decentering our approach to Welles, but some recentering may also be useful. In particular, if researchers shift from an overriding concern with espousing or contesting such subjects as Welles's supposed fear of completion, and substitute sustained attention to his real and demonstrable lifelong fear of fascism and commitment to progressive politics, we may at last get a clear view of one of the elusive Rosebuds of Welles's life and works. Tracing a portrait of Welles in deep and sharp focus will always be a work in progress, and that is both daunting and exciting: there is—always—much more to be done, but the rewards are real. As we enter into his second hundred years and get closer and closer to the totality of Welles, we gain more and more insight into how "large" he was: by himself, with the help of others, and often in the service of others.

NOTES

1. Personal communication with Joseph McBride at Indiana University's Orson Welles Centennial Symposium and Celebration, Bloomington, IN, 2015.

2. Robin Pogrebin. "'Vertigo' Tops Sight and Sound Poll of Greatest Films." *The New York Times*. August 1, 2012, accessed May 23, 2017, https://artsbeat.blogs.nytimes.com/2012/08/01/vertigo-tops-sight-and-sound-poll-of-greatest-films/?_r=0.

3. Recent biographies of Welles include Simon Callow, *Orson Welles*, Vol. 3: *One-Man Band* (New York: Viking, 2016) and Patrick McGilligan, *Young Orson: The Years of Luck and Genius on the Path to* Citizen Kane (New York: HarperCollins, 2016).

1

THE DEATH OF THE *AUTEUR*
Orson Welles, Asadata Dafora, and the 1936 *Macbeth*

MARGUERITE RIPPY

In 1936, at the age of twenty, Orson Welles directed *Macbeth* for the Federal Theatre Project's (FTP) Negro Theatre Unit. Undaunted by his youth, Welles facilitated a sensational success, an adaptation that infused Shakespeare's iconic work with music and dance from African indigenous cultures.[1] But the role of his collaborators, particularly the central influence of dancer/choreographer Asadata Dafora, has been overlooked. Acknowledging Dafora's contributions to the production replaces the binary question of whether Welles exploited or supported African American artists with a more productive paradigm, one that inquires into the complexity of intercultural exchange. Such a paradigm shift opens Welles's work to new audiences by illuminating his process of collaboration and challenging the auteurist focus on isolated creative genius.

Critics and scholars alike often privilege Welles's name over the names of his collaborators, in part because of his success as a charismatic storyteller and promoter of his entertainment brand. But his stories of the production illuminate and distract in equal parts and often work in tandem with cultural forces to obscure his collaborative process. On the centenary of Welles's birth, it is time to embrace the death of the auteur and acknowledge instead the polyvocal nature of creative genius. This approach turns away from questions of individual genius and toward inquiries into the collaborative nature of performance—replacing the idea of sole authorship with that of collaboration. The question then becomes not whether Welles is an auteur, but rather how the concept of auteur is itself culturally constructed, often at the expense of the identities of the many contributors to any given performance. Specifically, this chapter focuses on the contributions of Asadata Dafora and his colleague, musician Abdul Assen, whose musical performance and choreography created the sound and mood of the show, in particular through the witches' scenes.[2]

The 1936 *Macbeth* fulfilled two distinct roles for "Negro theater": first, to celebrate African indigenous arts; second, to showcase the talents of African Americans within Western art forms. In 1934, the *New York Amsterdam News* published an article titled, "Where's the Negro Theatre?" In this article, pitched primarily to African American readers, Romeo Dougherty lamented the lack of theater that fostered a sense of black pride. He pointed to Asadata Dafora's Shogola Oloba dance troupe and their African dance piece *Kykunkor* (1934) as a positive example of such theater (fig. 1.1). FTP director Hallie Flanagan saw the performance, and decided Dafora and the influential Shogola Oloba fit the FTP mission of the Negro Theatre Unit well, and would bring needed experience with African dance form to *Macbeth*.[3]

In contrast to FTP Negro Theatre "folk" productions like *Green Pastures*, the 1936 *Macbeth* blended Western European and African diasporic forms. Welles's concept for *Macbeth*, set in Haiti, employed classical Shakespearean verse spoken against a background of traditional African dance and drums. A daring risk, "Welles's canny use of simplified elements from various black cultures," in tandem with Shakespeare's verse, had the "dualistic, perhaps even contradictory result" of satisfying both black and white audience members.[4] Although the black community had expressed anxiety that Welles would produce *Macbeth* as a minstrel burlesque, this was not the result, in part due to Dafora's choreography and the music for jungle scenes.[5] As the *Pittsburgh Courier* noted, audiences came "to jeer, stay[ed] to cheer."[6] The negotiation among African, American, and European artistic traditions succeeded in part because

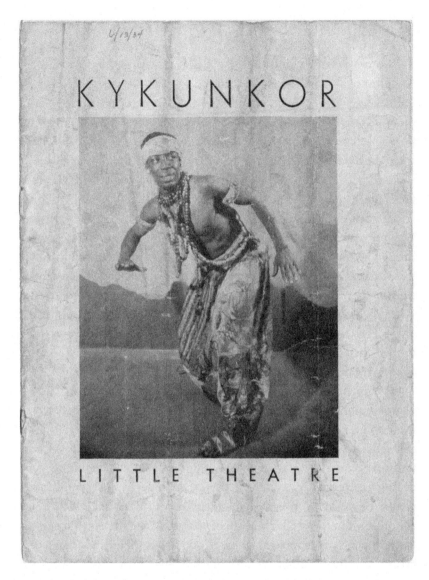

Figure 1.1. Photo of Asadata Dafora for *Kykunkor* (1934).
Courtesy of Asadata Dafora Photograph Collection, New York
Public Library, Schomburg Center for Research in Black Culture.

Welles and Dafora worked together to create a new and dynamic blend of performance.

Dafora's choreography and his connection with dancer/drummer Abdul Assen—who reprised his role as a witch doctor from *Kykunkor* ("The Witch Woman")—created a powerful sense of authentic Haitian "voodoo" for the audience, despite little evidence of direct Haitian influence. Assen's work as the lead drummer and witch doctor received widespread critical praise, and he became one of the figures most associated with the production, in part because of an oft-retold tale of his conjuring a curse that killed critic Percy Hammond following his unfavorable review. This tale was retold over the years by John Houseman, Hallie Flanagan, and Eric Burroughs, as well as repeatedly by Welles himself.[7] Assen's contributions are central to understanding this performance, because in 1936, voodoo practice was advertised as a central element of this *Macbeth*. In this analysis, the spelling *voodoo* refers to staged performance of ritual and *vodou* to off-stage community ritual practice. Assen himself was careful to distinguish between the two—the former a harmless representation produced for entertainment, the latter a powerful spiritual tool.[8]

Although Dafora and Assen are often referred to in stories and reviews simply as "drummers," by 1936, they were both established artists from different African performance traditions. Dafora emigrated from Sierra Leone, and was from a family who blended European and African traditions; Assen was a Nigerian immigrant who celebrated his connections to ritual dance and vodou. Both men described themselves as practicing Muslims on at least one program for *Kykunkor*.[9] But the roles of both men in the production are obscured by both active and passive cultural practices of racism—what is said about them, and what is left unspoken or unrecorded. As with many actors of color in the era, they are often grouped rhetorically into composite characters, unnamed or renamed along the way. Welles is an active participant in this process, often referring to Assen and Dafora by nicknames, exoticizing rather than professionalizing them, or combining them into a composite African character.

One example of Welles's ability to acknowledge the influence of Dafora and Assen, even as he diminishes their professional stature, comes in episode two of Welles's 1955 *Sketch Book* television program. In this fifteen-minute episode, twenty years after the performance, Welles recognizes the artistic contributions of Dafora and Assen, even as he fails to recognize them as equal colleagues. Welles encapsulates their contributions in a tale he told often, that of Percy Hammond's death via a "voodoo curse." In part because of his fascination with magic, Welles was drawn to *Macbeth*'s supernatural darkness, both in its Shakespearean context (after all, Macbeth was cursed long before this production) and in the voodoo elements highlighted in this specific adaptation.[10] As Welles recounts, he chose to set *Macbeth* in Haiti because "above all the witches, translated terribly well into witch doctors."[11] Despite his acknowledgment of Dafora's and Assen's contributions, Welles refers to Assen only as "Jazbo" in this version of the Percy Hammond story, although in other versions he refers to him by name, as Abdul. It is worth quoting from this version of the Hammond curse at length, in order to capture the nature of Welles's storytelling:

> Witch doctors were specially imported from Africa because the governments in the West Indies took the view that there was no such thing as voodoo. So we had to go all the way to the Gold Coast and import a troupe. And they were quite a troupe, headed by a fellow whose name was Asadata Dafora. The only other member of the coven who had any English was a dwarf with gold teeth by the name of Jazbo. At least we called him Jazbo up in Harlem; I don't know what his African name was. He had a diamond in each one of those gold teeth. He was quite a character. Fairly terrifying. The other members of the troupe not only spoke no English, but didn't seem to want to speak at all. They confined their communications to drumming. . . . Finally the drums were ready, and the drumming began, the legend grew backstage—and indeed all over the community of Harlem—that to touch the drums, was to die. And indeed, one poor stagehand did touch a drum and did fall from a high place and break his neck. And after that, Asadata and his rhythm boys were treated with a little respect. And then we opened with *Macbeth*, and the drummers were fine, and the voodoo sequences—that is the witch scenes—went very well indeed, and everybody seemed to like the show. Critics were very kind to us, except . . . for Mr. Percy Hammond. . . . I was approached by Jazbo, who said to me, [heavy accent] "This critic bad man." And I said, [offhandedly] "Yes, he's a bad man."
>
> [Jazbo] "You want we make beri-beri on this bad man?" (All this dialogue's very much like the native bearers in Tarzan and so on, I apologize for it, but it's really what went on.)
>
> I said, "Yes, go right ahead and make all the beri-beri you want to."

He said, "We start drums now."

I said, "You go ahead and the start the drums, just be ready for the show tonight." . . . Woke up next morning, proceeded on ordinary course of work, and bought the afternoon paper to discover that Mr. Percy Hammond for unknown causes had dropped dead in his apartment. I know this story is a little hard to believe, [slight chuckle] but it is circumstantially true.[12]

This story demonstrates how Welles's engaging anecdotes often sacrifice literal truth for the sake of a good story, as well as how his dominant personality can interfere with a full understanding of his collaborative entertainment products. While it is true that Hammond wrote a negative review on April 16 and that he died of pneumonia on the 25th, the story is striking in both Welles's casual acknowledgement of his self-conscious blackface ventriloquism and for the contextual details he omits regarding Dafora and Assen as artists. By 1955, when Welles told this story on Sketch Book, Dafora had worked with Katherine Dunham, Pearl Primus, and Esther Rolle. He and Abdul Assen had both performed in Carnegie Hall before Eleanor Roosevelt as part of the African Academy programs in 1943, 1945, and 1946.[13] Welles's description of both men diminishes their professionalism and neglects to mention that Dafora was well-versed in both Western theatrical practice and African indigenous arts.

Dafora, truly a product of disaporic education, had studied opera in Europe as well as native dance rituals in West Africa, and had written the popular Kykunkor as an African opera two years before Welles staged Macbeth. Kykunkor, featuring the choreography and drumming of Dafora, and starring Assen as a witch doctor who issues an authentic voodoo curse on stage, embodies several parallels to the witch scenes of the 1936 FTP Macbeth.[14] Although Welles suggests that both men were "imported" for the 1936 performance, Dafora had been in the United States since 1929, had founded the Shogola Oloba dance troupe, and had worked separately with Assen to craft multiple performances of African dance for a wide variety of audiences. Welles's performance in Sketch Book creates personas that conform to stereotypes rather than reality and fails to acknowledge the depth and complexity of artistic collaboration. The story itself functions as a type of entertaining magic trick. It situates Welles at the center, as he literally speaks for his collaborators and draws their images for the viewer; he then disappears from the center of the story, making voodoo witchcraft the agent of the tale.

This *Sketch Book* episode effectively deploys the Hammond story both as an iconic representation of the 1936 *Macbeth* and to explain Welles's own failure to complete and commercially distribute his Brazilian project, the ironically named *It's All True*. He flows smoothly from the Hammond tale into a similar anecdote of being cursed himself by a disgruntled witch doctor on *It's All True*, thus resulting in the film's lack of distribution. The reality of this project's fate is far more complex, driven by commercial and intercultural factors that are studied in detail by Catherine Benamou in *It's All True: Orson Welles's Pan-American Odyssey*.[15] Welles crafts his stories to generate a mythology of himself as an artist working under crossed stars, and his story of the Hammond curse repeatedly works in tandem with media coverage and historical discourse to obscure the intercultural collaborative work that underpinned this *Macbeth*.

Welles's story of the Hammond curse had strategic implications for both Welles and Dafora, and became the defining story of this performance. The tale makes its way into not just Welles's memory of the show, but into biographers' records, critics' reactions, and then into a new generation of stories about the 1936 *Macbeth*, in online listings like Wikipedia, and in graphic novelist Norris Burroughs's account based on his father's memories.[16] The legend of the "Voodoo" *Macbeth* thus generates its own history, and this legend calls for some demystification and grounding in what VèVè Clark calls an "archaeological approach" to black performance history.[17] As Clark points out, commercial and cultural practices create the context for exclusionary politics, and their complex interaction often serves multiple stakeholder interests, including those of the excluded or marginalized party. The oral histories surrounding this production are entertaining, but they are also strategic, as is silence. Dafora himself rarely referred publicly to his role in *Macbeth*, and his own discomfort with the sensationalized production may have contributed to the lack of connection between his body of work and Welles's.

For Welles's part, the rhetorical self-aggrandizing stems less from racism—although racist practices of the time in terms of salary, credit,

and production contribute to the erasure—than from his love of an entertaining story and his aptitude for capitalist brand building. He loved
a good story and wasn't above changing details to make the story better,
and he consistently situated himself as the ringmaster in his productions
through a process Scott Newstok has referred to as "re-fabularization."[18]
Scholars continue to struggle with how to credit collaborators from Herman Mankiewicz to John Houseman to Gary Graver and Oja Kodar, and
this struggle goes to the heart of auteurist theories of creation. To some
extent, fully crediting collaborators diminishes the value of directorial
brands, and thus lessens the income from the works themselves for all
involved. Welles was a highly collaborative artist, often hiring colleagues
in multiple productions and using performances in one medium (radio,
for example) to fund ongoing projects in another (film, for example). As
Simon Callow has argued, Welles "stole anything that was germane to
his purpose. He was not, in fact, a great innovator at all; he was a great
fulfiller."[19] A major limitation of the auteur approach is that it awards
genius status as an individual attribute, rather than a collaborative result.
Auteurism, along with modern conventions of salary contracts, industry
awards, and intellectual copyright, rewards the myth of isolated artistic creation, even in the highly collaborative field of performance. In
Welles's case, his cooperative production practices resulted in prolonged
debates over ownership of performance products and screening rights,
and the 1936 *Macbeth* predicts patterns of creative partnership that he
retained throughout his career.

The distinctive drumbeat and choreography of the jungle scenes
that Dafora and Assen created were widely recognized, and became hallmarks of the production and focal points of reviewers' praise. Welles
took full advantage of the soundtrack that Dafora provided, using the
drumbeat as "the equivalent of a film dissolve."[20] Reviewers ranging from
the influential Brooks Atkinson of the *New York Times* to lesser-known
journalists in regional newspapers noted the distinctive sound and look
of the jungle scenes, referring to Assen as a "torso twisting witch doctor," noting the "shrieking sable slatterns of horrific men" and praising
the "savagery and voodooism [that create] the uncanny atmosphere."[21]
Yet neither man is fully credited in most reviews—Assen is listed on the
program itself only as "Abdul." Dafora, while credited as the choreogra-

pher of the jungle scenes on the program, is rarely mentioned by name in reviews. This anonymity starkly contrasts his treatment in reviews of *Kykunkor*, which widely celebrated him by name. He was equally praised in the media for his later work with Assen at Carnegie Hall, and for his 1940 African dance piece *Zunguru*. The contributions of both men would surely have merited greater public credit had they been white.

Despite the lack of recognition for Dafora, he was essential to the production. Without Dafora, Welles would not have had access to the Shogola Oloba African musicians and dancers, nor would he have been able to tap into traditions of African indigenous performance with the same level of detail. His vision of Haiti would have lacked the physical sensations of African diasporic art.

AN ARGUMENT FOR COAUTHORSHIP:
ASSEN, DAFORA, AND WELLES

Welles and Dafora worked well together in part because they shared several artistic values. Both envisioned the role of theater as means to educate and entertain, adapted performance to connect with contemporary themes, recycled parts of previous performances, and had an aptitude for promoting their work through media spectacle. In addition, both men had an interest in the portrayal of ritual magic on stage, and both were superstitious (or spiritual, depending on your perspective). Welles wanted to transform *Macbeth*'s witches into Haitian voodoo witches, and Dafora's own prior work with this theme in *Kykunkor* proved useful. Welles substituted African arts for Haitian arts and focused on Hecate, the witches, and a voodoo witch doctor, fascinating audiences and critics in New York and on the road tour. *Macbeth*'s combination of African rhythm and dance with African American performance of Shakespearean verse provoked a national media conversation regarding integration in the cities it toured, since the art itself was seen as a type of miscegenation. This integrated art form spurred debate from Dallas to Indianapolis to Chicago to Cleveland. The show was a provocative cultural act, and proved a highlight of the FTP Negro Unit's work, in no small part because of its genre-crossing, culture-blending combination of African and European diasporic arts.

Dafora, like Welles, was experienced in the art of public self-con-
struction, although not much record of Dafora's voice or performance
remains. Just a few snippets exist in newspaper interviews or program
biographies that provide direct quotations regarding his aesthetic
views. A large body of critical work exists, however, tracing his influential dance career, which reached its apex in the 1930s and 1940s. Based
on Dafora's papers, held in New York Public Library's Schomburg Collection, he regards *Macbeth* as a minor event in his thirty-year career.
His archive holds numerous clippings from projects of this era, but none
from *Macbeth*.[22] Like Welles, he prefers to emphasize work for which
he claimed artistic control as director, composer, and performer. He
particularly celebrates his efforts to bring African dance to audiences
through educational or ethno-musical frames. Dafora remains silent on
his full role in Welles's production, despite the fact that he remained in
contact with Welles through at least 1940, when he inquired about a role
in Welles's proposed *Heart of Darkness*.[23] He gives several interviews
surrounding Shogola Oloba performances, but either chooses not to
give interviews or is not asked to talk about his performance in *Macbeth*.
His papers do, however, reflect constant concerns with funding and promoting Shogola Oloba. Like Welles, Dafora used lucrative acting roles
to subsidize his own company. Overall this approach worked. Dafora
went on to become a leader in the study and practice of African dance
and directly or indirectly influenced later dancers like Pearl Primus,
Esther Rolle, and Alvin Ailey, and is widely studied for his influence
on modern dance.[24]

Unlike Welles, who used his commercial appearances to build name
brand recognition, Dafora's and Assen's contributions are difficult to
trace, in part due to Dafora's adherence to the common practice of the era
to change the names of actors and dancers between performances in order to appeal to specific audiences. The variety of programs for Dafora's
performances between 1933 and 1947 reflect how he adapted his own
name and those of his players to suit various audiences.[25] Depending
on the context of the performance, Dafora assigned performers names
that would connote Africa or America. Abdul Assen, the central source
of the voodoo in the "Voodoo" *Macbeth*, is difficult to trace, in part because his name often changes from program to program. Abdul can be

listed as Abdul Assen, Abdul Essen, Frank Abdul, or just Abdul.[26] In their memoirs, Welles and Houseman tend to refer to him as Jazbo or Abdul. Renaming reflects strategic use of rhetoric by marginalized artists to adjust from one setting to another. It also, however, obscures their contributions, making the kind of name brand recognition rewarded by commercial practice more difficult.

While Dafora shaped the look and sound of *Macbeth*'s jungle scenes to sell to the audience, Assen provided the feeling of "authenticity" within the performance. Assen was singled out for critical praise in his role as Witch Doctor, if not by his name. Both contemporary reviewers and later scholars cite his body and aptitude for creating a stylized voodoo presence as key to the show's success. Assen's Witch Doctor role often extends off-stage, and he is central to the story of the Hammond curse that comes to define this production. Assen was appreciative of the vodou practice of "white magic," and promoted himself in program bios and media coverage for *Kykunkor* as one of a line of practicing witch doctors (fig. 1.2). Assen embodied African cultural, religious, and artistic elements. Mainstream press focused on Assen's performance of supernatural possession and his powerful drumming, whereas black press tended to address the totality of the black-cast production. But media accounts from both audiences describe a musical form that conjured "(pan)-national identity fully reliant on rhythmic appeal."[27]

Despite the major contributions of Assen and Dafora, their connection to *Macbeth* remains largely unacknowledged, even though Assen continued to receive acclaim during the FTP national tour of Dallas, Chicago, Indianapolis, Detroit, and Cleveland. Most media accounts—by both mainstream and traditionally African American newspapers—accept Welles as the primary author of the performance. Assen's last name is never credited on the program, and reviews refer to him in terms of his role, rather than by his name. There is no mention in mainstream critical or media accounts that Dafora and Assen worked together in Dafora's preexisting dance troupe (first named the Asadata African Opera and Dramatic Company, then later the Shogola Oloba Dancers and Singers) or that they had fully realized professional dance careers. Dafora was well known through *Kykunkor*'s success, at least within New York, but he remains largely unnamed in press accounts of *Macbeth*.[28]

Figure 1.2. Abdul Assen in *Kykunkor*. Photo by Maurice Goldberg. Photographs and Print Division, New York Public Library, Schomburg Center for Research in Black Culture.

When newspaper reviews focused on Welles's collaborators, they tended to credit Nat Karson's costume design and Abe Feder's lighting for creating the sensational effect of the show, and they rarely mention the African artists, despite praise for the "jungle" soundtrack and dance numbers. In an extreme example, the *Dallas Morning News* credits the show's success at the segregated Texas Centennial Celebration entirely to Welles, Karson, Virgil Thomson, and Feder.[29] When the show moved north, historically black press in Chicago, Indianapolis, and Cleveland tended to focus on African American stars Jack Carter and Edna Thomas or the controversies surrounding the show in terms of African American racial empowerment and civil rights. The cultural context of the play changed with each stop, but Dafora and Assen remained unmentioned, even when their contributions in terms of music and dance receive praise.[30]

AFRICA AND WELLES: THE IMPACT OF A DIASPORIC *MACBETH*

The work of Dafora and Assen had a lingering effect on Welles, and he remembered the central nature of their contributions even twenty years after the staging of *Macbeth*. In the same *Sketch Book* episode in which he recounts the Percy Hammond story, Welles remembers the voodoo elements of the production as being essential to its success, and acknowledges the long-term impact on him artistically. Setting up the role of the FTP Negro Theatre Unit, Welles outlines the twin goals of the production: to celebrate African diasporic art, and to adapt a classic Shakespearean work to appeal to a mass audience:

> We were anxious to give to Negro artists, who are so very talented, an opportunity to play in the sort of thing that's usually denied them . . . the parts that fall to Negroes are too often old mammies with bandannas and watermelon eating pickaninnies and Uncle Rastuses and so on, so we did quite a number of shows from classical repertory. We began with a Gilbert and Sullivan . . . Hot Mikado we called it. And encouraged by that success, we went on to Shaw and then backwards into literature, and finally dared a production of Macbeth.[31]

Michael Anderegg notes that the production succeeded in these goals. It reinvigorated Shakespeare and paved the way for Welles's *Caesar* the following year, and its success "encouraged other experiments in non-traditional casting."[32]

Welles and Dafora shared the view that performance should be used for edification as well as entertainment. Welles appropriated the classic *Macbeth* to generate contemporary political discussion, a move he demonstrates repeatedly in adaptations of classic literature for mass consumption—*Faust, Caesar*, and Kafka's *The Trial* to name a few.[33] Similarly, Welles's early career projects, including *Everybody's Shakespeare/ Mercury Shakespeare* and his formation of the Mercury Theatre, shared the goal of bringing classics to the masses through engaging, inventive performances. These goals parallel Dafora's desire to bring an understanding of African communal dance and music to the masses. Dafora observed that *Kykunkor* challenged the "old stereotype of the African arts" in its efforts to bring authentic indigenous African forms to the stage.[34] His approach relied on bringing these details of indigenous performance into American performance, leading him to import "rare stringed instruments and drums of Africa."[35] In large part, the 1936 *Macbeth* succeeded in exposing audiences who had yet to see either Shakespeare or African indigenous art to both art forms.

Macbeth was politically progressive in terms of artistic outreach and employment—it employed more than 125 African and African American actors during the Great Depression, which is no small feat. It also bridged an artistic rift within the African diasporic community of Harlem, since indigenous African music and dance held twin meanings in American culture at the time, both celebrating African culture and selling a fantasy of Africa to mainstream audiences. On the one hand, fantastic adaptations of the exotic underpinned the movement now labeled modernist primitivism, which reflected a middle-class fascination with exotic, indigenous cultures and contributed to the stereotypes of African performance to which Dafora refers above.[36] Welles experimented with modernist primitivism in a number of his radio broadcasts of the era, a movement in which the African American community also participated by juxtaposing "primitive" African music and dance against "modern" African American art forms.[37]

The term *primitivism* in modern dance, however, holds a less pejorative connotation, one tied to intellectual expression through bodily movement. This use of dance as interpellation, an invitation to the audience to create meaning with the dancer, meant that modern dance could "conjugate body and feeling in diverse and opposed understandings of 'authentic' cultural identities," and thus could integrate indigenous arts within contemporary experimental form.[38] Dance as interpellation was a central feature of the 1936 *Macbeth*, allowing audience members and performers to participate in active construction (and destruction) of diasporic, postcolonial identity, and to create a vision of African art that was neither authentic nor stereotyped. Dafora's choreography brought African indigenous practice into Shakespeare's Western narrative framework, allowing audiences to experience both forms simultaneously. Both Welles and Dafora were fascinated by this type of blending of indigenous and staged arts, and of African and European form.[39]

In 1936, Dafora was a more experienced director than Welles in terms of intercultural performance, in part due to his success in 1934 with *Kykunkor*. *Kykunkor* can be regarded as a direct influence on Welles's production as well as a success in its own right, and it was widely known by the time Dafora worked with Welles. It was well reviewed in the *New York Times*, played for sixty-five performances, and featured a voodoo plot similar to that of *Macbeth*. Many of the Shogola Oloba dancers also worked with the FTP Negro dance company. *Kykunkor* was a popular success: Maureen Needham suggests that it may have influenced Gershwin's score for *Porgy and Bess*.[40] Susan Manning describes *Kykunkor* as "an intercultural fusion of African and Western influences" that played to packed crowds.[41] *Kykunkor* reflected a combination of African communal and Western dance forms—it removed African dance from its ritual context and placed it in a Western narrative form, with beginning, middle, and end to be performed on a proscenium stage.[42] A ritual dance performed on stage an ocean away from its original setting, *Kykunkor* was created by artists from multiple cultures, thus providing a template for diasporic collaboration in the later *Macbeth* (fig. 1.3).

Like Welles, Dafora staged performances that infused the supernatural into the social world of the audience—works that implied vodou could get one a job or kill one's harshest critic. In addition, both were savvy media manipulators, using showmanship to generate publicity. The Percy Hammond curse represents a collaborative marketing effort.

Figure 1.3. Invitation to Shogola Oloba performance (1934).
Courtesy of Asadata Dafora Collection, New York Public Library,
Schomburg Center for Research in Black Culture.

In an era where fascination with African voodoo (the fantasy of vodou)
was at a premium, both Welles and Dafora used Assen's identity as a
practitioner of white magic as a valuable promotional tool. Dafora staged
a 1934 publicity stunt that featured Assen capturing evil spirits atop the
Empire State Building and offering to use his magic to get bystanders a

job.[43] This incident presages the Hammond story, connecting voodoo art with vodou practice. After *Macbeth*, Dafora again used Assen in a similar 1940 publicity event to promote his dance piece *Zunguru*.[44] Like Welles, Dafora was not averse to creating publicity when needed, and he shared Welles's interest in showmanship.

The artistry of Dafora and Assen informed several of Welles's projects of this era, and the 1936 *Macbeth* radicalized Welles in a way that his worldly travels had not. Aesthetically, Welles's work on the 1936 *Macbeth* influenced early radio productions and film proposals, and he often wove elements of African ritual music into productions over the next decade. Shows like his radio *Heart of Darkness* (1938; 1945), *Algiers* (1939), *The White God* (1938) and *Hello Americans* (1942–43) all featured soundtracks that evoked indigenous music, and thematically, all were preoccupied with the convergence of indigenous and colonizing cultures. He recast key actors in future productions: Jack Carter in his first film proposal for *Heart of Darkness*; Carter again as his Mephistopheles in *Doctor Faustus* (1937), with Clarence Yates in a minor role; and Canada Lee as Bigger Thomas in *Native Son* (1941). Welles's film of *Macbeth* (1948) opens with the destruction of a voodoo doll of Macbeth, mimics elements of the stage production, and features a similar use of drumbeats at several points, most notably the execution of Cawdor.[45] His interest in African diasporic music prompted him to begin the Pan-American study *It's All True*, which originated as a proposal to study the evolution of jazz. According to the Dance Heritage Collection, Welles and Dafora even coauthored a radio show, "Trangama-Fanga," in 1941.[46]

This raises the question of why, for so long, critics and scholars have privileged the image of Welles's solo authorship over his highly collaborative process. The answer may lie in cultural practices that surround performance as an entertainment product, as well as in the personal practices of his collaborators, and finally in institutionally racist practices regarding artists of color. While Dafora's creative process overlapped with Welles's in many ways—recycling material, using it to educate and entertain, and preferring to run his own production companies rather than be managed by others—his approach to this performance starkly contrasts Welles's in his reluctance to give interviews or keep chronicles of his work. Even less of Assen's work remains, due to the ephemeral and unscripted nature of indigenous dance performance, but also due to the institutional neglect of artists of color. A brief video clip of Dafora at the Jacob's Pillow dance festival in 1942 demonstrates how his drums may have sounded in *Macbeth*, but his music has been all but erased from history, despite his importance to African music and dance, and more broadly to contemporary dance.[47]

Dafora's contributions to the powerful soundtrack of *Macbeth* influenced Welles aesthetically, just as Welles's relationships with cast members like Jack Carter and Canada Lee influenced him politically. Welles emerged from the production committed to racial equality in concept, if not always in practice. Despite Welles's participation in practices like racially biased pay scales, he was a steadfast advocate for racial equality, and his failure to properly credit collaborators needs to be balanced against the very public, progressive work he did for racial equality. Welles's 1936 black-cast production underpinned his continued interest in civil rights, an interest represented through his series of editorials and commentaries throughout the 1940s, 1950s, and 1960s.

A week after the *Sketch Book* episode in which he recounted the Percy Hammond story, Welles took as his topic the beating of African American veteran Isaac Woodard in *Orson Welles' Sketch Book*, Episode 3. It was a topic he had covered earlier, at great risk to his commercial appeal, in his *Hello Americans* broadcasts. He also became interested in African rhythms, an influence that appears in several of Welles's productions in both radio and in film.[48] His progressive antisegregationist politics informed his production of *Native Son* (1941) as well as his subsequent political writings and radio broadcasts. His interest in hybridized forms of regional popular music helped fuel his evolving proposals for *It's All True*, as his interest in jazz as an intercultural, diasporic form evolved toward a study of Brazilian samba music and culture. His work with African American artists is worthy of further exploration, including his casting of Eartha Kitt as Helen of Troy in the Parisian *Faustus* adaptation (1950), accompanied by a Duke Ellington score.

The 1936 black-cast *Macbeth* was a popular and critical success, in no small part due to Welles's collaboration with the cast of performers and musicians pieced together through the WPA Negro Theatre and

Dance units. The 1936 FTP *Macbeth* incorporated the sounds of African diaspora as they merged into American culture, critically offering audiences "proof that black actors could perform" Shakespeare even as it conformed to modernist interests in intersections between indigenous and experimental art forms.[49] Dafora's choreography and Assen's performance challenged stereotypes of African music and dance, replacing, for at least some viewers, a sense of the fantastic with a sense of communal connection. In 1943, Edward Perry, the casting director of Welles's *Macbeth*, even went so far as to hope that Welles would "keep an oft-made promise—to return to New York to aid in the establishment of a permanent Negro Theater."[50] This was not to happen, but the 1936 *Macbeth* had a profound, lasting, and far-reaching impact: on theatrical practice, on African American diasporic theater art and culture, and on Welles's own subsequent creative work.

Like so many of Welles's works, the 1936 *Macbeth* invites and rewards further study, especially if we reorient our approach. It takes nothing away from Welles's abilities and accomplishments to say that we should no longer regard it narrowly as Welles's *Macbeth*. Identifying the numerous threads of collaboration in its construction, recognizing the broad cultural, transindigenous, and multinational context of its origin, articulation, and meaning, and specifically crediting and celebrating the extensive contributions of artists like Dafora and Assen deepens our understanding of how the 1936 *Macbeth* came to be, and how it connected with its contemporary audiences, participants, and numerous contributors. Identifying webs of collaboration connects the 1936 *Macbeth* with new generations of critics, performers, and enthusiasts that are increasingly aware of art as a source of cultural exchange, as a matrix of communal and collaborative as well as personal and individual elements. Each act of reinterpretation expands rather than challenges Welles's legacy if one is willing to trade the notion of solo authorship for communal creativity.

MARGUERITE RIPPY is Professor in the Department of Literature and Languages at Marymount University. She is author of *Orson Welles and the Unfinished RKO Projects: A Postmodern Perspective* and coauthor of *Welles, Kurosawa, Kozintsev, Zeffirelli: Great Shakespeareans*.

NOTES

1. For further discussion of the production relative to the process of adapting Shakespeare, see Richard France, "The 'Voodoo' Macbeth of Orson Welles," *Theatre* 5, no. 3 (1974): 66–78; Susan McCloskey, "Shakespeare, Orson Welles, and the 'Voodoo' *Macbeth*," *Shakespeare Quarterly* 36, no. 4 (Winter 1985): 406–16; Scott Newstok and Ayanna Thompson, eds. *Weyward Macbeth*, (New York: Palgrave, 2010).

2. Assen also sometimes appears in credits as Abdul Essen or Frank Abdul, and often just as Abdul. In earlier scholarship, I have listed him as "Essen," since that is the name most frequently appearing in media and other Welles scholarship. However, in programs and contracts of his work with Dafora, he is most often listed as "Assen," indicating it as a preferred spelling.

3. Marcia E. Heard and Mansa K. Mussa, "African Dance in New York City," in *Dancing Many Drums: Excavations in African American Dance*, ed. Thomas DeFrantz (Madison: University of Wisconsin Press, 2002), 144. Patrick McGilligan suggests Welles saw Dafora perform *Kykunkor* in Carnegie Hall during his tour with Katharine Cornell, but timelines and locations for both shows suggest this would not have been possible; see *Young Orson: The Years of Luck and Genius on the Path to* Citizen Kane (New York: HarperCollins, 2015), 335.

4. Zanthe Taylor, "Singing for Their Supper: The Negro Units of the Federal Theater Project and Their Plays," *Theater* 27 (Spring/Summer 1997): 49.

5. For a further examination of the relationship of this performance to modernist primitivism, including historical connections to minstrelsy, see Marguerite Rippy, *Orson Welles and the Unfinished RKO Projects: A Postmodern Perspective* (Carbondale: Southern Illinois University Press, 2009), 72–74.

6. "N.Y. 'Macbeth' Glamorous Presentation," *Pittsburgh Courier*, April 25, 1936, A7.

7. Biographers and contemporaries of Welles alike mythologize Assen, connecting him with mythic Africa rather than with Dafora's Shogola Oloba troupe. Houseman refers to Assen only in a collective sense, dwelling on "the drummers" in terms of witchcraft and animal sacrifice in *Unfinished Business: A Memoir* (London: Chatto & Windus, 1986), 97. Welles repeats similar stories, which appear in the 1955 *Sketch Book* television episode and in biographies. See Simon Callow, *Orson Welles*, Vol. 1: *Orson Welles: The Road to Xanadu* (New York: Penguin, 1997), 234; Barbara Leaming, *Orson Welles: A Biography* (New York: Viking, 1985), 108–9; and McGilligan, *Young Orson*, 348–49.

8. For a survey of critical responses to *Macbeth*'s dark magic, see Marguerite Rippy, "Black Cast Conjures White Genius: Unraveling the Mystique of Orson Welles's 'Voodoo' *Macbeth*," in *Weyward Macbeth*, ed. Scott Newstok and Ayanna Thompson (New York: Palgrave, 2010), 83–90. For further discussion of the voodoo vs. vodou distinction, see Marguerite Rippy, "Welles's 'Voodoo' *Macbeth*: Neither Vodou nor Welles? Discuss." *Shakespeare Bulletin* 32, no. 4 (2014): 687–92.

9. The Asadata Dafora collection at the Schomburg branch of the New York Public Library (NYPL) holds multiple programs for *Kykunkor*.

10. Celia Daileader argues that the witches have far more to do with Jacobean playwright Thomas Middleton's vision than with Shakespeare's, but that they were irresistible to Welles as a showman. Celia Daileader, "Weird Brothers: What Thomas Middleton's *The Witch* Can Tell Us about Race, Sex, and Gender in *Macbeth*," in *Weyward Macbeth*, ed. Scott Newstok and Ayanna Thompson, 11–20.

11. Orson Welles, *Orson Welles' Sketch Book*, Episode 2, originally broadcast on April 30, 1955, http://www.wellesnet.com/Sketchbook_episode2.htm.

12. A video of this episode is available on YouTube at https://www.youtube.com /watch?v=NL3ZoUJ-Tek. I am indebted to Wellesnet for the transcription of this episode, which I have updated with minor edits.

13. Thanks to Rebekah Kowal for confirming this through archival programs from Carnegie Hall.

14. For detailed analysis of *Kykunkor*, see Mark Franko, "Nation, Class, and Ethnicities in Modern Dance of the 1930s," *Theatre Journal* 49, no. 4 (December 1997): 487–88; and Pamyla Stiehl, "The Curious Case of *Kykunkor*: A Dansical/Musical Exploration and Reclamation of Asadata Dafora's *Kykunkor, or the Witch Woman*," *Studies in Musical Theatre* 3, no. 2 (2009), 143–56. Programs and supporting materials for *Kykunkor* are held in the Dafora collection at Schomburg New York Public Library.

15. Catherine Benamou, *It's All True: Orson Welles's Pan-American Odyssey* (Berkeley: University of California Press, 2007).

16. Callow, *Road to Xanadu*, 234–39; Leaming, *Orson Welles*, 108–9; McGilligan, *Young Orson*, 348–49; Norris Burroughs, *Voodoo Macbeth: A Graphic Novel* (London: Engine Comics, 2010), 57–65, at Norrisburroughs.com.

17. VèVè Clark, "The Archaeology of Black Theater," *The Black Scholar*, no. 10 (July–August 1979): 43–56.

18. Scott Newstok, "Welles, Othello, Verdi," unpublished lecture (2011).

19. Callow, *Road to Xanadu*, 242.

20. France, "Voodoo *Macbeth*," 68.

21. Len G. Shaw, "Negro Players Give *Macbeth*," *Detroit Free Press*, September 15, 1936; William F. McDermott, "Colored Actors Take *Macbeth* to Tropics," *Cleveland Plain Dealer*, September 30, 1936; Robert Tucker, "New *Macbeth* Presented at Keith's," *Indianapolis Star*, August 26, 1936, 11. For surveys of media responses, see Callow, *Road to Xanadu*, 240, and Rippy, "Black Cast," 87–89.

22. Dafora is similarly reticent about his role as the witch doctor opposite Paul Robeson in an *Emperor Jones* revival in 1939. For an account of this production, see Sheila Tully Boyle and Andrew Bunie, *Paul Robeson: The Years of Promise and Achievement* (Amherst: University of Massachusetts Press, 2005).

23. Asadata Dafora papers, Schomburg Collection, New York Public Library, New York, NY, October 10, 1940.

24. John O. Perpener, *African American Concert Dance: The Harlem Renaissance and Beyond* (Urbana: University of Illinois Press, 2001); Julia Foulkes, *Modern Bodies: Dance and American Modernism from Martha Graham to Alvin Ailey* (Chapel

Hill: University of North Carolina Press, 2002), 183; Rebekah J. Kowal, *How to Do Things with Dance: Performing Change in Postwar America* (Middletown, CT: Wesleyan University Press, 2010).

25. Asadata Dafora papers, Schomburg Collection.

26. The spelling "Essen" appears on the Little Theatre program in 1934. *The New York Times* lists him as "Assen" in a John Martin review of "Zunguru," but as "Essen" on April 14, 1946 in "A Tale of Old Africa." A March 24, 1934 program for *Kykunkor* refers to him as Frank Abdul, and lists the troupe as "HORTON'S PRIMITIVE African Artists known as the Shogola Aloba Group Singers" (see fig. 1.3).

27. Franko, "Nation, Class," 490.

28. An exception would be the *Variety* review (April 22, 1936), which at least credits Dafora, although it doesn't link him to the jungle scenes in its discussion.

29. The *Dallas Morning News* explicitly attempts to erase all contributions by performers of color, calling it "a Nordic achievement of vaulting imagination and magnificent execution." John Rosenfield, "Provocative Distortion of 'Macbeth' Given," *Dallas Morning News*, August 14, 1936.

30. To get a sense of how the reactions to African indigenous performance and vodou ritual might be framed differently, one can look at a version of the Percy Hammond curse as told by the son of Eric Burroughs, the actor who played Hecate. In the graphic novel *Voodoo Macbeth*, Norris Burroughs shows the savagery of African and American cultures in equal parts, portraying Jack Carter's brushes with mafia violence equal in proportion to Abdul's curse. Burroughs's representation of the curse doesn't sensationalize Assen. Rather, Burroughs emphasizes Welles's naïveté about the power of vodou and his desire to project "authenticity," even at the risk of self-destruction. The lesson is to respect an unfamiliar indigenous art form and the artist's explanation of its power, rather than to fear these men themselves.

31. Welles, *Orson Welles' Sketch Book*, Episode 2, originally broadcast on April 30, 1955; transcript: http://www.wellesnet.com/Sketchbook_episode2.htm. Wellesnet also contains links to a four-minute film clip of the stage production and archival materials housed at the Library of Congress at http://www.wellesnet.com/voodoo-macbeth-turns-80-photos-and-video/.

32. Michael Anderegg, *Orson Welles, Shakespeare, and Popular Culture* (New York: Columbia University Press, 1999), 26.

33. Welles's adaptations of the Faust legend pull from several sources, although he explicitly references Marlowe's *Doctor Faustus*. For his 1950 adaptation, Alberto Anile points out, he "mixed Goethe, Dante, Milton, and Marlowe"; see *Orson Welles in Italy* (Bloomington: Indiana University Press, 2013), 192.

34. Quoted in Maureen Needham, "*Kykunkor, or the Witch Woman*: An African Opera in America, 1934," in *Dancing Many Drums: Excavations in African American Dance*, ed. Thomas DeFrantz (Madison: University of Wisconsin Press, 2002), 237.

35. Asadata Dafora papers, Schomburg Collection.

36. For an extensive discussion of this movement relative to this production, see chapter 3 in Rippy, *Orson Welles and the Unfinished RKO Projects*. For an overview

of the movement as a whole, see Marianna Torgovnick, *Gone Primitive: Savage Intellects, Modern Lives* (Chicago: University of Chicago Press, 1990).

37. For one concurrent example of this, see Heppie Ross' recital/lecture at the YMCA Little Theatre, described by H. Lawrence Freeman in "Lecture Recitalist Proves that Africa Gave us Rhythm," *Afro American*, March 7, 1937.

38. Franko, "Nation, Class," 476.

39. For an explanation of how we might approach such "TransIndigenous," performances not just from the perspective of national identities, but from a global/historical perspective that acknowledges nonnational identities, see Ric Knowles, "Editorial Comment: TransIndigenous Performance," *Theatre Journal* 67, no. 3 (October 2015): ix–xv.

40. Needham, *Kykunkor*, 247–48.

41. Susan Manning, *Modern Dance, Negro Dance: Race in Motion* (Minneapolis: University of Minnesota Press, 2004), 55.

42. Perpener, *African American Concert Dance*, 109–10.

43. E. K. Titus, n.d., Asadata Dafora papers, Schomburg Collection.

44. "Jungle Drums Sound as Africans Wed atop Skyscraper," *The Sun*, April 19, 1940. Asadata Dafora papers, Schomburg Collection.

45. Marguerite Rippy, "Orson Welles," in *Welles, Kurosawa, Kozintsev, Zeffirelli*, by Mark Thornton Burnett, Courtney Lehmann, Marguerite H. Rippy, and Ramona Wray (London: Bloomsbury, 2013), 17–24.

46. I have been unable to verify this, but it would fit Dafora's interest in Fanga dance and Welles's documentary broadcasts of the era.

47. "Asadata Dafora," Dance Heritage Coalition website, accessed January 16, 2016, http://www.danceheritage.org/dafora.html.

48. As James Naremore has pointed out, Welles's interest in expressionist drumming emerges even in his youthful *Bright Lucifer* project, but his use of drums acquires a more purposeful sense after the "Voodoo" *Macbeth*; see *The Magic World of Orson Welles*, 2nd ed. (Dallas, TX: Southern Methodist University Press, 1989), 12.

49. Taylor, "Singing for Their Supper," 49.

50. Edward Perry, "Actor Lauds Orson Welles for Work in Negro Theatre," *LA Tribune*, October 25, 1943.

2

REVISITING "WAR OF THE WORLDS"

First-Person Narration in Golden Age Radio Drama

SHAWN VANCOUR

One of the most celebrated broadcasts in the history of Golden Age radio, Orson Welles's October 30, 1938, "War of the Worlds" production for the Columbia Broadcasting System's *Mercury Theatre on the Air*, has been the subject of numerous studies, from Hadley Cantril's work on the social "panic" it incited to scriptwriter Howard Koch and journalist Alan Gallop's accounts of its production and reception, John Gosling's study of its international success, Brad Schwartz's analysis of its "fake news" aesthetic, and a seventy-fifth anniversary volume on its continued significance for understanding present-day media.[1] By this point in his career, Welles was no stranger to radio, having appeared on CBS's *School of the Air, March of Time,* and *Columbia Workshop,* adapted a radio version of *Les Misérables* for the Mutual Broadcasting System, and starred as the eponymous hero of the popular Mutual series, *The Shadow.* However, as Welles biographers have observed, it was his *Mercury* broadcasts that cemented his reputation as a radio artist, with the controversy surrounding "War of the Worlds," in particular, placing him squarely in the national spotlight.[2] The eighth installment in *Mercury*'s fall run, after an inaugural summer season as *First Person Singular,* "War of the Worlds" continued the series' tradition of unorthodox adaptations of popular literary works anchored by first-person narration delivered in character by Welles. Although "War of the Worlds" is better known today for its use of the fake news style, this essay argues that the techniques of first-person narration used in this and other *Mercury* productions had a much more profound impact on broadcasting history, contributing to formative shifts in the dominant production culture of Golden Age radio.

While previous analyses of this broadcast have focused on aesthetic innovations in its dramatized scenes of Martian invasion during the program's first act, I argue that the post-invasion sequences of the program's neglected second act warrant equal, if not greater attention. In contrast to the first act's rapid scene changes, dramatic sound effects, and use of fake news reportage, the second act relies primarily on first-person narration delivered by Welles in the role of Princeton professor Richard Pierson. Analyzing scripts in Koch's personal papers, I suggest this second act was revised to foreground its first-person style, which formed a key marker of *Mercury*'s larger series identity and a means by which Welles sought to differentiate his program from mainstream radio fare. However, this style was not a distinctly Wellesian innovation, with Welles, instead, contributing to much broader shifts in the dominant culture of radio production during the late 1930s and 1940s, which increasingly embraced once-maligned techniques of voice-over narration as newly valued tools of radio storytelling. Seeking to recover the importance of the neglected second act of "War of the Worlds" for its use of *Mercury*'s signature first-person style, I argue that this style should itself be understood in relation to broader shifts in production norms with which Welles scholars and media historians in general have yet to adequately reckon.

"WAR OF THE WORLDS" AND THE FIRST-PERSON SINGULAR STYLE

If mentioned at all in Welles scholarship, the second act of "War of the Worlds" is typically dismissed as an aesthetic failure, with blame attributed to Koch's inexperience as the newly appointed series writer. Noting that "nobody then or now has paid much attention to the second half," James Naremore argues that the success of the program "depends on the manipulation of sounds, silences, and accurate vocal imitations of radio news bulletins in the first half," and that "anyone who has heard a recording of the entire broadcast must realize that the second half, which switches to a conventional first-person narration, is pretty lame writing."[3] Paul Heyer similarly disparages the narration in the second act as "maddeningly slow," while Schwartz's book-length analysis of the broadcast devotes only a few lines to the second act, stating that "Koch struggled to inject drama into this largely impersonal chronicle," whose narrator was "a passive character . . . an observer of monumental events rather than a direct participant in the action" like the protagonists of preceding *Mercury Theatre* broadcasts.[4] Affirming Welles's contributions to the "literary" turn in radio drama and efforts to exploit "the novel . . . [as] an untapped 'form' that might enrich radio's content," Jeff Porter likewise focuses his own analysis of "War of the Worlds" on the broadcast's first act. Treating news reporter Carl Phillips as the main narrator, he argues that interrupting Phillips's on-the-scene reports with accounts from other characters destabilizes his position of narrative authority and denies listeners "the comfortable certainty of one monologic perspective," but ignores the second act's focus on Pierson, who narrates without interruption and maintains his position of narrative authority for the full act.[5]

It was, in fact, this second act, not the first, that distinguished "War of the Worlds" as a *Mercury* production, showcasing its signature first-person style. Welles had already made use of the technique in his earlier production of *Les Misérables* for Mutual and was lauded in promotional coverage for incorporating it as the centerpiece of his new CBS series.[6] A 1939 article in *Radio Guide*, for instance, promising to reveal "more about that man Orson Welles—who invented 'First Person Singular,'" explained that the "technique, admirably suited to radio . . . employed a narrator whose narration is broken by dramatic episodes," adding that "Welles loves to serve as narrator [and] does it on every occasion except when, as with 'Jane Eyre,' the part requires a woman."[7] In an August 1938 interview with the *New York Times*, published at the end of the series' initial run as *First Person Singular* and promoting its fall premiere as the retitled *Mercury Theatre*, Welles described the technique as an "experiment . . . based on a distinct belief that an original treatment of microphone drama is better than the old haphazard method of clinging to a technique designed for the stage." "Broadcast drama," he continued, "must stand on its own feet": "There is nothing that seems more unsuited to the technique of the microphone . . . than to tune in a play and hear an announcer say: 'The curtain is now rising on a presentation of—' and then for him to set the stage, introduce the characters and go on with the play. The curtain is not rising at all, as everybody well knows, and this method . . . seems hopelessly inadequate and clumsy."[8]

His first-person singular technique, he continued, was intended as a less alienating alternative that could better draw the listener into the story, featuring narration by one of the main characters: "When a fellow leans back in his chair and begins, 'Now this is how it happened'—the listener feels that the narrator is taking him into his confidence; he begins to take a personal interest in the outcome." Combined with what he claimed was a more sparing use of music and sound effects, which "are overdone in most radio plays" and "clutter up the action," his first-person technique strove to free radio from the shackles of stage drama and help it take its place "as a new art form."[9]

As Porter notes, mounting criticism of radio's low-brow programming and crass commercialism in the 1930s spurred network investment in "prestige" dramas, repositioning radio as a "writer's theater" that would yield a new "literature of the air."[10] Welles's rejection of established techniques of radio drama worked to set *Mercury* apart as a prestige production, accruing signs of distinction and building career capital for himself as an innovative auteur.[11] This claim to distinction lay in asserting his series' literary qualities, realigning radio drama as an art form that drew on the creative resources of the novel instead of the theater. While his adaptations of classic novels were accessible to a mass audience, he explained that they were especially for "lovers of literature" who held an appreciation for the original works; if "highbrows are still sniffing at [radio]," he continued, this use of literary properties and techniques would win it newfound cultural acceptance as a legitimate writer's medium.[12] As Pierre Bourdieu remarks in his work on the sociology of art, new artists seeking to usurp dominant producers typically do so through rejection of techniques associated with established artists and embrace of techniques that those established artists have themselves rejected.[13] For Welles, the path to autonomy lay not simply in rejecting the theatrical, but in embracing a literary style itself rejected by previous industry authorities as unfit for radio.

Use of the first-person singular style in the opening forty-minute act of "War of the Worlds" is limited to a brief introductory narration by Welles, who in the character of Pierson sets up the scenes of Martian invasion that will consume the remainder of the act. Shuttling the listener rapidly from one narrative location and character perspective to another, this act exemplifies what Neil Verma has called a "kaleidosonic" style that stands in stark contrast to what he labels the more "intimate" aesthetic of the second act, which positions the listener alongside Pierson for its duration and includes extensive passages of first-person narration that offer direct access to his inner thoughts.[14] Replacing the British setting of H. G. Wells's novel with more familiar US landmarks, this act follows Pierson across a postapocalyptic New Jersey countryside and through the Holland Tunnel to the ruins of New York, where he finds the ground littered with dead Martians that have succumbed to human disease.[15] Unlike the radically reworked style of the first act, the second act is remarkably faithful to the original novel, whose story is rendered through the first-person narration of its protagonist and explicitly framed as an act of writing. Following the invasion scenes in book 1 of the novel, the narrator, at the start of book 2, hides out with a curate whom he will shortly sacrifice to the Martians. His shameful act of inhumanity, he explains, is painful to record: "It is disagreeable for me to recall and write these things, but I set them down that my story may lack nothing. Those who have escaped the dark and terrible aspects of life will find my brutality, my flash of rage in our final tragedy, easy enough to blame . . . But those who have been under the shadow, who have gone down at last to elemental things, will have a wider charity."[16]

Act 2 of the radio adaptation is similarly rendered as a written recollection, opening with Welles in the role of Pierson reading from his diary. "As I set these notes on paper," he begins, "I'm obsessed by the thought that I may be the last living man on earth. I have been hiding in this empty house . . . [living a] furtive existence of the lonely derelict who pencils these words on the back of some astronomical notes bearing the signature of Richard Pierson."[17] This narration continues for over five minutes, as Pierson searches for food, leaves the house, encounters a squirrel and several dead cattle, then makes his way slowly to Newark, where he is hailed by a stranger. A dialogue sequence follows, running nearly six minutes, with Pierson then resuming his narration for another four-and-a-half minutes to close out the act. No sound effects are heard throughout this second act, and the only music comes at the closing curtain.

While present-day Welles scholars have disparaged these lengthy first-person sequences as bogging down the broadcast, in his *Handbook of Radio Writing* (1939), veteran dramatist and historian Erik Barnouw argued that the episode's "long unbroken stretches of narration . . . sometimes a page or two long" were typical of Welles's technique and "might occasionally lead to only three or four lines of dialogue" before lapsing back into further narration. Consistent with the goals Welles had laid out for the series in his 1938 interview, this technique, Barnouw explained, "took radio drama far away from the forms of stage and screen drama, and made it resemble much more closely the forms of the novel."[18] What observers today dismiss as uncharacteristically poor writing, in other words, was recognized by Welles's contemporaries as exemplifying the series' signature style, refusing conventional modes of radio dramatization in favor of more literary alternatives. Analysis of successive versions of the script for this episode substantiate this view, indicating an effort not to correct perceived failings of the act's first-person style but to instead further concentrate and actively foreground its literary qualities through a protracted narration sequence that moved the script even closer to the original novel and provided opportunities for an extended star turn by Welles in his role as Pierson.

"War of the Worlds" was only the fourth script that Koch undertook for the series, with the draft written in scarcely two days' time.[19] It is easy, therefore, to blame any perceived failings of the second act on the writer—a tendency exacerbated by anecdotal evidence suggesting Koch's initial draft for the production was less than satisfactory. Drawing on producer John Houseman's memoirs, Schwartz summarizes the run-through of this initial script as an "unmitigated disaster," which Welles condemned as too "dull" to hold listeners' attention and sought to improve by having producers Houseman and Paul Stewart play up the fake news portions.[20] This required, Schwartz explains, trimming the second act to remove the scene with the curate from Wells's novel, leaving the script "somewhat lopsided," with its first act nearly double the length of the second.[21] The implication here is clear: the material in the second act is seen as more dispensable than the first and received less creative attention by the show's senior producers, remaining largely in the state Koch wrote it; faced with an immutable deadline, producers focused their efforts on salvaging Koch's script for the first act, while compressing the second act to minimize the damage.

However, inspection of this earlier draft preserved in Koch's personal papers suggests a different story. The original five-page dialogue sequence between Pierson and the curate effectively splits Pierson's opening narration in half and is replete with sound effects.[22] Beginning with Martians crashing through the house in which the two men hide and narrowly avoid discovery, it then features intermittent "hooting" noises of machines outside of the house that continue under much of the dialogue, the sound of Pierson crawling through debris to peer outside, sounds of a scuffle in which Pierson knocks the hysterical clergyman unconscious, and the subsequent sound of Martian tentacles scraping across the floor and dragging the man's limp body out of the house.[23] The revised script, by contrast, joins the two formerly separate stretches of Pierson's voice-over narration into a continuous monologue, while removing all sounds other than human speech.[24] Were the damage-control hypothesis offered by Schwartz to hold, we might expect the exact opposite strategy, preserving the conflict-heavy scene with the curate and rich use of sound effects consistent with the style of the episode's first act. However, this style, in fact, violates Welles's professed aesthetic commitments to a sonic parsimony that eliminates all but the most essential sound effects and privileges the affective power of first-person narration (a device disrupted and significantly diluted in the initial draft by the scene with the curate). Rather than an unfortunate compromise born of last-minute necessity, the alterations in the second act of "War of the Worlds" suggest a deliberate decision to strip the drama to its barest elements and foreground its first-person style in a manner consistent with the broader *Mercury* series. Scholarly emphasis on the first act of the broadcast may in this sense occlude more than it illuminates, emphasizing the exceptional at the expense of the typical and downplaying qualities of the broadcast that producers themselves sought to amplify.

From a historical perspective, it is these more seemingly prosaic and unremarkable aspects of "War of the Worlds" that prove most vital for understanding not only *Mercury*'s larger series identity but also its place within the broader production culture of Golden Age radio drama. Just as Schwartz notes that the fake news aesthetic of "War of the Worlds" had ample precedent in other programs ranging from *The March of Time* to Archibald MacLeish's *Columbia Workshop* production, "The Fall of the City" (1937), the first-person style was by no means the singular innovation of Welles.[25] Rather, Welles's interventions were part of a broader transformation in dominant production practices that would recuperate first-person narration and voice-over in general as valued tools of radio writing.

CHANGING INDUSTRY ATTITUDES TOWARD AND USES OF VOICE-OVER NARRATION

To place Welles's own interventions within the context of broader shifts in industrial uses and valuation of voice-over narration, I here consider not only changes in period programming but also guidelines set forth in a growing body of radio writing manuals. These texts provided a space for industry members to engage in acts of "industrial self-theorizing," making sense of shifting practices within their profession.[26] As Jay David Bolter and Richard Grusin have observed, new media regularly "remediate" earlier media forms, with producers incorporating familiar techniques but also striving to play up the medium's "newness" and uniqueness.[27] Discussion of voice-over narration in period production manuals reflected this double logic of remediation, acknowledging the value of techniques with proven success in other media but revealing anxieties over their appropriateness for radio. While manuals at the start of the decade expressed suspicion of voice-over narration as a technique tied too closely to the "old" medium of the novel, manuals from the late 1930s and 1940s marked a shift to more permissive attitudes. Consistently praised for his demonstrations of voice-over's aesthetic viability for radio and the value of first-person narration, in particular, Welles was one of several radio dramatists to pursue these formerly taboo devices, which were soon in regular use across a wide range of programming genres.

Initial suspicions of voice-over narration were frequently lodged within larger discourses of medium specificity promulgated by workers struggling to legitimate their craft and ensure their industry's long-term success.[28] One of the decade's first published guidebooks was a volume by NBC producers Katharine Seymour and John Martin titled *How to Write for Radio* (1931), which devoted a full chapter to the subject of adaptations.[29] While noting that adaptations were an important programming staple, the authors warned that they were also a risky endeavor for the radio writer, who had to find equivalent expressive resources in his own medium to match those of other media. Radio drama, they insisted, was by necessity much faster paced than other forms of storytelling. "From the end of the opening announcement to the beginning of the closing announcement," they explained, "radio drama must *move*," avoiding any slow spots or scenes that did not directly contribute to "advancing the action or developing the characters." For this reason, they continued, "explanations of time changes [and] changes of setting . . . must be kept short" and used sparingly.[30] Unlike literature, in radio "there will be no fine descriptive passages to relieve the monotony of the working out of a hackneyed plot, no rhythm or music of words and phrases to make up for the lack of action, of real character development in a long scene."[31] In conclusion, they advised, "[when] adapting printed fiction to radio, a complete transformation must be brought about," as the expressive demands and resources of the medium were wholly distinct from those of the novel or short story.[32]

Some writing guides continued to echo these cautions against the use of literary devices through the end of the decade, but others adopted a more accepting stance and singled out the work of Welles and others for special praise. On the conservative end of the spectrum lay CBS director Max Wylie, whose widely read *Radio Writing* (1939) addressed both third-person and first-person narration, advising aspiring writers to steer well clear of these techniques. Third-person narration during scene changes and other transitional moments, he conceded, could prove tempting, "as much ground can be got over and got over quickly," but "its single disadvantage is so disturbing that it makes a very debatable issue of the whole thing," disrupting the narrative and destroying "continuity of illusion."[33] First-person narration, or "monologue," was similarly problematic, "giv[ing] away the author and show[ing] him as having stumbled into a quagmire that is the result of bad leakage in his structural plan. . . . The listener's illusion evaporates instantly."[34] Especially problematic in this regard, he warned, was "the one-man story," which "takes place substantially within a man's mind." While effective in print, "here is the radio problem in all stories of this nature: to whom is the man going to talk?"[35] For third-person narration, Wylie recommended the writer simply "do your narrating at the beginning and be done with it," while character monologue was to be avoided in all but the most exceptional of cases and an interlocutor added wherever possible.[36]

If Wylie remained suspicious of literary techniques, Barnouw was more accepting and pointed to Welles's role, among others, in proving voice-over's viability for broadcast drama. In his *Handbook of Radio Writing* (1939), Barnouw explained that the figure of the narrator was initially regarded as "merely an evil makeshift," with writers "only gradually . . . realiz[ing] that narration might become to radio as valuable and flexible a tool as to the printed page."[37] This discovery, he continued, owed much to the work of Welles.[38] Repeating this point in an introduction to one of Welles's scripts in his subsequent volume, *Radio Drama in Action* (1945), he explained that the *Mercury* series was perhaps Welles's best-known work, remembered by most "because of the Martian invasion" in "War of the Worlds," but was "far more important in its general impact on radio writing," having proven narration's value for broadcast drama.[39] "Welles gave a series of brilliant demonstrations of what could be done with the [first-person singular] device—and with narrators in general." "In the field of adaptations," he concluded, "radio had . . . looked mostly to the stage for material," but Welles "made clear that the novel was a far richer source."[40] If Wylie continued to eye the use of literary techniques with caution, Barnouw embraced them as a source of welcome innovation, highlighting Welles's work, in particular, as a demonstration of their efficacy for radio drama.

However, Welles was not the only innovator in this area, with successive editions of Barnouw's *Handbook* documenting an increasingly

diverse range of voice-over techniques across a variety of genres. Alongside Welles's contributions, Barnouw's 1939 manual highlighted three
additional techniques: (1) stream-of-consciousness narration used by
NBC dramatist Arch Oboler, (2) inclusion in programs such as *Tom
Mix* (1933–50) and *Death Valley Days* (1930–51) of a "proxy listener" who
"represents the listening audience" and prompts the narrator for further
information, and (3) "split narration" handed off from one character to
another, in a kind of "vocal relay race" seen most prominently in work
by *Columbia Workshop* director Norman Corwin. These innovations,
he explained, "banish[ed] completely the cumbersome expositions of
old-time drama."[41] Addressing the continued development of voice-
over techniques in the 1940s, Barnouw's revised, second edition of his
Handbook (1947) preserved his earlier sections on the proxy listener and
split narration, then organized the remaining methods into categories
of first-, second-, and third-person narration. First-person narration, he
explained, included established techniques such as stream of consciousness and Welles's style, plus newer devices that ranged from characters
reading diaries and personal letters to addressing a jury or delivering
a deathbed confession.[42] Second-person narration, although rare, had
been used to good effect in several CBS sustaining series to create a
sense of "exceptional immediacy," drawing listeners into the story and
making them feel part of the action, while writers pursuing third-person
narration now favored "characterized" narrators (whether fictional characters or "actual person[s]," such as public officials) who could better
engage the audience than the anonymous, "uncharacterized" narrator
of earlier dramas.[43] Despite these innovations, Barnouw's 1947 edition
noted lingering "prejudice against narration" in some quarters, but his
third, 1949 edition declared the debate finally closed: thanks to the work
of Welles and others, "The device of the narrator [now] fits radio almost
as naturally as it fits the printed page."[44]

Barnouw's emphasis on the contributions of auteurist producers
associated with prestige anthology series was in part a prescriptive strategy, promoting work he felt exemplified best practices in radio writing;
however, this emphasis also reflected the real historical trajectory of
first-person narration, which was initially adopted by a small cadre of anthology writers in the late 1930s, then gradually moved into more popular

genres during the 1940s and 1950s. Prior to Welles's own experiments with first-person narration, MacLeish had embraced the technique in his *Columbia Workshop* production, "The Fall of the City," featuring an intradiegetic narrator (played by Welles himself) whose first-person plural address helped to place the listener alongside him within the play's narrative world.[45] Norman Corwin also incorporated single-character monologue in his own *Columbia Workshop* productions, with his "Soliloquy to Balance the Budget" (1941) representing by far his most sustained use of the device. A one-man show starring House Jameson in the role of the Soliloquist, the production moved breathlessly between direct, second-person address (Jameson hailing his audience with lines such as, "Well—can you take it, Listener") and competing modes of first-person narration (from musings on human mortality delivered in first-person singular to a guided tour in first-person plural that positioned the listener alongside the Soliloquist as he moved past exotic statues in yawning catacombs).[46] Oboler's experiments with stream of consciousness narration, for their part, included productions ranging from prestige dramas such as NBC's *Arch Oboler's Plays* (1939–40) and *Everyman's Theatre* (1940–41) to the popular thriller, *Lights Out* (1934–47), while CBS's own thriller series, *Suspense* (1942–62), also made extensive use of the technique to expose the deranged psyches of protagonists from Agnes Moorehead's hysterical murder victim in "Sorry, Wrong Number" (1943) to confirmed criminals and other social misfits.[47]

A crucial component of Welles's first-person singular style was its shifts between more subjective sequences with internal monologue narrated in the past tense (from a position several years in the future) and action sequences allowing the listener to bear direct witness to those events unfolding in the present. This device figures prominently in most *Mercury* productions, including "War of the Worlds," which moves from Pierson's first-person singular narration at the start of the second act to the present-tense dramatization of Pierson's encounter with the stranger, then back to past tense, first-person narration to close the act. This same technique was deployed by Oboler in his debut radio production, "Ugliest Man in the World" (1939), which used extensive sequences of stream of consciousness narration to communicate protagonist Paul Martin's recollections of traumatic childhood scenes with his mother;

lines delivered in past tense as Paul thinks to himself, "How old was I? Nine or ten? She kept me home away from the others," segue into present-tense dramatizations of the recollected events.[48] As Verma notes, although such action sequences seemingly offer more objective modes of storytelling than the character's subjective internal monologue, they typically continue to align listeners' experiences of events with the main character through microphone positioning (what Verma calls "audio-position"), encouraging sustained and in-depth identification with the protagonist.[49]

While initially limited to the experimental dramas of auteurist producers such as Welles and Oboler, by the late 1940s and 1950s these techniques were in widespread use across a diverse range of popular programming genres. CBS's *Suspense*, for instance, regularly moved between first-person singular narration delivered in past tense to present-tense stream-of-consciousness narration. "The Yellow Wallpaper" (1948), for example, starring Agnes Moorehead as a mentally unhinged heroine who is convinced a woman is hiding in her wallpaper, slips fluidly from one mode of narration to the next with lines such as, "I'd locked the door and thrown the key down into the front path. I don't want anyone to come in. . . . If the woman gets out from behind the pattern. . . . There! There she is!"[50] While police shows of the 1930s such as CBS's *Gangbusters* relied on third-person narration by a "characterized" narrator such as local or federal law enforcement officials, shows like NBC's *Dragnet*, in the 1940s and 1950s, increasingly abandoned this style in favor of first-person narration by their protagonists.[51] This technique was a defining characteristic of the noir genre, as well. Detective shows like *Adventures of Philip Marlowe* (1947–51) and *Barrie Craig, Confidential Investigator* (NBC, 1951–55) adopted the familiar Wellesian approach, moving between first-person singular narration by the main character in past tense to present-tense action sequences and back again, while *The Adventures of Sam Spade* (ABC, 1946; CBS, 1946–49; NBC, 1949–51) and *Yours Truly, Johnny Dollar* (CBS, 1949–62) employed the personal letter device, framing their first-person narration as dictated accounts of newly completed cases. By the 1950s, first-person narration had even crept into radio Westerns, such as *The Six Shooter* (NBC, 1953–54) and *Frontier Gentleman* (CBS, 1958), which moved in the same manner as *Mercury* productions two decades before, from first-person singular narration in the past tense to present-tense dramatizations.

If emphasizing the fake news aesthetic in the first act of "War of the Worlds" risks favoring the exceptional at the expense of the typical, analysis of Welles's first-person singular style in this and other *Mercury* broadcasts should not treat the technique in isolation but rather connect it to the larger production culture of which it was a part. Often regarded as its chief innovator, Welles was in fact one of a growing number of radio producers to explore the possibilities of first-person narration in the late 1930s, which by the late 1940s and 1950s had gained widespread acceptance as a valued tool of Golden Age radio drama.

CONCLUSION: AUTHOR STUDIES AND INDUSTRIAL CONTEXT

While best remembered for the fake news aesthetic in its celebrated first act, it was the first-person singular style in the neglected second act of "War of the Worlds," I have argued, that marked it as a *Mercury* production. Recovering the dynamics of the first-person style in this and other Welles productions restores a lost balance in scholarship on his radio work, while also opening pathways for understanding its migration across media into subsequent film works such as *Citizen Kane* (1941) and *Lady from Shanghai* (1947).[52] At the same time, I have argued that these techniques were not exclusively Wellesian innovations, to which end Welles scholarship must look beyond Welles himself to consider the larger production culture in which he operated. Author-oriented studies may in this manner be enriched through a project of what David Bordwell describes as "historical poetics," addressing "the principles according to which [texts] are constructed" and reasons "these principles [have] arisen and changed in particular empirical circumstances."[53] While these principles may be reverse-engineered from programs themselves, they were also the subject of frequent and explicit discussion by producers in promotional texts surrounding those broadcasts, and in production literature aimed at guiding the aesthetic choices of creative agents. Strategically decentering Welles, I have sought to call these other voices into presence, locating the techniques he espoused within a much broader shift in and reevaluation of dominant aesthetic norms for Golden Age radio broadcasting. Treating techniques of voice-over narration not only at the level of individual innovators but also at this larger systems level helps us understand the industrial rationales for and conditions in which resulting radio styles could gain currency—appreciating, in other words, both the extent of Welles's own influence on radio technique and reasons that the style he popularized successfully spread throughout the industry, instead of falling on deaf ears. Production studies in this sense offer an important complement to author studies, placing the actions of individual creators in relation to the broader industrial contexts of which they were a part and into which they sought to actively intervene.

SHAWN VANCOUR is assistant professor of Media Archival Studies in the Department of Information Studies at University of California, Los Angeles. He is author of *Making Radio: Early Radio Production and the Rise of Modern Sound Culture.*

NOTES

For earlier thoughts on some of the issues addressed in this essay, see Shawn Van-Cour, "A Hard Act to Follow: War of the Worlds and the Challenges of Literary Ad-aptation," *Antenna: Responses to Media and Culture,* October 14, 2013, http://blog .commarts.wisc.edu/2013/10/14/from-mercury-to-mars-a-hard-act-to-follow-war -of-the-worlds-and-the-challenges-of-literary-adaptation-2/.

    1. Hadley Cantril, *The Invasion from Mars: A Study in the Psychology of Panic* (Princeton, NJ: Princeton University Press, 1940); Howard Koch, *The Panic Broadcast: The Whole Story of Orson Welles' Legendary Radio Show, Invasion from Mars* (New York: Avon Books, 1970); Alan Gallop, *The Martians Are Coming! The True Story of Orson Welles's 1938 Panic Broadcast* (Gloucestershire, UK: Amberly, 2012); John Gosling, *Waging the War of the Worlds: A History of the 1938 Radio Broadcast and Resulting Panic* (Jefferson, NC: McFarland, 2009); A. Brad Schwartz, *Broadcast Hysteria: Orson Welles's War of the Worlds and the Art of Fake News* (New York: Hill & Wang, 2015); Joy Elizabeth Hayes, Kathleen Battles, and Wendy Hilton-Morrow, eds., *War of the Worlds to Social Media: Mediated Communication in Times of Crisis* (New York: Peter Lang, 2013).

    2. For a full discussion of Welles's radio career, see Paul Heyer, *The Medium and the Magician: Orson Welles, The Radio Years, 1934–1952* (New York: Rowman & Lit-tlefield, 2005). As Heyer explains, despite his growing success in the theater, much of Welles's early radio work was uncredited, with *First Person Singular* and *Mercury*

Theatre on the Air being the first programs specifically crafted as Welles vehicles to capitalize on his growing reputation (Heyer, 46–47).

3. James Naremore, *The Magic World of Orson Welles*, rev. ed. (Urbana: University of Illinois Press, 2015), 31, 10.

4. Paul Heyer, "America Under Attack I: A Reassessment of Orson Welles' 1938 *War of the Worlds* Broadcast," *Canadian Journal of Communication* 28, no. 2 (2003): 158; Schwartz, *Broadcast Hysteria*, 49.

5. Jeff Porter, *Lost Sound: The Forgotten Art of Radio Storytelling* (Chapel Hill: University of North Carolina Press, 2016), 63, 73–82.

6. *Les Misérables* aired over the Mutual Broadcasting Systems in seven installments on Friday evenings from July 23 to September 3, 1937.

7. Francis Chase, Jr., "He Scared Us to Death!," *Radio Guide*, October 20, 1939, 9.

8. Orson Welles, quoted in Richard O'Brien, "'The Shadow' Talks," *New York Times*, August 14, 1938, reprinted in *Orson Welles: Interviews*, ed. Mark Estrin (Jackson: University of Mississippi Press, 2002), 3–4.

9. Quoted in O'Brien, "'The Shadow' Talks," 4–5.

10. Porter, *Lost Sound*, 37–61.

11. On the importance of interviews and promotional texts for building career capital, see John Thornton Caldwell, *Production Culture: Industrial Reflexivity and Critical Practice in Film and Television* (Durham, NC: Duke University Press, 2008), 3, 37–58.

12. Quoted in O'Brien, "'The Shadow' Talks," 5.

13. Pierre Bourdieu, *The Rules of Art: Genesis and Structure of the Literary Field*, trans. Susan Emanuel (Stanford, CA: Stanford University Press, 1996), 160.

14. Neil Verma, *Theater of the Mind: Imagination, Aesthetics, and American Radio Drama* (Chicago: University of Chicago Press, 2012), 63–68.

15. The original publication of Wells's novel was in serialized form for *Pearson's Magazine* in 1897, with the completed story then published as a full novel the following year; H. G. Wells, *The War of the Worlds* (London: William Heinemann, 1898). For the present essay, I use the World Library Classics edition (Franklin Park, IL: J. S. Paluch, 2009).

16. Wells, *War of the Worlds*, 102.

17. "War of the Worlds," *Mercury Theatre on the Air*, directed by Orson Welles, original airing October 30, 1938 (New York: Columbia Broadcasting System, 1938).

18. Erik Barnouw, *Handbook of Radio Writing: An Outline of Techniques and Markets in Radio Writing in the United States* (Boston: Little, Brown & Co., 1939), 22.

19. Koch's first *Mercury* script was for the October 9, 1938 broadcast of "Hell on Ice," which was followed by a broadcast of "Seventeen" on October 16 and "Around the World in Eighty Days" on October 23. For a discussion of these early Koch scripts, see Heyer, *The Medium and the Magician*, 68–71. On the timetable for Koch's initial draft, see Koch, *The Panic Broadcast*, 13, and John Houseman, *Run-Through: A Memoir* (New York: Simon & Schuster, 1972), 393.

20. Schwartz, *Broadcast Hysteria*, 58–59. For Houseman's account, see Houseman, *Run-Through*, 393.

21. Schwartz, *Broadcast Hysteria*, 59 and 254, n. 98.

22. Additional sound effects are indicated for the closing scene, which specifies the inclusion of "The unearthly howl of the Martians: 'Ulla Ulla Ulla' at first distant and then nearer" as Pierson approaches New York; "Working Script," 44, Howard E. Koch Papers, box 1, folder 3, Wisconsin Historical Society, Madison, Wisconsin. However, this was cut by CBS censors, who found the effects "too terrifying" for the network's general prime-time listenership; see Frank Brady, *Citizen Welles: A Biography of Orson Welles* (New York: Creative Publishing, 2015), 163.

23. "Working Script," Koch Papers, box 1, folder 3, Wisconsin Historical Society; for crashes, see p. 31; hooting, 33; crawling, 34; scuffle and scraping, 35.

24. "Final Script," 32–35, Koch Papers, box 1, folder 2, Wisconsin Historical Society. Koch donated both a "Working Script" and "Final Script" for the broadcast (box 1, folders 3 and 2, respectively). Thanks to Brad Schwartz for his assistance in locating these materials, and to Jennifer Wang for her help in procuring them.

25. See Schwartz, *Broadcast Hysteria*, 20–32 (for *March of Time*) and 36–37 (for "Fall of the City").

26. Caldwell, *Production Culture*, 346–47.

27. Jay David Bolter and Richard Grusin, *Remediation: Understanding New Media* (Cambridge, MA: MIT Press, 2000), 3–15.

28. For a sustained discussion of medium specificity and its role in modern theories of art, see Noël E. Carroll, *Philosophical Problems of Classical Film Theory* (Princeton, NJ: Princeton University Press, 1988).

29. Katharine Seymour and J. T. W. Martin, *How to Write for Radio* (New York: Longmans, Green, 1931), 154–67.

30. Seymour and Martin, *How to Write for Radio*, 162–64; emphasis in original.

31. Seymour and Martin, *How to Write for Radio*, 164.

32. Seymour and Martin, *How to Write for Radio*, 164.

33. Max Wylie, *Radio Writing* (New York: Farrar & Rinehart, 1939), 72–73.

34. Wylie, *Radio Writing*, 37.

35. Wylie, *Radio Writing*, 219.

36. Wylie, *Radio Writing*, 72–73 (for dispensing with narration at beginning), 219 (for inclusion of an interlocutor).

37. Barnouw, *Handbook of Radio Writing* (1939), 21.

38. Barnouw, *Handbook of Radio Writing* (1939), 22.

39. Erik Barnouw, ed., *Radio Drama in Action: Twenty-Five Plays of a Changing World* (New York: Farrar & Rinehart, 1945), 2.

40. Barnouw, *Radio Drama in Action*, 2–3.

41. Barnouw, *Handbook of Radio Writing* (1939), 50–55.

42. Barnouw, *Handbook of Radio Writing* (1947), 64–66.

43. Barnouw, *Handbook of Radio Writing* (1947), 66–68.

44. Barnouw, *Handbook of Radio Writing* (1947), 57, and Erik Barnouw, *Handbook of Radio Production: An Outline of Studio Techniques and Procedures in the United States* (Boston: Little, Brown, 1949), 13.

45. "The Fall of the City," *Columbia Workshop*, directed by Archibald MacLeish, original broadcast April 11, 1937 (New York: CBS, 1937). On the episode's use of an intradiegetic narrator, see Verma, *Theater of the Mind*, 50–51.

46. "Soliloquy to Balance the Budget," *Columbia Workshop: Twenty-Six by Corwin*, directed by Norman Corwin, original broadcast June 15, 1941 (New York: CBS, 1941).

47. "Sorry, Wrong Number," *Suspense*, directed by Norman MacDonald, May 25, 1943 (New York: CBS, 1943). For further discussion of this and related *Suspense* broadcasts, see Allison McCracken, "Scary Women and Scarred Men: *Suspense*, Gender Trouble, and Postwar Change, 1942–1950," in *Radio Reader: Essays in the Cultural History of Radio*, ed. Michele Hilmes and Jason Loviglio (New York: Routledge, 2002), 183–207, and Neil Verma, "Honeymoon Shocker: Lucille Fletcher's 'Psychological' Sound Effects and Wartime Radio Drama," *Journal of American Studies* 44, no. 1 (2010): 137–53.

48. "The Ugliest Man in the World," *Arch Oboler's Plays*, directed by Arch Oboler, original broadcast March 25, 1939 (New York: NBC, 1939). Script available at The Generic Radio Workshop, *Vintage Radio Script Library*, accessed May 14, 2016, http://www.genericradio.com/.

49. Verma, *Theater of the Mind*, 61.

50. "The Yellow Wallpaper," *Suspense*, directed by Anton Leader, original broadcast July 29, 1948 (New York: CBS, 1948). The play was adapted by Sylvia Richards from the 1892 short story by Charlotte Perkins Gilman, which, like the radio version, is narrated in first person by the story's heroine.

51. Despite their use of first-person narration, as J. Fred MacDonald notes, shows like *Dragnet* did not encourage as strong an identification with their protagonists, who were a generally unlikeable "group of disillusioned, embittered men who reluctantly went about their professions"; see *Don't Touch That Dial! Radio Programming in American Life from 1920–1960* (Chicago: Nelson-Hall, 1979), 183.

52. *Citizen Kane*, directed by Orson Welles (RKO Pictures, 1941) and *Lady from Shanghai*, directed by Orson Welles (Columbia Pictures, 1947). Rick Altman has attempted to explore intermedial affinities in Welles's radio and film productions but focuses chiefly on microphone distance; see Rick Altman, "Deep-Focus Sound: *Citizen Kane* and the Radio Aesthetic," *Quarterly Review of Film and Video* 15, no. 3 (1994): 1–33. Robert Spadoni takes up the use of first-person narration in Welles's aborted *Heart of Darkness* film for RKO but focuses on efforts to translate the style into visual terms through point of view shots, ignoring the more straightforward incorporation of the technique through voice-over narration; see Robert Spadoni, "The Seeing Ear: The Presence of Radio in Orson Welles's *Heart of Darkness*," in *Conrad on Film*, ed. Gene Moore (Cambridge, UK: Cambridge University Press, 1997), 78–92.

53. David Bordwell, "Historical Poetics of Cinema," in *The Cinematic Text: Methods and Approaches*, ed. R. Barton Palmer (New York: AMS Press, 1989), 371.

3

OLD-TIME MOVIES
Welles and Silent Pictures

MATTHEW SOLOMON

On July 22, 1939, Orson Welles signed the two-picture contract with RKO that would eventually result in the production of *Citizen Kane* (1941) and the release of a severely truncated *The Magnificent Ambersons* (1942).[1] But before the first of these two films was undertaken, Welles explored a number of other possible projects. In the six months after signing with RKO, Welles made considerable progress on film adaptations of two novels, Joseph Conrad's *Heart of Darkness* and Nicholas Blake's *The Smiler with the Knife*. Though neither was produced, each of these two projects generated a critical mass of preproduction documents.[2] What does not seem to have survived from this period, however, are any traces of an unproduced film project about silent filmmaking that Welles mentioned many years later during the course of an extended interview by Peter Bogdanovich, which was published in thoroughly revised and greatly abbreviated form as the book *This is Orson Welles*, edited by Jonathan Rosenbaum.[3]

"When I first came to Hollywood," Welles is paraphrased as saying in the version of the interview published in the book, "I wanted to make a movie about the great days of the silents." He was inspired by meeting a number of directors who had made silent films: "They weren't all of them so old then, of course—but at that epoch they looked a bit old-timey to me."[4] This must have been around the time of an August 4, 1939, letter to his wife Virginia Nicolson in which Welles wrote: "The old fashioned movie people who grew up with the industry and who know what makes a picture move on the screen are all very nice."[5] A few days later, Welles was quoted in the *Los Angeles Times* praising the timeless appeal of silent cinema: "It would be well, incidentally, if we had some silent films from time to time. That form was great in itself."[6] He appears to have begun to nurture an interest in film history: "After I came out to Hollywood," Welles told Bogdanovich, "I began to read movie books."[7]

Welles's arrival in Hollywood coincided with a surge of popular interest in film history that preceded the celebration of American cinema's fiftieth birthday during the second week of October 1939. According to film historian Terry Ramsaye, Thomas A. Edison's first successful motion picture demonstration took place on October 6, 1889.[8] Though few subsequent film histories have corroborated that specific date, in 1939, the American film industry "observed its Golden Jubilee, officially commemorating the 50th anniversary of the Kinetoscope of Thomas A. Edison."[9] According to the *Motion Picture Herald*, "Film exchanges were overwhelmed with orders for old time pictures . . . while 'Old Time Movie Parties' were held in many theatres . . . with old silent pictures, with slides, a piano player, or song plugger, forming part of the show."[10] The commemoration of this anniversary made the film that Welles considered making about silent filmmaking somewhat timely.

Just a few months earlier, the July 1939 installment of *The March of Time* newsreel had been entirely devoted to film history. The two-reel "The Movies March On!" provides a brisk audiovisual account of the history of American cinema, bracketed by shots of Museum of Modern Art Film Library director John Evans Abbott and curator Iris Barry seated in a darkened movie theater and illuminated by the light of a film projector—shots that anticipate the newsreel projection room scene in *Citizen Kane*. Much of the rest of "The Movies March On!" is made up of excerpts from a dozen silent films accompanied by music, sound effects, and authoritatively delivered explanatory narration by Westbrook Van Voorhis. He notes, "So young is Hollywood that many of its earliest pioneers are still active in the industry," as successive shots show D. W. Griffith and Hal Roach "back in the studios" at work on the film *One*

Million B.C., then Buster Keaton and Mack Sennett "at work again" on the film *Hollywood Cavalcade*, both of which were forthcoming, and then a shot of "RKO's President, capable George Schaefer" seated at his desk, Van Voorhis explains, "meeting the growing demand for important drama."[11]

Welles never did make a film about the days of silent movies, although he told Bogdanovich, "I love movie stories; they're my favorite thing."[12] He may not have gotten very far with the project in 1939. Welles's biographers make no mention of him working on a story of silent-era filmmaking. Nor does Marguerite H. Rippy allude to it in her study of what she terms "the unfinished RKO projects."[13] To my knowledge, no other comment on it appears elsewhere. Unlike a plethora of other film projects that Welles began but never completed, not even a provisional title survives for this story about silent movies.

This chapter uses Welles's aborted project about silent-era filmmaking as the point of departure for considering how Welles engaged with silent cinema during his career. While Welles wrote many scripts that were never ultimately realized, he also came up with ideas for many more film projects that remained more or less hypothetical. Some of these hypothetical projects may have left no material traces not so much because they were unfinished but because they were not started. Although imagined by Welles, many of these hypothetical films were not even attempted. While Welles's death left his dozens of unrealized and incomplete films perpetually suspended in the future tense, so to speak, his many more hypothetical films have existed mainly, if not entirely, in the subjunctive. These include a film about silent moviemaking and another, somewhat closely related, idea for "a whole movie about" Charlie Chaplin's unconsummated romance with fellow silent film star Pola Negri.[14]

I have drawn much from what Welles said about silent movies during the course of a long interview by Peter Bogdanovich, while supplementing the transcription of their discussions of silent films and filmmakers with quotations from the filmed introductions Welles made for *The Silent Years*, a series of silent feature films broadcast on American public television stations during the early 1970s. Cinematographer Gary Graver shot a dozen introductions (as well as a number of brief filmed epilogues) with Welles, who typically speaks to the camera directly in close-up shot against a red background, often while smoking a cigar. According to Graver, the various segments were filmed in a "very small soundproofed recording studio in London . . . in about three days."[15] All of the films broadcast in the series were American feature films drawn from the collection of Paul Killiam.[16] All but one, *Intolerance*, dated from the 1920s. Welles's remarks are seemingly improvised, highly anecdotal, and often quite personal, but his discussion of silent film actors and his comments about silent cinema in *The Silent Years* serve as a useful complement to the parts of his conversation with Bogdanovich that turned to the silent screen.

When it came to silent cinema, Welles "was much more interested in movie actors than in movies or movie directing," he told Bogdanovich, claiming, "It was just the great kind of vehicle for star personalities."[17] Thus, in a number of introductions for *The Silent Years* broadcasts, Welles recounts lively stories of 1920s silent film stars like Rudolph Valentino, Douglas Fairbanks, Buster Keaton, John Barrymore, and W. C. Fields, many of whom he met, and nearly all of whom he claims to have remembered. Welles's first-person accounts of these stars of the silent screen suggest the mystique that certain silent films evidently had for him.

"AN AFFECTIONATE KIND OF MOCKERY"

Welles never made a film about the silent period, but he did make several silent films. Among the earliest was *The Hearts of Age*, the silent 16mm short that Welles filmed with several classmates at the Todd School in Woodstock, Illinois, in 1934.[18] Welles, who appears in the film in grotesque expressionist make-up, is quoted in *This is Orson Welles* calling it a "put on," a "send-up" of films "considered . . . great," namely *The Cabinet of Dr. Caligari*, "the cinéaste's dream picture. . . . You saw it every time you went to New York."[19] By the mid-1930s, the Museum of Modern Art was one of few places where silent films were still screened. There, selected silent films were treated as museum objects worthy of historical study and as sources of aesthetic edification.[20]

Welles had no such pretensions, telling Bogdanovich with dismay about a Greenwich Village screening of *Citizen Kane* at which "a packed audience . . . sat in there in reverent silence as though they were in church" despite "all these jokes in it."[21] Welles was skeptical of "art cinema," whether silent or sound, and his taste in silent films was decidedly popular.[22] Welles's appropriations of silent cinema emphasized the humor that contemporaneous audiences could derive from the archaic idioms of silent films without deriding the medium itself. Thus, Welles's appropriations of silent cinema are strikingly different from *Flicker Flashbacks*, the series of short subjects RKO produced beginning in 1943. In an installment of *Flicker Flashbacks* found in the David Bradley Collection at Indiana University, part of a silent short starring Snub Pollard that appears to be from the 1910s is accompanied by sarcastic running commentary on the action of the film and the actors (and rote readings of the intertitles) in a voice-over that is regularly punctuated by the commentator's cackling laughter.[23]

Welles made a number of silent films that were meant to be projected as part of his live theatrical productions of *Too Much Johnson* in 1938 and *Around the World* in 1946. These films were shot in a deliberately anachronistic style that evoked cinema of the 1910s. Welles's allusions to silent cinema tend to refer to films released before he was born in 1915 or while he was still too young to have been taken to a movie theater. Welles told Bill Krohn: "The directors . . . whom I admire, have in my view spent too much time in their childhood at the movies. They're all to[o] fascinated with whatever period represented their childhood in the movie theatre."[24] Welles himself, by contrast, seems to have been especially fascinated by films from the period immediately before he remembered starting to watch movies.

Writing in the 1960s, Seymour Stern contended that sometime after World War II, the "distinction . . . in the public mind between the earlier silent-film period of 1915 . . . and the later one of 1928" had ceased to exist. "All silent films had been relegated well before 1950 to the limbo of an archaic, if not a dead, art. To the so-called average patron of the filmhouses, . . . [they were all] 'just old silent movies,' and the once important chronological separation . . . was buried."[25] During the late 1930s and early 1940s, however, when Welles became re-interested in silent cinema, this distinction was still operative and at least partly recognizable to the general public. Welles borrowed selected characteristic elements of 1910s cinema—including slapstick performance, the iris, and a flickering effect—precisely because those distinctive tropes gave his silent movies the archaic quality of a dead art.

This was the era, Welles recalled, when movies were "picture shows" and movie actors were "photo-players." The thought of these outmoded terms delighted Welles, but when Bogdanovich interrupted him with what he believed was a comparable example from a 1929 movie magazine, Welles cut him short: "Yeah, well that's not so long ago but 1915 is when it's funny."[26] In his films and theatrical productions of the 1930s and 1940s, Welles mobilized what he imagined American cinema of the 1910s looked like to conjure up a time that appeared disproportionately dated yet was not too far into the past. Just as the "old fashioned movie people who grew up with the industry" that Welles met after moving to Los Angeles—King Vidor, John Ford, Frank Capra, Victor Fleming, Lewis Milestone, and W. S. Van Dyke among them—seemed "a bit old-timey" to him, so too did the films they made in the 1910s.[27] Just twenty years later, these films looked "old-timey," meaning "out of date . . . something that is old-fashioned."[28]

For Welles and his audiences, films made before the institutionalization of the Hollywood style in the mid-1910s represented an especially striking visual anachronism. Welles represented this anachronism through largely obsolete modes of performance, cinematic transition, and film projection. Welles's consistent choice to allude to films of the 1910s creates a disproportionately greater effect of historical displacement while also invoking humor. Welles explained: "I think people always look back on things with that—Americans tend to look back on the immediate past or fairly near past . . . the past that isn't historical but is still in dim memory as being faintly comic. It's an American attitude toward the past . . . quaint and somewhat comical and yet it's an affectionate kind of mockery."[29]

Welles's affectionate mockery of silent cinema is manifest in the films he made to be screened as part of his live theatrical production of *Too Much Johnson*, which he described as "an imitation silent comedy done . . . with subtitles and everything . . . with a great chase over the roofs of the chicken market in New York."[30] Ultimately, Welles did not screen these films in his production of the play—much less edit them into coherent segments or add intertitles. He acknowledged that the films "make

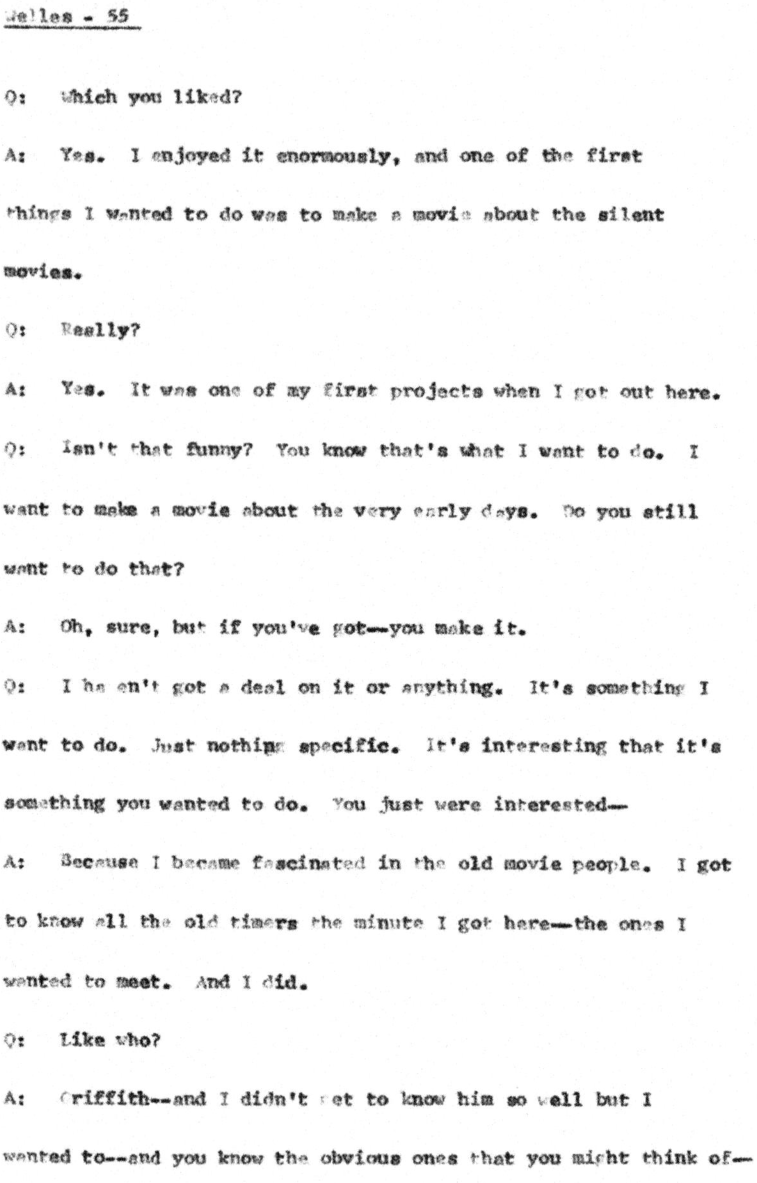

Q: Which you liked?

A: Yes. I enjoyed it enormously, and one of the first things I wanted to do was to make a movie about the silent movies.

Q: Really?

A: Yes. It was one of my first projects when I got out here.

Q: Isn't that funny? You know that's what I want to do. I want to make a movie about the very early days. Do you still want to do that?

A: Oh, sure, but if you've got—you make it.

Q: I hasn't got a deal on it or anything. It's something I want to do. Just nothing specific. It's interesting that it's something you wanted to do. You just were interested—

A: Because I became fascinated in the old movie people. I got to know all the old timers the minute I got here—the ones I wanted to meet. And I did.

Q: Like who?

A: Griffith—and I didn't get to know him so well but I wanted to—and you know the obvious ones that you might think of—

Figure 3.1. Welles-Bogdanovich interview transcription, box 1, folder 1, p. 55, Richard Wilson-Orson Welles Papers, University of Michigan Library (Special Collections Library).

no sense without the play after."[31] But the recently rediscovered footage (which includes numerous outtakes) shows actors Joseph Cotten, Arlene Francis, and Edgar Barrier performing exaggerated parodies of silent film acting. Joseph McBride describes these films as a "sophisticated . . . pastiching [of] bygone film style," noting that "the comical elaboration of gesture by the actors . . . helps add to the sense of a knowing and loving pastiche rather than an ignorant mockery." McBride concludes, "Welles loves the silent medium, just as he loves the old costumes, cars, ships, horses, and buildings he films."[32] The imitation silent movies that Welles shot for *Too Much Johnson* parody acting styles that continue to be misjudged as unnaturally excessive, even "inappropriate" by the standards of more recent, more rigidly naturalistic, standards of screen acting.[33]

A HYPOTHETICAL "MOVIE ABOUT THE SILENT MOVIES"

One year after *Too Much Johnson*, Welles appears to have returned to silent movies with a hypothetical film about silent-era moviemaking. Glossed in just four lines in *This is Orson Welles*, the interview transcription on which the book was based (fig. 3.1) supplies crucial context and additional detail about the project. To begin with, Welles described the project as having been about "the silent movies"—not, as it was paraphrased editorially, "the great days of the silents." Partially excerpted below, the full transcription of this part of Welles and Bogdanovich's conversation takes up two full typewritten pages, but it is rendered in only four sentences in *This is Orson Welles*. Much was omitted, some of what was retained was altered, and the context for the exchange was changed altogether. In conversation with Bogdanovich, Welles related this unrealized project both to his initial arrival in Hollywood as well as to his eventual production of *Citizen Kane*:

> And it was the golden days still—there was a sort of a glitter of the old nonsensical circus Hollywood left. It was very amusing. . . . I enjoyed it enormously, and one of the first things I wanted to do was to make a movie about the silent movies. . . . It was one of my first projects when I got out here. . . . Because I became fascinated in the old movie people. I got to know all the old timers the minute I got here—the ones I wanted to meet. And I did . . . And I listened to all the stories I could. It was still close enough then to those days so it was awfully easy

to get to the sources of it all. And it sounded to me like it was a fascinating set-up and a wonderful movie to be made about it, you know. . . . That's why I began to want to make a movie about it—because they'd talk about it and talk about their first beginnings and all that. I became very interested in the early Hollywood only when I got here. It never struck me before as being fascinating. And in a way, you know, *Kane* was part of that because—not the very early Hollywood but pretty early. This town began to be dominated by Hearst, and it was partly from that road that I came to it.[34]

Both William Randolph Hearst's influence in Hollywood and the power his newspaper syndicate wielded over the film industry have been well documented.[35] While Hearst's attempts to suppress *Citizen Kane* are likewise well known, Welles told Bogdanovich that earlier versions of the script contained even more sensational allusions to Hearst that overlapped with the history of silent-era Hollywood (but insisted that his account of the eliminated scene not be included in *This is Orson Welles*): "In the original script we had a scene in which a murder was committed on a yacht . . . It comes from history. . . . Hearst stood on a yacht and shot a man dead in front of Chaplin and everybody else. The man was . . . Thomas Ince. . . . If I'd kept it in I would have had no trouble from Hearst. He wouldn't have dared to admit it was him."[36]

Compared with the omission from *Citizen Kane* of a scene based on the legendary murder of Thomas Ince, the editorial choice to change Welles's recollection of "a movie about the silent movies" to the more specific phrasing "a movie about the great days of the silents" in *This is Orson Welles* seems relatively inconsequential. But Welles's wording specifies "first beginnings" and "early Hollywood"—phrases that suggest the project was about the period when Hollywood was only just emerging as an important site for film production. This was the generation of "old fashioned movie people," as Welles put it in 1939, "who grew up with the industry." *Le Silence est d'or* (1947) is French filmmaker René Clair's homage to "the artisans who, between 1900 and 1910, gave birth, in France, to the first cinema industry in the world."[37] Welles, by contrast, was less interested in the "birth" of the film industry during the first decade of the twentieth century than in the first generation of Hollywood filmmakers who "grew up with" the American film industry during the 1910s.

After hearing about Welles's silent movie project, a surprised Bogdanovich interjected (in a passage understandably omitted from *This is*

Orson Welles) that he too "want[ed] to make a movie about the very early days."[38] As the conversation continued, Bogdanovich made clear that, for him, the "very early days" of filmmaking meant the 1910s. He told Welles that his long interview with Allan Dwan had inspired him: "That's what made me want to do the early days because he was there since 1909, . . . since the same time as Griffith. He started making pictures the year after Griffith."[39] Later in the interview, Bogdanovich recalled Dwan's response to a question about silent filmmaking techniques that became obsolete: "We dropped all that when we grew up."[40]

The most conspicuous allusions to silent cinema in *Citizen Kane* appear in the "News on the March" segments that were altered in postproduction. In his detailed account of the making of *Citizen Kane*, Harlan Lebo reports, "To give some of the footage in the newsreel a tattered, archival quality, [editor Robert] Wise and assistant editor Mark Robson copied segments repeatedly to simulate age, dragged negatives across a concrete floor to inflict actual damage on the film," going so far (according to Wise) as "running pieces of film through cheesecloth filled with sand to age it."[41] Welles told Bogdanovich that in Italy these parts of the film were mistaken for "a very primitive American picture with bad quality."[42]

Welles recalled filming the fake newsreel in an improvisational process that was memorably enjoyable:

> We did a piece of the newsreel every day depending on what make-up I had on. And then we'd go and steal it from someplace on the back lot . . . and do a little piece of that depending on which age I was made-up for. We'd just run out and grab a piece. . . . End of the day or during the day. You see there was a big back lot . . . and as we were moving from one place to another. . . . It was all kind of half-improvised—all the newsreels. It was great fun doing—tremendous fun doing it.[43]

Welles's account of filming the components of "News on the March" resonates with Bogdanovich's description of "those more carefree times" during the early days of Hollywood cinema in his book on Allan Dwan.[44] The sense of spontaneity evoked by Welles's memories of freely roaming the RKO lot in Culver City with a crew, filming pickup shots of various kinds, also corresponds with his assistant Kathryn Trosper's recollection that "Orson created much of the film on the fly."[45]

Narrator	
Twice married --	RECONSTRUCTION of very old silent news-
	reel of wedding party on the back lawn
	of the White House. Many notables,
to Emily Norman, debutante	including the bridegroom, the bride,
and President's niece, on	Thatcher Sr., Thatcher Jr. and recog-
the White House lawn.	nizably Bernstein, Stevens, et al,
	among the guests.
Sixteen years later, two	RECONSTRUCTED SILENT NEWSREEL. Craig,
weeks after his divorce, to	Susan and Annenberg emerging from side
Susan *Alexander,* singer, at	doorway of City Hall into a ring of
the Town Hall in Trenton,	press photographers, reporters, etc.
New Jersey.	Craig looks startled, recoils for an
	instant, then charges down upon the
	photographers, laying about him with
	his stick, smashing *whatever he can hit-*

Figure 3.2. "American" draft script, box 26, folder 1, p. 19, Richard Wilson-Orson Welles Papers, University of Michigan Library (Special Collections Library).

Filmmaking during the silent period, Welles and Bogdanovich seem to have imagined, had allowed for forms of spontaneity and improvisation that the Hollywood studio system had largely foreclosed. Welles conveyed some semblance of this rough-and-ready approach by foregrounding the visible imperfections of scratched and jerky ersatz silent films. In an early script of *Citizen Kane*, which was then entitled "American," shots of the two weddings in "News on the March" are described as "RECONSTRUCTION of very old silent newsreel" and "RECONSTRUCTED SILENT NEWSREEL," respectively (fig. 3.2).[46]

THE MAGNIFICENCE OF TRANSITION

Among Welles's completed feature films, *The Magnificent Ambersons* is the one that alludes most frequently to silent cinema. The anachronistic techniques of silent films help suffuse the first part of *The Magnificent*

Ambersons with a sense of nostalgia—and more precisely, with the feeling of how irrevocably and just how lamentably the past is lost to the present. In an illuminating 2014 blog post, David Bordwell argues that *The Magnificent Ambersons* is not just "a film about the past" like various "other films [that] have sought to present the past, recreating the settings and costumes and props of an era," but also a film "about past*ness*." Bordwell contends that "Welles enhances the aura of pastness through specific film techniques . . . choices that are, historically, anachronistic . . . noticeable old-time technique[s]."[47]

The most iconic of these "old-time techniques" is the iris out that closes around Eugene Morgan's motorcar as he drives off through the snow into the distance with a carload of passengers merrily singing "The Man Who Broke the Bank at Monte Carlo." In this elegiac moment, the halcyon days of the Ambersons and all they represent are summarily brought to a close. Many writers (including Bogdanovich) have characterized this iris out as an "homage" to silent cinema, but Welles recoiled at the use of this term, telling Bogdanovich,

> Well, we didn't know about hommage in those days, thank God. But it was just —it seemed to me it was a shame that people didn't use it anymore. I had happened to see a silent movie, and I thought "that's nice and let's use it." . . . I think it's a beautiful thing, the iris-out. You know, it's a marvelous invention. There are a lot of silent things that should be revived. But I didn't really mean it as a[n] homage; I just wanted to use it cause I liked it. . . . Yes, it was deliberately evoking movies' innocent times and all that, because in the end of the picture which nobody's seen which had nothing to do with innocent days and you couldn't have irised-out at all.[48]

As Bordwell observes, "Welles'[s] visual techniques aren't faithful to the period when the story action takes place. Assuming that the snow idyll occurs around 1904, the iris wouldn't have appeared in films of that time. . . . But by 1942, these techniques were associated with silent film generally and give a cinematic tinge of 'oldness' to the action."[49] In his encyclopedic chronology of the historical development of film style, Barry Salt writes, "use of the iris-in and iris-out . . . begins during 1913," noting that "irising rather than fading became . . . popular for a few years after 1914."[50] Eileen Bowser adds, "Later, however, when emphasis was placed on making cuts as inconspicuous as possible, . . . the use of these early devices lessened."[51]

Another set of allusions to silent cinema in *The Magnificent Amber-sons* is visible in the lengthy tracking shot that shows George Amberson Minafer (Tim Holt) and Lucy Morgan (Anne Baxter) walking downtown. After crossing paths, they walk along National Avenue shoulder to shoulder on the sidewalk amidst a bustle of pedestrian, automobile, and horse-drawn traffic that gets busier as they pass through the business district. George and Lucy walk by a series of storefronts, including an interior decorator, several drapers, and a haberdasher, before passing the Bijou Moving Pictures theater, which is showing a variety program of one-reelers. According to a cutting continuity dated March 12, 1942, the sequence of George and Lucy walking along National Avenue takes place in 1905.[52] Yet, hanging in front of the Bijou are posters for *The Bugler of Battery B*, a 1912 Kalem war film; *The Cow-Boy Girl*, a 1910 musical stage show; *Ghost at Circle X Camp*, a 1912 Gaston Méliès Western produced in southern California (and starring Francis Ford); *Her Husband's Wife*, a 1913 Lubin comedy; and "Jack Holt in 'Explosion,'" an apocryphal film poster put outside the theater, Welles told Bogdanovich, as an "in-joke" for Tim Holt.[53] Additionally, there are advertisements for *Ten Days with a Fleet of U.S. Battleships*, a 1912 Edison actuality; *The Mis-Sent Letter*, a 1912 Essanay melodrama; and what looks like a poster for the stage play *Jesse James, The Missouri Outlaw*, first performed in 1902.[54] Welles was likely not trying very hard to be absolutely faithful to the 1905 date specified in the cutting continuity, but the selection of film posters outside the Bijou seems potentially significant. The movie posters span a range of genres and nearly all date from 1912–13.

Instead of a storefront location converted into a nickelodeon (something that entrepreneurs did increasingly after 1905), National Avenue contains what appears to be a purpose-built movie theater, complete with a recessed entrance and an enclosed ticket booth. And, instead of a Georges Méliès film, which would have been quite common in the United States in 1905, we see a film produced by his older brother Gaston, who began making his own films after obtaining a license from the Motion Pictures Patent Company.[55] Apart from two theatrical posters and an ersatz poster for an apocryphal film, the posters outside of the Bijou situate the historical movie-going experience firmly within what film historians have described as "the most profound transformation in American film history to date."[56] The years between 1908 and 1917 or so marked a period when exhibition and production practices were only beginning to normalize and could vary widely. During this period of transition, moving pictures were ensconced in the cultural landscape, but the widespread predominance of the feature film was still several years in the future.

Welles's consistent choice to allude to films of the early 1910s, made before he was born, harks back to a period when some of the hallmarks of classical filmmaking—feature length, star-centered film discourse, continuity editing, verisimilar acting—were not fully institutionalized. Instead, what we get is production companies and genres, as the posters outside of the Bijou indicate. Cinema of the early teens, before many of the constituent features of the so-called classical Hollywood studio system were yet in place, signals a more distant "past-ness."[57]

CINEMATIC "PRIMITIVES"

In his introduction to *The Silent Years* broadcast of *Blood and Sand*, Welles explained, "I can't pose as any sort of expert or authority on silent movies. What I've tried to supply is the odd personal note from one who's . . . old enough to have seen most of these movies when they first came out." And, in conversation with Bogdanovich, he recalled seeing several silent films in particular, including Rex Ingram's *The Four Horsemen of the Apocalypse* ("I remember the picture very well . . . I was about six"); Lon Chaney in *The Hunchback of Notre Dame* ("I think the movie I liked best from the point of view of an actor"); John Ford's *The Iron Horse* ("I remember . . . what effect it had on me as a little child. I was mad about it"); and D. W. Griffith's *The Birth of a Nation* ("a revival . . . with a big symphony orchestra in the pit. It frightened and depressed me.").[58] Welles described himself to Bogdanovich as having been a "true . . . movie fan . . . with no interest in it as an art form. . . . Just loved to go to the movies without taking them very seriously."[59] He also emphatically denied having seen many German silent films: "there's a whole section of . . . old movies, that I never saw which are supposed to have influenced me which are the German expressionist movies. I've never seen them. . . . Even till now. . . . I always stayed away from . . . what were then called 'artistic movies,' . . . And I never have seen these pictures that are supposed to have influenced me so much, these German ones."[60] Welles held onto memories of going to the movies frequently during the 1920s: "I went to the movies that my mother or father wanted me to go see, and they liked Flaherty and low comedy and—I never heard about German movies or that kind of thing. They either didn't know about them or didn't care about them." Welles noted, however, that he "saw some German expressionist *theatre*," adding that, "except for Flaherty, I never was conscious of the movie-maker as being all that interesting."[61]

Patrick McGilligan reports, "It was his mother who took Orson to Robert Flaherty's pioneering *Nanook of the North*" while noting that, a few years later, in 1925, Welles and his father went to a Dixon, Illinois "theater where the comedies and Westerns were interspersed with vaudeville acts," and that together they saw *The Gold Rush, Ben-Hur,* and *Tumbleweeds.*[62] Between films like *Nanook of the North*—"among the most sophisticated of their era," according to McGilligan—and what Welles himself called "low comedy," I argue that Welles's "nostalgia for … early silent moving pictures" centered on the latter.[63] Indeed, Welles's most lasting cinematic "influences" (which Bogdanovich was eager to identify, despite Welles's continued objections), I conclude, were decidedly lowbrow as well as explicitly paternal: the anarchic comedies of Mack Sennett and his ilk. Additionally, stage productions like *Too Much Johnson, The Green Goddess, Around the World,* and *The Unthinking Lobster* indicate that Welles's privileged mode of combining theater and cinema was to integrate film projections into live performances— what Gwendolyn Waltz terms "alternation format stage-and-screen hybrids."[64] This was common practice in early film exhibition.

Welles relished filming comic chases in the style of Sennett's Keystone Cops, which he could insert into live performances. Vincent Longo's research reveals that the films made to be projected between acts of Welles's production of *Too Much Johnson* were originally "publicized on flyers as being in the Mack Sennett tradition" (fig. 3.3) and that the performers in the films made to be screened as part of Welles's Broadway show *Around the World* were supposed to "waddle jerkily 'ala Essanay'"— an allusion to the short films Charlie Chaplin made for the Essanay studio in Los Angeles in 1915, immediately after he left Sennett's Keystone Film Company.[65] Welles's fascination with 1910s slapstick continued un-

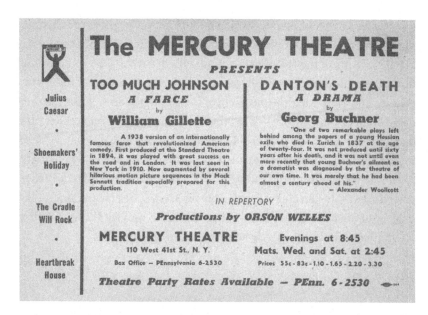

The MERCURY THEATRE

PRESENTS

TOO MUCH JOHNSON
A FARCE

by
William Gillette

A 1938 version of an internationally famous farce that revolutionized American comedy. First produced at the Standard Theatre in 1894, it was played with great success on the road and in London. It was last seen in New York in 1910. Now augmented by several hilarious motion picture sequences in the Mack Sennett tradition especially prepared for this production.

DANTON'S DEATH
A DRAMA

by
Georg Buchner

"One of two remarkable plays left behind among the papers of a young Hessian exile who died in Zurich in 1837 at the age of twenty-four. It was not produced until sixty years after his death, and it was not until even more recently that young Buchner's ailment as a dramatist was diagnosed by the theatre of our own time. It was merely that he had been almost a century ahead of his."
— Alexander Woollcott

IN REPERTORY

Productions by ORSON WELLES

MERCURY THEATRE
110 West 41st St., N. Y.
Box Office — PEnnsylvania 6-2530

Evenings at 8:45
Mats. Wed. and Sat. at 2:45
Prices 55c - 83c - 1.10 - 1.65 - 2.20 - 3.30

Theatre Party Rates Available — PEnn. 6-2530

Julius Caesar

•

Shoemakers' Holiday

•

The Cradle Will Rock

•

Heartbreak House

Figure 3.3. Flyer for *Too Much Johnson* and *Danton's Death*, box 23, Richard Wilson–Orson Welles Papers, University of Michigan Library (Special Collections Library).

til the very end of his career. In one segment of *The Magic Show*, a film that Welles was still working on when he died in 1985, "two policemen in the style of the Keystone Cops went around the theater" trying to restore the body of a woman who had been sawed in half.[66]

Welles's comic tastes were unapologetically "primitive" and thus he was most enthusiastic about the "low comedy" that had flourished during the silent period. The critical establishment had uniformly lionized Chaplin since the 1920s, but Welles thought Chaplin "isn't very funny. I never smiled at Chaplin in my life," while acknowledging that Chaplin was "one of the greatest artists I ever watched. . . . He's brilliant. You just say, 'How does he do such a wonderful, beautiful thing?' But he never makes me laugh."[67] Welles was more effusive about comics who made him "sick with laughter"[68]—comedians like W. C. Fields, Laurel and Hardy, and Jerry Lewis in his prime, who "went too far . . . way too far and it just made you sick."[69] Welles valued laughter for its own sake and, among "the silent clowns," praised Harold Lloyd as "the fellow who doesn't correspond to what the highbrows want."[70]

Welles's continuing interest in the "primitive" years of film history ran counter to an emerging historiographic orthodoxy that tended to privilege films of the twenties—the so-called "mature" period of silent film history. Indeed, most subsequent film critics, theorists, and historians would claim that the pinnacle of the silent period—if not the pinnacle of all of film history—was "the late silent era" (as one recent film history textbook terms the period between 1919 and 1929).[71] Welles's taste in silent films was often at odds with critics and historians who sought to elevate the medium and imbue it with value as an art. Indeed, Welles placed great value on cinema's relationship to the popular audience, telling Bogdanovich at one point, "what has saved movies is the fact that movies have not been entirely accepted as an art form."[72]

ECHOES OF SILENTS

Welles's hypothetical film about silent filmmaking left very few traces, but he continued to be fascinated by legendary silent filmmakers Erich von Stroheim, Rex Ingram, and D. W. Griffith, each of whom Welles appears to have identified with to varying degrees late in his career. Like Welles, von Stroheim was an actor-director who acquired a reputation for being difficult and excessive. Welles told Bogdanovich: "when I used to read about his career . . . I began to decide that I had ahead of me . . . before I ever made a picture—years like Von Stroheim and the others. . . . I was sure that was going to be my future. I saw it clearly before I ever got behind a camera."[73] Several of von Stroheim's films were notoriously mangled by the studios, including *Greed*, which was reduced to less than half its length before being released.[74] If Welles envisioned "years like Von Stroheim," who sustained a film career as an actor long after he had lost favor as a director through a series of idiosyncratic character roles in films like *The Great Gabbo* (1929), *Grand Illusion* (1937), *The Great Flamarion* (1945), and *Sunset Boulevard* (1950), by the late 1960s, it might have seemed to Welles that his own career was running a similar course.

"If there was one director who gave Louis B. Mayer almost as much trouble as Erich von Stroheim, it was certainly Rex Ingram," film historian Richard Koszarski writes.[75] During the silent period, Ingram was celebrated as one of Hollywood cinema's most artistic directors, and he has a special place in Victor Oscar Freeburg's 1923 book *Pictorial Beauty on the Screen*.[76] According to Jonathan Rosenbaum, in *The Other Side of the Wind*, another of the unfinished films Welles was working on at the time of his death, the character Jake Hannaford (played by sound-era film director John Huston in the footage Welles shot) was partly based on Ingram.[77] After Ingram's Hollywood career peaked during the early 1920s, directing his wife Alice Terry and Rudolph Valentino in *The Four Horsemen of the Apocalypse* and *The Conquering Power*, Ingram set up his own movie studio in Nice in 1924.[78] Although Welles thought that Ingram was "over-rated" (and says he told King Vidor as much on the set of *Citizen Kane*), the trajectory of Ingram's career from celebrated Hollywood director to semi-independent émigré filmmaker may have resonated with Welles.[79]

One of the few Hollywood directors more renowned during the silent period than Ingram or von Stroheim was Griffith. Welles met Griffith on December 23, 1939, at a holiday party in Hollywood, and later wrote a brief account of their meeting, which he called "the best thing I ever wrote about anybody in movies," insisting it be reprinted in *This is Orson Welles*.[80] In that brief piece, Welles ruminates on the Hollywood legend who, by the 1930s, had become "an exile in his own town"—forgotten by the industry that he had helped to found in the 1910s.[81] A few years after Welles met Griffith, journalist Ezra Goodman managed to interview Griffith "in a hotel room in the heart of Hollywood guzzling gin out of a water glass . . . attired in pajamas and a patterned maroon dressing gown . . . at the age of seventy-two."[82] He told Goodman, "I loved *Citizen Kane* and particularly loved the ideas he [Welles] took from me."[83] For Welles, Griffith was a living reminder of early Hollywood glory who had become painfully obsolete less than fifteen years later. Yet, Griffith was also, as Richard Watts Jr. pointed out in 1936, a "social crusader" who was, as he put it, "the pioneer in the conception of the screen as a medium for social ideas."[84]

In response to one of Bogdanovich's frequent queries about influence, Welles replied, "I suppose he created influence on anybody who's ever made a movie."[85] But Griffith was also an especially old-timey figure from the cinematic past, even if his use of cinematic technique was modern. In his introduction to *The Silent Years* broadcast of *Intolerance*, the only film in the series made during the 1910s, Welles characterized it as a Janus-faced landmark of film history: "It was made just a year after I was born. And there is almost nothing in the entire vocabulary of the cinema that you won't find in this film. There's also a lot of it which is terribly old-fashioned. And it was old-fashioned, I'd like to point out, even at the time when this film was shown." In his introduction to *Orphans of the Storm*, another Griffith film in *The Silent Years* series, Welles expanded upon this idea, noting, "They seem to be more dated than in fact they are. . . . When I first saw Griffith films as a little boy . . . those pictures seemed to me to be old-fashioned." It is a similar sense of movies "seem[ing] more dated than in fact they are" that Welles tried to create by employing filmmaking idioms of the silent period, and especially those that dated to the 1910s.

Griffith's obsolescence was hardly only stylistic. As Lewis Jacobs claimed in a chapter on "the decline of D. W. Griffith" in *The Rise of the American Film*, which was published in October 1939, in time for the commemoration of the movies' Golden Jubilee: "Revolutionary changes in moral attitudes during these years were irreconcilable with Griffith's nineteenth-century orthodoxy. He clung to a moral code which was disdained and mocked as 'old-fashioned.' Even when he chose up-to-date themes, his outmoded and deep-seated prejudices were obvious; all his films appeared stilted, forced, ludicrously colored by pre-war ideals. Griffith's great weakness was his inability to move with the times."[86] As Jacobs's account suggests, Griffith's legacy was very much in dispute by the time Welles arrived in Hollywood. In December 1939, a heated debate over Griffith's already infamous film *The Birth of a Nation* began, Melvyn Stokes explains, when "David Platt published a series of articles in *The Daily Worker*, the main newspaper organ of the communist party, advancing the thesis that *The Birth of a Nation* had been part of a deliberate attempt by Hollywood, in collaboration with capitalist interests, to rule both blacks and whites by dividing them. However, the timing of this assault . . . meant that *The Birth of a Nation* would now become both a symbol and a focus of the wider disagreements among American communists and ex-communists."[87] As far as I know, Welles wrote no account of *The Birth of a Nation*'s relationship to American racial politics, but he was likely aware of the highly politicized disagreements over the film at the time.[88]

When Bogdanovich mentioned to Welles that he really only began the history of movies with *The Birth of a Nation*, which was only twenty-five years before Welles came to Hollywood, Welles was stunned: "To me *Birth of a Nation* must have been about—in my mind—was fifty years before I began. . . . It seemed to me fifty years ago, you know, and I think it's twenty-five years now what have they done?"[89] Welles continued, "But it seemed fifty years ago then. Believe me. Because talkies did that, and brought in all those people. Really changed the town as completely as air travel has changed the world. I'm not putting myself well, but it absolutely—it really did seem. There was Griffith, you know, in full possession of his faculties—with no job. No jobs."[90] Asked specifically about *The Birth of a Nation*, Welles said, "It's great. No doubt about it. But I haven't anything great, bright to say. I just loved it, that's about all."[91] But, when Bogdanovich started to hold forth on the watershed historical importance of the film (which Welles saw as a ten-year-old boy in 1925 with his mother) by saying "*The Birth of a Nation* summed up everything that had gone before. It brought everything to a head," Welles cut him short: "All right. You say that in the book. Don't say that to me."[92]

Welles's hesitation may have signaled his impatience with clichés of film history: "You find out that history is just repetition of a series of slogans and cliches that have got imbedded [*sic*] into people's thinking," since movie histories "keep fee[d]ing on each other . . . they just rewrite the books so that the[y] . . . keep feeding on each other."[93] But it may have signaled something else as well, given what a contentious film *The Birth of a Nation* was when Welles came to Hollywood as well as when Bogdanovich interviewed him some thirty years later. It would likely have been impossible for broadcast public television stations to include *The Birth of a Nation* in *The Silent Years* series. Instead, *Intolerance* seems to have been substituted. Welles described it as "a bit too complicated for the 1916 audiences—maybe it's too complicated for an audience today" in his filmed epilogue.

Welles's one and only meeting with Griffith occurred just as the controversies over *The Birth of a Nation* were being revived with a new political valence that typically pitted leftist calls to suppress and/or boycott the film against overweening defenses of the film on aesthetic grounds, but Welles entirely elided these controversies in his account of meeting Griffith as well as in his recorded conversations with Bogdanovich. Given his longtime activism around issues of racial injustice, his impatience with Bogdanovich's apotheosizing of *The Birth of a Nation* suggest that he regarded this particular Griffith film with some degree of ambivalence.[94] Ambivalence was in fact a general feature of Welles's attitude toward silent filmmakers and their films, which inspired him both to laughter and to wistfulness.

Although Welles never made a feature-length film about silent movies, they were nevertheless a key touchstone for him throughout his career. Often, they serve as a compelling way to mark the unbridgeable chasm that separates the past from the present. Welles alluded frequently to silent cinema in his films—including the films he made to be screened as part of live theatrical productions and several that were unfinished or unrealized, if not entirely hypothetical—as well as in his recorded comments about films and film history. In *The Magnificent Ambersons*, Eugene Morgan (Joseph Cotten) says, "There aren't any old times. When times are gone, they're not old, they're dead." This line is also in Booth Tarkington's novel *The Magnificent Ambersons* and in Welles's 1939 radio adaptation for *The Campbell Playhouse* series. It epitomizes Welles's relationship to silent cinema, which was the source of his childhood love of movies, but by his adolescence had become a "dead" medium, and, by the time he began making movies himself, had been relegated to the "quaint and somewhat comical" status of old-time movies.

MATTHEW SOLOMON is associate professor in the Department of Screen Arts and Cultures at the University of Michigan. He is author of a 2015 BFI Film Classics monograph on *The Gold Rush* and of *Disappearing Tricks: Silent Film, Houdini, and the New Magic of the Twentieth Century*, which won the Kraszna-Krausz award for best moving image book in 2011; he is also editor of *Fantastic Voyages of the Cinematic Imagination: Georges Méliès's* Trip to the Moon.

NOTES

This chapter emerged from a series of lively conversations with Vincent Longo, whose groundbreaking research on Welles has spurred my interest and efforts. I would also like to thank Philip Hallman, Film Studies field librarian at the University of Michigan, and the undergraduate students in my winter 2015 "Authorship and the Archive" course in the Department of Screen Arts and Cultures at the University of Michigan, especially Natalie Grove, Nicholas Sheehan, and Joseph Pecoraro. Kathleen Dow and Kate Hutchens helped with illustrations, while François Thomas and James Gilmore generously shared their research with me. My thanks go to the editors of this volume, James Gilmore and Sidney Gottlieb, for their interest in my presentation at the 2015 Welles conference at Indiana University, for their helpful and encouraging feedback in revising it for publication, and for their patience. Any deficiencies are, of course, mine.

1. Orson Welles to Virginia Nicolson, July 22, 1939, p. 2, box 1, Orson Welles-Chris Welles Feder Collection, Special Collections Library, University of Michigan.

2. Welles modified the titles of these two novels slightly; his adaptations were titled "The Heart of Darkness" and "The Smiler with a Knife," respectively, box 26, Richard Wilson-Orson Welles Papers, Special Collections Library, University of Michigan (hereafter cited as Wilson-Welles Papers).

3. Orson Welles and Peter Bogdanovich, *This is Orson Welles*, rev. ed., ed. Jonathan Rosenbaum (New York: Da Capo Press, 1998). Wherever possible elsewhere, I have drawn upon a transcription of Peter Bogdanovich's interview with Orson Welles, which survives mostly intact as a typescript of more than 1,300 pages in folder 1, box 1, and folders 2–10, box 2, Wilson-Welles Papers, Special Collections Library, University of Michigan (hereafter Welles-Bogdanovich interview transcription). Additionally, it is worth noting, there were a number of points during the course of the interview when the tape recorder was turned off so that particularly sensitive parts of the conversation were not recorded. While a fully systematic comparison of the Welles-Bogdanovich interview transcription with *This is Orson Welles* is beyond the scope of this chapter, the thorough revisions to their conversations appear comparable to the pervasive changes François Truffaut's interview with Alfred Hitchcock underwent before publication. See Janet Bergstrom, "Lost in Translation? Listening to the Hitchcock-Truffaut Interview," in *A Companion to Alfred Hitchcock*, ed. Thomas Leitch and Leland Poague (Malden, MA: Wiley-Blackwell, 2011), 387–404.

4. Welles and Bogdanovich, *This is Orson Welles*, 21–22.

5. Orson Welles to Virginia Nicolson, August 4, 1939, p. 2, box 1, Orson Welles-Chris Welles Feder collection.

6. Quoted in "Welles Sees Television Boon to Dramatic Arts," *Los Angeles Times* (August 6, 1939): C2. Thank you to Vincent Longo for bringing this article to my attention.

7. Welles-Bogdanovich interview transcription, box 2, folder 3, p. 642.

8. Terry Ramsaye, "The First Preview," *Motion Picture Herald* (October 7, 1939): 7–8; Ramsaye, *A Million and One Nights: A History of the Motion Picture*, Vol. 1 (New York: Simon & Schuster, 1926), 65–73. Ramsaye cites personal correspondence with Thomas Edison and W. K. L. Dickson. Compare Paul Spehr, *The Man Who Made Movies: W. K. L. Dickson* (New Barnet, UK: John Libbey, 2008), 148–49.

9. "'Jubilee' Observed on Radio and in the Field," *Motion Picture Herald* (October 14, 1939): 52. See also "50th Birthday of the Movies," *Los Angeles Times* (October 1, 1939): H12.

10. "'Jubilee' Observed on Radio," 52. See also Wilbur Morse, "The First 50 Years," *Hollywood* (April 1939): 20–21; "The Cinema Observes Its Golden Jubilee This Year," *Washington Post* (June 6, 1939): 6; C. M. Withington, "New Vistas," *Motion Picture Herald* (June 17, 1939): 7.

11. See "Movies March On," *The March of Time,* https://archive.org/details/HistoryOfTheMotionPictureTheMoviesMarchOn.

12. Welles-Bogdanovich interview transcription, box 2, folder 3, p. 655.

13. Marguerite H. Rippy, *Orson Welles and the Unfinished RKO Projects: A Postmodern Perspective* (Carbondale: Southern Illinois University Press, 2009).

14. Welles-Bogdanovich interview transcription, box 2, folder 9, pp. 50–53. Compare David Robinson, *Chaplin: His Life and Art*, 2nd rev. ed. (London: Penguin Books, 2001), 42–49.

15. Gary Graver, with Andrew J. Rausch, *Making Movies with Orson Welles: A Memoir* (Lanham, MD: Scarecrow Press, 2008), 19.

16. The films broadcast as part of *The Silent Years* series were *The Gold Rush, Son of the Sheik, Intolerance, The Mark of Zorro, The General, The Beloved Rogue, The Extra Girl, The Thief of Bagdad, Orphans of the Storm, Sally of the Sawdust, Blood and Sand,* and *The Hunchback of Notre Dame.*

17. Welles-Bogdanovich interview transcription, box 1, folder 1, pp. 60–61.

18. Welles had also previously filmed a dress rehearsal for a 1933 production of *Twelfth Night* at the Todd School that survives as a fragment. See Frank Brady, *Citizen Welles: A Biography of Orson Welles* (New York: Anchor Books, 1990), 44.

19. Welles and Bogdanovich, *This is Orson Welles,* 41–42. Set designs for the funhouse sequence of *The Lady from Shanghai* were at least partly inspired by *The Cabinet of Dr. Caligari.* In the script, "Michael wakes up to find himself alone in one of the queerest rooms ever built by man. . . . The floor is raked at an angle of the sheerest vertigo, the walls and ceilings are pure 'Cabinet of Dr. Caligari.'" "The Lady from Shanghai" script, December 20, 1946, box 30, folder 4 of 4, p. 139 (ellipsis in original), Wilson-Welles Papers. Thank you to Nicolas Ciccone for this reference.

20. See especially Haidee Wasson, *Museum Movies: The Museum of Modern Art and the Birth of Art Cinema* (Berkeley: University of California Press, 2005).

21. Welles-Bogdanovich interview transcription, box 2, folder 2, pp. 332–33.

22. For an account of Welles's negotiations of high and low culture, see Michael Anderegg, *Orson Welles, Shakespeare, and Popular Culture* (New York: Columbia University Press, 1999).

23. Thank you to Rachael Stoeltje for making this 16mm print accessible to me remotely.

24. "My Favourite Mask is Myself," interview with Orson Welles by Bill Krohn, February 19–20, 1982, in *The Unknown Orson Welles*, ed. Stefan Drössler (Munich: Filmmuseum München, Belleville Verlag, 2004), 68.

25. Seymour Stern, *D. W. Griffith's 100th Anniversary: The Birth of a Nation*, ed. Ira H. Gallen (Victoria, BC: Friesen Press, 2014), 600.

26. Welles-Bogdanovich interview transcription, box 2, folder 2, p. 317, and folder 10, p. 10.

27. Welles and Bogdanovich, *This is Orson Welles*, 22.

28. Frederic G. Cassidy and Joan Houston Hall, eds. *Dictionary of American Regional English*, Vol. 3: I–O (Cambridge, MA.: Belknap Press, 1996), 872.

29. Welles-Bogdanovich interview transcription, box 2, folder 3, p. 546. Compare Welles and Bogdanovich, *This is Orson Welles*, 104.

30. Welles-Bogdanovich interview transcription, box 1, folder 1, pp. 156–57. Compare Welles and Bogdanovich, *This is Orson Welles*, 40–41.

31. Welles-Bogdanovich interview transcription, box 1, folder 1, p. 159. Compare Welles and Bogdanovich, *This is Orson Welles*, 40–41. This remark was borne out by the multimedia staged reading of *Too Much Johnson* performed by University of Michigan students at the Detroit Institute of Arts, June 7, 2015.

32. Joseph McBride, "*Too Much Johnson*: Recovering Orson Welles's Dream of Early Cinema," *Bright Lights Film Journal*, April 7, 2014; rev. August 24, 2014, http://brightlightsfilm.com/too-much-johnson-orson-welles-film-recovering-orson-welless-dream-of-early-cinema/#.V4vHH74rJ8e. See also Patrick McGilligan, *Young Orson: The Years of Luck and Genius on the Path to* Citizen Kane (New York: HarperCollins, 2015), 472–80.

33. See especially David Mayer, "Acting in Silent Film: Which Legacy of the Theatre?," in *Screen Acting*, ed. Alan Lovell and Peter Krämer (London: Routledge, 1999), 10–30. Compare Roberta E. Pearson, *Eloquent Gestures: The Transformation of Performance Style in the Griffith Biograph Films* (Berkeley: University of California Press, 1992).

34. Welles-Bogdanovich interview transcription, box 1, folder 1, pp. 54–56.

35. See especially Louis Pizzitola, *Hearst Over Hollywood: Power, Passion, and Propaganda in the Movies* (New York: Columbia University Press, 2002).

36. Welles-Bogdanovich interview transcription, box 2, folder 2, p. 436. For another version of this story, see Kenneth Anger, *Hollywood Babylon* (New York: Dell, 1975), 97–104. On the inclusion of this incident in an early version of *Citizen Kane*, see Robert L. Carringer, *The Making of* Citizen Kane, rev. ed. (Berkeley: University of California Press, 1996), 21, 155n10. In an early script not yet titled *Citizen Kane*, the allusion to Ince's murder is much less direct since the character's death takes place offscreen during a Wild West costume party; this is followed by a scene aboard a yacht. "American," draft screenplay, April 16, 1940, box 26, folder 5, pp. 282–93, Wilson-Welles Papers. See also Harlan Lebo, Citizen Kane:

A Filmmaker's Journey (New York: Thomas Dunne Books, St. Martin's Press, 2016), 44, 228.

37. René Clair, "Foreword to *Le Silence est d'or*," *Four Screenplays*, trans. Piergiuseppe Bozzetti (New York: Orion Press, 1970), 6.

38. Welles-Bogdanovich interview transcription, box, folder 1, p. 55. Bogdanovich returned to the milieu of silent cinema in the films *Nickelodeon* (1976) and *The Cat's Meow* (2001), the latter which is set aboard Hearst's yacht the night of Ince's death. Thank you to an anonymous reader of this manuscript and Sidney Gottlieb, respectively, for these two film references.

39. Welles-Bogdanovich interview transcription, box 1, folder 1, p. 60.

40. Welles-Bogdanovich interview transcription, box 2, folder 2, p. 295. Bogdanovich was paraphrasing from the extended interview he conducted with Dwan in 1968–69, an edited version of which makes up most of Peter Bogdanovich, *Allan Dwan: The Last Pioneer* (London: Studio Vista, 1971), 14. The text of Bogdanovich's edited interview with Dwan was reprinted as chapter 1 of Bogdanovich, *Who the Devil Made It: Conversations with Robert Aldrich, George Cukor, Allan Dwan, Howard Hawks, Alfred Hitchcock, Chuck Jones, Fritz Lang, Joseph H. Lewis, Sidney Lumet, Leo M. McCarey, Otto Preminger, Don Siegel, Josef von Sternberg, Frank Tashlin, Edgar G. Ulmer, Raoul Walsh* (New York: Ballantine, 1997), 49–123.

41. Lebo, Citizen Kane: *A Filmmaker's Journey*, 164, quoting personal interview with Wise.

42. Welles-Bogdanovich interview transcription, box 1, folder 1, pg. 75. Compare Welles and Bogdanovich, *This is Orson Welles*, 76. In early scripts of *Citizen Kane*, the newsreel sequence, which was titled "The March of Time," was considerably longer because it was intended to replicate the two-reel format of weekly installments of *The March of Time* newsreel; "American," draft screenplay, April 16, 1940, box 26, folder 1, pp. 5–24, Wilson-Welles Papers. Thank you to Vincent Longo for pointing this out to me. See also Lebo, Citizen Kane: *A Filmmaker's Journey*, 62, 163–65, 252.

43. Welles-Bogdanovich interview transcription, box 2, folder 2, pp. 273–74.

44. Bogdanovich, *Allan Dwan*, 6.

45. Quoted in Lebo, Citizen Kane: *A Filmmaker's Journey*, 60. Trosper appears in *Citizen Kane* as the female reporter exploring Xanadu after Kane's death (Lebo, Citizen Kane: *A Filmmaker's Journey*, 76).

46. "Houseman's Edit of American," draft screenplay, n. d., box 26, folder 1, p. 19, Wilson-Welles Papers.

47. David Bordwell, "*The Magnificent Ambersons*: A Usable Past," *Observations on Film Art* blog, May 30, 2014, http://www.davidbordwell.net/blog/2014/05/30/the-magnificent-ambersons-a-usable-past/. Bordwell describes *The Magnificent Ambersons* as "the most downbeat of the 'nostalgia' cycle of the 1940s, which includes *Strawberry Blonde* (1941), *Meet Me in St. Louis* (1944), and *Centennial Summer* (1946)."

48. Welles-Bogdanovich interview transcription, box 2, folder 2, pp. 283–84. Compare Welles and Bogdanovich, *This is Orson Welles*, 126–27. See also James Naremore, *The Magic World of Orson Welles*, 2nd ed. (Dallas, TX: Southern Methodist

University Press, 1989), 103, and V. F. Perkins, *The Magnificent Ambersons* (London: British Film Institute, 1999), 51.

49. Bordwell, "*The Magnificent Ambersons.*"

50. Barry Salt, *Film Style and Technology: History and Analysis*, 3rd ed. (1983; London: Starword, 2009), 92.

51. Eileen Bowser, *The Transformation of Cinema, 1907–1915* (Berkeley: University of California Press, 1994), 244.

52. "The Magnificent Ambersons," Cutting Continuity, March 12, 1942, box 27, p. 12, Wilson-Welles Papers. See also Robert L. Carringer, The Magnificent Ambersons: *A Reconstruction* (Berkeley: University of California Press, 1993), 39–41.

53. Welles-Bogdanovich interview transcription, box 2, folder 9, p. 36. Welles added, "It's the wrong period. . . . We gave Tim a little pleasure . . . because his father was coming to lunch . . . we put it on as a joke." Jack Holt's first credited film role dates from 1914, and elsewhere Welles acknowledged, "It was too early. . . . Of course it was an anachronism." Welles-Bogdanovich interview transcription, box 1, folder 3, p. 556. Compare Welles and Bogdanovich, *This is Orson Welles*, 127. See also Bordwell, "Breaking *Ambersons* News: Did You Say Buried?" and "The *Ambersons* Poster Mystery: The Clincher," *Observations on Film Art* blog, August 18, 2014 and August 20, 2014, http://www.davidbordwell.net/blog/2014/08/18/breaking-ambersons-news-did-you-say-buried/ and http://www.davidbordwell.net/blog/2014/08/20/the-ambersons-poster-mystery-the-clincher/.

54. Bordwell writes, "There were several Jesse James films circulating in 1911–1912, but one two-reeler named for the bandit . . . seems a likely candidate" ("*The Magnificent Ambersons*"). I think this is a poster for a stage play described in Roger A. Hall, *Performing the American Frontier, 1870–1906* (Cambridge, UK: Cambridge University Press, 2001), 132.

55. Compare Welles and Bogdanovich, *This is Orson Welles*, 127. On the films of Gaston Méliès, see Frank Thompson, *The Star Film Ranch: Texas' First Picture Show* (Plano: Republic of Texas Press, 1996). On the exhibition of French films in the United States during this period, see Richard Abel, *The Red Rooster Scare: Making Cinema American, 1900–1910* (Berkeley: University of California Press, 1999).

56. Charlie Keil and Shelley Stamp, Introduction to *American Cinema's Transitional Era: Audiences, Institutions, Practices*, ed. Charlie Keil and Shelley Stamp (Berkeley: University of California Press, 2004), 1. See also Bowser, *The Transformation of Cinema.*

57. On "classical Hollywood," see David Bordwell, Janet Staiger, and Kristin Thompson, *Classical Hollywood Cinema: Film Style and Mode of Production to 1960* (New York: Columbia University Press, 1985), who date its formation around 1917.

58. Quotations from, respectively, Welles-Bogdanovich interview transcription, box 2, folder 11, pp. 12–13; box 1, folder 1, p. 57; box 1, folder 1, p. 63; Welles and Bogdanovich, *This is Orson Welles*, 37.

59. Welles-Bogdanovich interview transcription, box 1, folder 1, p. 55.

60. Welles-Bogdanovich interview transcription, box 1, folder 1, pp. 58, 61. Compare Welles and Bogdanovich, *This is Orson Welles*, 37–38.

61. Welles-Bogdanovich interview transcription, box 1, folder 1, pp. 58–61.

62. McGilligan, *Young Orson*, 89–90, 118.

63. McGilligan, *Young Orson*, 118.

64. Gwendolyn Waltz, "Half Real-Half Reel: Alternation Format Stage-and-Screen Hybrids," in *A Companion to Early Cinema*, ed. André Gaudreault, Nicolas Dulac, and Santiago Hidalgo (Malden, MA: Wiley-Blackwell, 2012), 360–80.

65. Vincent Longo, "Going *Around the World* with Orson Welles: A Multimedia Auteur" (B.A. honor's thesis, Department of Screen Arts and Cultures, University of Michigan, 2014), 24. See also Richard de Cordova, *Picture Personalities: The Emergence of the Star System in America* (Champaign: University of Illinois Press, 1990). Longo notes another reference to an early film production company in descriptions of the films made for *Around the World*, described as "a typical Vitagraph movie set of a London street" (Longo, "Going *Around the World*," 24) See also Longo, "Multimedia Magic in *Around the World*, Orson Welles's Film-and-Theater Hybrid," in this volume for a detailed description of the five silent films included in *Around the World* and how Welles used them interactively with the live action on stage. On Chaplin's Essanay period, see Robinson, *Chaplin*, 139–62.

66. Drössler, ed., *The Unknown Orson Welles*, 110.

67. Welles-Bogdanovich interview transcription, box 2, folder 2, pp. 277–78. Compare Welles and Bogdanovich, *This is Orson Welles*, 135. See also Matthew Solomon, *The Gold Rush* (London: Palgrave BFI, 2015), 30–33.

68. Welles-Bogdanovich interview transcription, box 2, folder 2, p. 279.

69. Welles-Bogdanovich interview transcription, box 2, folder 5, p. 92. Compare Welles and Bogdanovich, *This is Orson Welles*, 38–39.

70. Welles-Bogdanovich interview transcription, box 2, folder 9, p. 61.

71. Kristin Thompson and David Bordwell, *Film History: An Introduction*, 3rd ed. (New York: McGraw-Hill, 2009), 68–174.

72. Welles-Bogdanovich interview transcription, box 2, folder 4, p. 112.

73. Welles-Bogdanovich interview transcription, box 2, folder 3, p. 642. See also Welles and Bogdanovich, *This is Orson Welles*, 147–48.

74. See Herman G. Weinberg, *The Complete Greed of Erich von Stroheim: A Reconstruction of the Film in 348 Still Photos Following the Original Screenplay, Plus 52 Production Stills* (New York: Dutton, 1973).

75. Richard Koszarski, *An Evening's Entertainment: The Age of the Silent Feature Picture, 1915–1928* (Berkeley: University of California Press, 1994), 236.

76. Victor Oscar Freeburg, *Pictorial Beauty on the Screen* (New York: Macmillan, 1923). See also Kaveh Askari, *Making Movies into Art: Picture Craft from the Magic Lantern to Early Hollywood* (London: Palgrave BFI, 2014), 111–28.

77. Jonathan Rosenbaum, "The Invisible Orson Welles: A First Inventory," in *Discovering Orson Welles* (Berkeley: University of California Press, 2007), 81. See

also Josh Karp, *Orson Welles's Last Movie: The Making of* The Other Side of the Wind (New York: St. Martin's, 2015), 47.

78. See especially Liam O'Leary, *Rex Ingram: Master of the Silent Cinema* (1980; reprint Pordenone: Le Giornate del Cinema Muto; London: British Film Institute, 1994).

79. Welles-Bogdanovich interview transcription, box 2, folder 10, p. 12.

80. McGilligan, *Young Orson*, 614–15; Welles-Bogdanovich interview transcription, box 2, folder 2, p. 298. See also Welles and Bogdanovich, *This is Orson Welles*, 20–21.

81. Welles and Bogdanovich, *This is Orson Welles*, 21.

82. Ezra Goodman, *The Fifty Year Decline and Fall of Hollywood* (New York: Simon & Schuster, 1961), 1.

83. Goodman, *The Fifty Year Decline and Fall of Hollywood*, 10.

84. Richard Watts Jr., "D. W. Griffith, Social Crusader," in *The Emergence of Film Art: The Evolution and Development of the Motion Picture as an Art, from 1900 to the Present*, ed. Lewis Jacobs (New York: Hopkinson and Blake, 1969), 80; originally published in *New Theatre* (November 1936).

85. Welles-Bogdanovich interview transcription, box 2, folder 4, p. 22. See also McGilligan, *Young Orson*, 102–03.

86. Lewis Jacobs, *The Rise of the American Film: A Critical History* (New York: Harcourt, Brace, 1939), 385. On the publication of Jacobs's book before the Golden Jubilee, see "Book Notes," *New York Times* (September 26, 1939): 33.

87. Melvyn Stokes, *D.W. Griffith's* The Birth of a Nation: *A History of "The Most Controversial Motion Picture of All Time"* (Oxford: Oxford University Press, 2007), 254. See also Janet Staiger, *Interpreting Films: Studies in the Historical Reception of American Cinema* (Princeton, NJ: Princeton University Press, 1992), 146–54, and David Platt, "Fanning the Flames of War," *Daily Worker* (December 20, 1939): 7, cited in Staiger, 242n28.

88. The Mercury Theatre manifesto, "Theatre and the People's Front," was published the previous year in *The Daily Worker*. See Michael Denning, *The Cultural Front: The Laboring of American Culture in the Twentieth Century* (London: Verso, 1996), 531n1, citing Welles, "Theatre and the People's Front," *Daily Worker* (April 15, 1938): 7.

89. Welles-Bogdanovich interview transcription, box 2, folder 2, p. 294.

90. Welles-Bogdanovich interview transcription, box 2, folder 2, p. 298,.

91. Welles-Bogdanovich interview transcription, box 2, folder 4, p. 23.

92. Welles-Bogdanovich interview transcription, box 2, folder 2, p. 299. Compare Welles and Bogdanovich, *This is Orson Welles*, 88–89.

93. Welles-Bogdanovich interview transcription, box 2, folder 5, p. 35.

94. At one point Welles did say, however, "Although my policies and feelings are liberal, I'm much more comfortable talking with reactionaries about everything but politics than I am talking with liberals about anything but politics"; Welles-Bogdanovich interview transcription, box 2, folder 4, p. 127.

4

ORSON WELLES'S ITINERARIES IN *IT'S ALL TRUE*

From "Lived Topography" to Pan-American Transculturation

CATHERINE L. BENAMOU

As with Orson Welles's oeuvre in general, the task of retrieving and interpreting *It's All True* is like entering a labyrinth, only to step out into an ever-expanding universe. The project, which was shot in Mexico and Brazil during World War II, consisted of four interlocking parts, spanned three continents, and engaged four film crews at a dozen rural, urban, and coastal locations. Infused with the work of some of the most talented cinematographers, photographers, composers, musicians, and screenwriters in the hemisphere, the film—at times documentary, at times reenactment, at times staged fictional drama—would have covered subjects as diverse as bull raising and bullfighting, jazz and samba music, youthful romance, artisanal fishing, urban renewal, and labor struggles. Over a period of ten months, beginning in September 1941, actors were cast and rehearsed, locations were scouted, dialogue written, diegetic music recorded, and scenes choreographed and performed before the cameras. Even though most of the Latin American episodes were shot on Technicolor and black-and-white film, RKO, the producing studio, decided to suspend the production in mid-1942, which, coupled with Welles's inability to secure the rights to the footage thereafter, left the film in a state of limbo.

The reasons for the suspension of the film are complex and cannot be disentangled from the limited box office returns for *Citizen Kane* from its US release, the projected losses related to *The Magnificent Ambersons* (after a largely negative response from a preview audience in Pomona, California, March 1942), and the misrepresentation by RKO executives of Welles's mission as "goodwill" ambassador to Latin America. These were concurrent with the location production of *It's All True* and the budget and expenditures for the film as of late April 1942, when a proposal was made to revoke Welles's contract at RKO—ironically, on the grounds of "material interference" and "loss of world markets" provoked by the war, when in fact, as of December 1941, the film had officially become a wartime assignment, to be coproduced by the Office of the Coordinator of Inter-American Affairs.[1] It is also worth noting the studio's discontent with Welles's open-ended, neorealist approach to shooting the Brazilian episodes, "Carnaval" and "Jangadeiros," with their deeply embedded elements of social critique and the adverse, inflammatory reaction by Welles's production manager Lynn Shores to what he perceived as Welles's repeated filming of "the Negro and low-class element in and around Rio," aggravated by the concern of at least one RKO executive back at the studio over how the "indiscriminate intermingling" of races in the film might be received by [white] audiences "south of the Mason-Dixon line."[2]

As a result of its suspension, the precise spatiotemporal dimensions, editing style, and ultimate plot structure that the film would have embodied if it had been completed at the time are a matter of conjecture. Would the film have included a fourth episode on the history of jazz, as viewed through the life story of Louis Armstrong, as outlined in contracts and correspondence? Would Welles have added a transitional sequence in a late screenplay draft between the Mexican episode, "My Friend Bonito," and the Northeast Brazilian episode, "Jangadeiros," that was set in the Peruvian Andes and focused on the anticolonial rebellion of Inca leader Atauhuallpa? What survives materially of the project is a 1986 assemblage of a "trailer," *Four Men on a Raft*, spearheaded by Welles's associate producer Richard Wilson; a 1993 documentary reconstruction, *It's All True: Based on an Unfinished Film by Orson Welles* (codirected by Wilson, Myron Meisel, and Bill Krohn), an eight-minute edited sequence of Technicolor footage for the "Carnaval" episode,[3] as well as over 200,000 feet of 35mm nitrate negative (most of which has yet to be preserved on safety film), 50,000 feet of sound negative recorded in Rio de Janeiro (still missing from Paramount studio archives), multiple treatments, a handful of screenplays, and hundreds of still photographs.[4] In this chapter, I will be drawing on a few of these surviving materials, along with oral histories I conducted with film participants, to shed new light on the original film event and the immaterial legacy of *It's All True*: its indelible traces in popular memory, the socially expansive possibilities of Welles's cinematic interventions, the film's alignment with, and foreshadowing of, the Latin American neorealist wave in the 1950s, and the connections between the production strategies and aesthetics of "place" in this project and Welles's later works.[5] My book on *It's All True* was primarily devoted to reconstructing the film text and its historical circumstances as it evolved from a North American to a Latin American version within the general context of World War II, as well as broadening our understanding of the project within Welles's film oeuvre. Here, I will be taking a step back to consider the linkage between geographic and textual itineraries pursued by Welles during preproduction and production, so as to highlight the extent to which *It's All True* served as a "rite of passage" that immersed Welles and crew in a process of transculturation with respect to Latin American cinema and popular culture. In contrast to other US filmmakers working in Latin America at that time, Welles emerged from this experience as a transnational *auteur* with lasting ties to modern film movements in Europe and Latin America. This transnationalism derives not merely from making a film for hemispheric distribution, nor from traveling across borders to shoot it, but from his ability to collaborate intensively with Mexican and Brazilian creative talent so as to produce a dialogical vision of cultural practices and social contrasts within those countries.[6] Welles's efforts and ability to collaborate and adapt only grew over time as he came into contact with diverse national cultures and production contexts once he became uprooted and had to reroute his sense of "home" (what Mette Hjort has referred to as a kind of "cosmopolitan transnationalism" that is reflected in the work of migrant or exilic directors) in Ireland, Spain, Yugoslavia, Morocco, Italy, and France.[7] Thus, in a way, *It's All True* can be seen as practical preparation, unbeknownst to Welles at the time, for his semi-exilic, peripatetic existence and experimentation with production techniques on location around the globe after 1947.

The key to this transformation, I will argue, can be found within the process of shooting the "Carnaval" episode in Rio de Janeiro and Minas Gerais between February and June 1942. In describing this as a process involving "dialogical vision," I am drawing on Mikhail Bakhtin's concept of dialogism, itself closely related to a theory of the carnivalesque, to refer to a textual representation that results from the cultivation and acknowledgment of the dynamic exchange that takes place between the filmmaker, profilmic protagonist, and creative collaborators during the creation of the work.[8] In the context of cross-cultural contact, such as the Good Neighbor project as a whole, a dialogical approach provides the basis (yet not of course the guarantee) for transculturation. As it was originally formulated by Cuban anthropologist Fernando Ortiz, transculturation occurs when the meeting of different cultural traditions results in the production of hybrid cultural forms.[9] Original cultural forms are not simply "lost" as a result of colonization, but continue to develop in a dynamic of contrast, tension, and hybridization with colonial (or in the twentieth century, neocolonial) forms. (For further elaborations of theories of transculturation in literary studies and in ethnographic film, see the work of Ángel Rama and David MacDougall, respectively.)[10] Here, I will be using *transculturation* to refer to (1) Welles's efforts during the making of *It's All True* to spark a process of transculturation as one of the desired outcomes of inter-American dialogue, and (2) the ways in which Welles and crew became effectively coinscribed with their film subjects in the work in progress, thereby creating "new links based on points of recognition among otherwise separated social groups," including members of disenfranchised or marginalized communities in both the United States and Brazil.[11]

Of the various episodes of *It's All True*, "Carnaval" exhibits most strongly the dialogism that Welles envisioned, and it registers a drift away from the strategies and themes of official wartime propaganda and toward a more place-based model, or *lived topography*, of cultural exchange and audiovisual expression.[12] According to a late screenplay draft for the film, "Carnaval" would have been the third episode, following

"My Friend Bonito" and "Jangadeiros" (a.k.a., "Four Men on a Raft"), even though it went into production in February, prior to "Jangadeiros" (which began shooting in mid-March in Rio). Consisting of a series of re-enactments based on what Welles was able to document in February and conversations with top local talent, "Carnaval" would have chronicled the various phases and modalities of the annual celebration through a spatial exploration, as well as close attention to the temporality of ritual. The episode also suffered the greatest dismemberment when thousands of feet of Technicolor footage were cast into the Pacific Ocean in the late 1960s. Only 5,481 feet of Technicolor negative and 35,530 feet of black-and-white negative survive, of which only about 7,000 feet have been preserved, necessitating a greater reliance upon oral accounts and the photographic archive for its reconstruction and interpretation.[13]

Transformed by Welles into a city symphony, "Carnaval" under-scores his attention to the spatialization of ethnic and class difference in his portrayal of Latin American societies. Its progressively nimble style (the physical displacement and, at times, swooping aerial move-ments and canted angles of the camera, and the penetration into dif-ferent social milieus) resonates with the recently rediscovered footage from Welles's *Too Much Johnson* (shot in 1938 on New York's West Side) and it brings into relief Welles's growing interest in reflexively utilizing film to capture and build, in individual sequences and entire episodes, a sociocultural dialogue among and within cities, regions, and nations.[14] For example, in recognition of the ethnic and class distinctions among Carnaval performance venues around Rio de Janeiro, Welles set up a "call-and-response" format that would feature Afro-Brazilian artist Grande Othelo, performing at a hilltop samba school rehearsal, call-ing out the phrase "I love to hear drumming in the hills," answered in reverse shot by the lighter-skinned, more mainstream vocalist Linda Batista's "ay, ay, ay" on the stage of the cosmopolitan shoreline Cassino da Urca.[15] Welles's approach to the portrayal of place and intraurban relationships in "Carnaval" opened up fertile ground for a new cross-cultural cinematic practice to emerge, but also led to serious challenges and problems. Welles faced what can be called representational and aesthetic crises as he attempted to devise strategies that would help him to link the margins of the city (and later, through "Jangadeiros," the margins of Brazil) to its center. And a deeper, more concrete crisis arose when, during the last month of the filming of "Carnaval," RKO began to withdraw its material and institutional support for the project. By concentrating in what follows on the interrelationship of the production history and the evolving film text I hope to shed new light on Welles's take on the poetics and sociodynamics of place, and his ability, despite the suspension of institutional support for the film, to demonstrate the potential for the cinema to serve as a medium of intercultural dialogue, helping to strengthen hemispheric relations from the inside out rather than the top down.

THE CHANGING VECTORS OF *IT'S ALL TRUE*

It's All True is best understood by taking multiple pathways to unravel its history and evolving narrative discourse and structure; indeed, Welles himself appears to have resisted adopting a single, programmatic pathway to documenting or understanding "Carnaval." As he openly acknowledged by devising the multipart structure of the film, no single event, no matter how hybrid, such as Carnaval, could embody the full complexity of Latin American culture as a whole. Here, I will be retracing the itineraries Welles pursued while working in Brazil, from the continental and urban itineraries prescribed for him as he embarked on his trip to Brazil, to his less visible itineraries as he familiarized himself with local cultural practices tied to the yearly Carnaval celebration. By linking literal points on the map to figurative representations, it is possible to capture Welles's and his crew's transition out of a state-commissioned, neocolonial framing of events, and into the foregrounding of place as a site of sociocultural resilience and remembrance.[16]

In various ways, the analysis of itineraries can help to illuminate the cultural politics and methods for making *It's All True*: they can clue us in to Welles's profilmic *choices*, choices that involve ethical considerations and political stances, and that, over time, might be indicative of a deeper shift within his creative mindset. As I aim to show, several places along Welles's itinerary were particularly charged with sociocultural meaning, and thus came to occupy a more central position within the plot of "Carnaval." Most of these places were "off the map"—not on the agenda provided for Welles by the Office of Inter-American Affairs (OIAA), and were discovered by way of informal networks. The challenge for Welles was how to enhance the significance of those places for North and Latin American audiences without losing the support of the very institutional structures (in complex wartime negotiations among themselves) that were planning to circulate the finished film under the aegis of the Good Neighbor policy.

Complicating this challenge was the tension among the various forces—individual, local, transnational—shaping the "Carnaval" itineraries. For example, one detractor in a Rio de Janeiro publication faulted Welles with seeking out the "wrong type" of Brazilian advice: "We should exploit the prestige of Orson Welles to show ourselves to the world as a civilized nation . . . Instead of showing him our possibilities, they [the advisers] let him film, to his delight, scenes of no good half-breeds."[17] Various kinds and amounts of power over the production of "Carnaval" were wielded by John Hay Whitney, director of the Motion Picture Division of the Coordinator of Inter-American Affairs; RKO Radio Studio executives (such as Vice President Phil Reisman), Adhemar Gonzaga, head of Cinédia Studio in Rio de Janeiro; Lourival Fontes, head of Brazil's Departamento de Imprensa e Propaganda (Department of Press and Propaganda, or DIP); and Welles's binational team of advisers and collaborators (screenwriter Robert Meltzer, photographer Genevieve Naylor, Brazilian journalist Edmar Morel, musical composers and performers Herivelto Martins and Grande Othelo), in addition to Welles himself. Of central interest is Welles's growing effort after the Carnaval celebration to find the local meanings and possible narratives within it and to add a new episode ("Jangadeiros") focused on the plight and courage of the northeastern *jangadeiros*, or raft fishermen, as they sailed down to Rio to petition Brazilian president Getúlio Vargas for inclusion in his new social security legislation.[18] The introduction of these new elements began to pull "Carnaval" away from the plan of the original sponsoring institutions and toward Welles and his Mercury collaborators and Brazilian experts, leading to a redefinition of the Good Neighbor policy in favor of grassroots efforts to achieve democracy, recognition, and cultural affirmation.

CIDADÃO WELLES VS. RKO AND THE OIAA

To appreciate the ramifications of the shift in the project's emphasis, it is important to remember that, for most of its production, *It's All True* was cosponsored by Nelson A. Rockefeller's Coordinator of Inter-American Affairs, an agency that was expressly established in 1940 to improve relations between the United States and Latin America and stave off Axis economic, political, and ideological influence through-out the hemisphere during World War II.[19] Although Welles and Mer-cury collaborators Norman Foster, José Noriega, and Dolores del Río launched "My Friend Bonito" during the Good Neighbor policy in Sep-tember 1941—and, like other US-sponsored projects in Mexico at the time, filming began with the approval and supervision of the Mexican government—production occurred largely in the central Mexican coun-tryside, off the radar of media scrutiny of both the North and South. The episode, directed by Foster, was to depict the friendship between a bull, "Bonito," and a young *mestizo* boy, Chico (played by nonprofessional Jesús Vásquez), from Chico's childhood to the moment when Bonito demonstrates his formidable bravery and is pardoned in the Plaza El Toreo in Mexico City.[20]

By contrast, "Carnaval" was initiated at the behest of the DIP and John Hay Whitney, head of the Motion Picture Division of the OIAA, as just one of the activities that Welles was to engage in as a goodwill ambassador to Latin America following his arrival in Brazil in early February 1942. As he would later tell a BBC reporter, Welles undertook the project of documenting the annual Carnaval as his "patriotic duty" for the war effort, rushing to finish shooting for both *The Magnificent Ambersons* (1942) and *Journey into Fear* (directed by Norman Foster, 1943) in time to attend the festivities in Rio de Janeiro, with a battalion of RKO and Mercury film professionals in tow.[21] He intended to resume production on "My Friend Bonito" on his way back from South America through Mexico to the United States, and to complete editing for *The Magnificent Ambersons* while in Rio de Janeiro. The "Carnaval" venture signaled a shift in the geographical emphasis of the multipart *It's All True* from North America to Latin America.[22] It also catapulted the project from relative public obscurity into the limelight of Brazilian, US, and hemispheric media. Parallel to working on the film, Welles presented lectures on Shakespeare and painting at the Instituto de Belas Artes in Rio de Janeiro (featured in a *Cinejornal* newsreel of the DIP), broadcast two live Pan-American radio programs on NBC's Blue Network (fig. 4.1), and gave scores of press interviews in cities across Brazil, followed by stops in South and Central America on his way back to the United States in July–August 1942.[23] Footage of Welles setting up the camera and reveling in the Carnaval ball at Rio's Teatro Municipal, captured by RKO cameras during the festivities, also appeared in a *March of Time* newsreel on the war effort, as well as in stills of the same in a *Life* magazine feature article.[24] Thus, at this juncture, *It's All True*, together with Welles's increasingly international presence as a radio personality and film celebrity, began to form part of the OIAA's "soft power" approach to strengthening relations with Latin America.[25]

The establishment of preset itineraries to be followed during hemispheric travel was central to the project of goodwill ambassadors, initiated by the OIAA in 1941. Itineraries could help to maximize propaganda efforts by generating media interest and coordinating media coverage in the Southern Hemisphere, as well as provide a means of effectively utilizing limited resources at a time of war: each ambassador was sent on a tour to key destinations, usually the capital cities of the larger Latin American nations, where they would be met by government dignitaries and artistic and scholarly luminaries, with their multiple public appearances documented by an eager and curious local press. Welles's Pan-American itinerary, as determined by the coordinator's office and advisory committee in Rio was ambitious, partly because of the precedent set by Walt Disney, who had traveled to the southernmost parts of South America and Brazil between August and October, 1941, and partly due to Welles's own notoriety, thanks to the release of *Citizen Kane* in South America in the fall of 1941. Indeed, soon after his arrival in Brazil, the local press dubbed him *Cidadão Kane*, easier for Lusophones to pronounce than "Orson Welles." When he departed from the United States for Brazil on February 4, 1942, Welles was scheduled to travel to San Juan, Puerto Rico, Uruguay, Argentina, Chile, Bolivia, Peru, Colombia, Panama,

Figure 4.1. Orson Welles and Brazilian Foreign Minister Oswaldo Aranha on the set of the Pan-American Day broadcast on NBC's Blue Network, April 14, 1942. Source: Richard Wilson-Orson Welles Papers, University of Michigan Library (Special Collections Library).

Guatemala, and Mexico in addition to Brazil. With the exception of Belém, Brazil (where his plane stopped to refuel), and the Bolivian jungle (where he accompanied a medical team on a special mission to treat leprosy), this was a largely cosmopolitan itinerary, revolving mainly around widely publicized events, such as receiving an award for *Citizen Kane* and attending a *parrillada* in Buenos Aires (in April 1942) or visiting major Carnaval venues including the Teatro Municipal, Cinelândia, Avenida Carioca, the Cassino da Urca, and the Yacht Club in Rio de Janeiro. The choice of these venues reflected a top down approach to representing the Brazilian public sphere, and a neat avoidance of locations that would bring issues of social inequality, religious diversity, and racial and ethnic "contact zones" to the fore.

While there is little question that Welles was eminently well suited for this multifaceted public agenda, especially given his background in radio production and his star performance in and direction of *Citizen Kane* (for which he received "best director" and "best actor" awards in more than one Latin American film competition), his exercise of artistic license and freedom of speech soon led to a strained relationship with RKO representatives in Rio (notably production manager Lynn Shores) and those in power within the Brazilian DIP. To begin with, in a synopsis for *It's All True*, dating most probably from mid-1942, Welles boldly stated that "Brazil is a Democracy in a hemisphere of Democracies, and among the Democracies neither peonage nor starvation need be tolerated by free men."[26] The inclusion of the *jangadeiros'* story helped Welles to direct attention to the popular struggle for recognition and socioeconomic justice under the populist dictatorship of Getúlio Vargas, while encouraging an appreciation for the dignity of the laborer, a theme that he and his screenwriters had explored in the North American version of *It's All True*.

While nearly all OIAA-sponsored and produced films placed a rhetorical emphasis on democratic ideals as the basis for Pan-American unity, few referred explicitly to the startling socioeconomic inequalities that persisted in the Southern Hemisphere, other than to showcase the benefits of US-supported efforts in the modernization of agriculture, infrastructure, healthcare, and hygiene. As a rule, modernization efforts were shown to be spearheaded by an educated, US-friendly Latin American élite, literally relegating the role and position of the laborer, the small farmer, or the newly arrived city dweller to the background of the *mise-en-scène*.[27] Given the headquartering of the OIAA-Hollywood "representational machine" in North America, Latin American participation in the hemispheric flow of audiovisual discourse tended to be limited to the provision of raw talent (such as Carmen Miranda, or Tito Guizar), landscapes, and folkloric traditions for the Hollywood screen and radio airwaves, and the expansion of an enthusiastic consumer base for North American product.[28] Any Latin American opinions voiced (usually off camera or in animated form) were either official or genteel, usually vetted for inclusion by a local OIAA-appointed committee. Welles, on the other hand, strove to incorporate Latin American voices and opinions into his multimedia agenda, from the voice of pro-Allies Brazilian foreign minister Oswaldo Aranha over the airwaves, to radio-turned-screen star Grande Othelo (voicing the lament of the largely Afro-Brazilian *carioca* working class in "Carnaval"), to *jangadeiro* leader Manoel "Jacaré" Olimpio Meira, whose sailing diary of the 1941 voyage was used to guide the plot and initial dialogue for "Jangadeiros."

What might have been upstaged, or carefully bracketed by the cameras of other OIAA-funded directors such as Julien Bryan or Walt Disney, began to take center stage in *It's All True*.[29] This happened first with Welles's decision to cover peripheral Carnaval festivities—across the bay from Rio in Niterói at the children's Carnaval, shown in figure 4.2, at working class dance clubs, such as the Teatro da República, in remote hillside neighborhoods (the customary *bandas*, followed by larger groupings, such as *ranchos*), and next, with the decision to reenact and structure a narrative around Carnaval at Cinédia sound studio, focusing on the roots and modern forms of samba music. At his own initiative, and assisted by various advisers—Robert Meltzer, Genevieve Naylor, Herivelto Martins, Grande Othelo, Anselmo Duarte—Welles rerouted the urban production itineraries to a pattern radiating outward from the sociopolitical center of Rio, which, combined with the staging of scenes at Cinédia Studio in São Cristovão and the decision to reenact the *jandadeiros*'s heroic voyage from Fortaleza (originally completed just six months before), significantly extended Welles's stay in Brazil. The initial media event, soft-propaganda approach to capturing local culture

Figure 4.2. *Caboclo* and children on beach in Niterói during Children's Carnaval.
Source: Richard Wilson-Orson Welles Papers, University of Michigan Library
(Special Collections Library).

was set aside for the painstaking work of ethnography. To the call for
hemispheric and national unity, Welles raised new questions and had
his own preliminary answers about the central concerns of *It's All True*:
whose Brazil would be represented? And which Americans would the
film effectively appeal to?

REDEFINING AND REPRESENTING A
CULTURAL POLITICS OF UBIQUITY

Upon witnessing Welles at work on the set of "Carnaval" at Cinédia Studio in Rio de Janeiro, Vinicius de Moraes, Brazilian poet, film critic, and
consul in Los Angeles following World War II, observed: "What energy,
what vitality, what *ubiquity* there is in this great *Brazilian*! Brazilian, yes;
Orson Welles begins to know Brazil, or at least an important side of the
Brazilian soul, better than many sociologists, many novelists, many crit-

ics, and many Brazilian poets out there. His perspective is at times *crude*, but it never errs on the side of injustice.[30]

De Moraes was not alone in this assessment; his sentiments have been echoed by many other Brazilians who met and worked with Welles in 1942, such as Chico Albuquerque (photographer) and Aloysio Pinto (musicologist), who recalled working with Welles in Fortaleza; samba musician Geraldo Caboré, who remembered teaching Welles to play the *pandeiro*, or tambourine, in a *favela* (hillside slum) overlooking Rio de Janeiro; Grande Othelo, and Pery Ribeiro (son of Herivelto Martins), who intimated, in the 1993 documentary *It's All True: Based on an Unfinished Film by Orson Welles*, that Welles's approach to shooting Carnaval would not have yielded a Hollywood version of Brazil, but rather a portrayal of Brazil "as it really was." Welles was, in their view, correcting the misrepresentations that had been made in previous North American audiovisual productions by becoming a dedicated participant observer, willing to sample the cultural riches that "insiders" were eager to share with him.[31] *It's All True* became, for Welles's local sympathizers, a bridge from Brazil out to the world, a feat only made possible by a director who had at least one foot planted solidly in Brazilian culture and society. Welles's "ubiquity" was greatly enhanced by his deviation from the official itinerary and decision to ad lib during and after the annual Carnaval, utilizing the second RKO unit as an exploratory device to document popular dancehalls, peripheral celebrations in the Rio suburbs, and the culmination of Lent in the neighboring state of Minas Gerais. Going further against the original plan, he brought his Technicolor cinematography from Rio's city center to its coastline to film the reenactment of the *jangadeiros'* arrival in Guanabara Bay (Rio de Janeiro), ending in a maritime procession of vessels of various types and sizes, from sailboats to fishing and ferry boats, flanking the São Pedro raft from multiple directions to escort it to safe harbor and a (fictive) integration into the Carnaval parade from Praça Mauá to Cinelândia. To the now distended ambassadorial itinerary, Welles added regional production itineraries (Minas Gerais, the coastal Northeast), and sketched a periphery-center construct that would show these regions in active conversation with Rio, the nation's capital. This structure also included microitineraries showing Carnaval as so many rivulets flowing from the

Figure 4.3. "Carinhoso," romantic couple and band in patio of "Rio Tennis Clube."
Source: Richard Wilson-Orson Welles Papers, University of Michigan Library
(Special Collections Library).

bandas down to the massive parade, surging like the Amazon down the
Avenida Carioca; samba composition and rehearsal reaching from the
"fountainhead" in weekly sessions atop the *favela* into an all-city jam
session in Praça Onze in downtown Rio (where the samba schools traditionally converged); and the tonal contrast during Carnaval between
boisterous whirls and conga lines in dancehalls and a quiet romantic
interlude, shot with *film noir* lighting, in a fictitious "Tennis Clube"
(fig. 4.3).

In March 1942, shortly after meeting Jacaré, the leader of the *jangada* expedition and spokesperson of the *jangadeiros*, Welles traveled to Fortaleza to visit the fishing colonies himself and begin planning the reenactment of the *raid* (expedition) to Rio, adding Good Neighbor stops in São Luiz (Maranhão), Recife (Pernambuco), and Salvador (Bahia). In April, the black-and-white second unit (cinematographers Harry Wild and Joseph Biroc, screenwriter Robert Meltzer, and associate producer Richard Wilson) was dispatched to Minas Gerais to document the Easter festivities (from Holy Thursday through Sunday), quite probably as a reminder to the audience that Carnaval is the Catholic prelude to Lent (which, from a social as well as spiritual viewpoint represents a "restoration of order"). Ouro Preto, the site of these festivities, is a colonial city known for its baroque culture and architecture, a form of expression that, in Brazil, reflects a deep transcultural process between African and European aesthetic traditions and belief systems as well as a certain ambivalence toward the erasures of vernacular culture brought about by modernity.

More than a showcase for tourists, then, Brazilian Carnaval could be revealed as having ecumenical value as part of the Christian calendar, while providing a high-profile conduit for the public expression and enjoyment of non-Christian elements of Afro-Brazilian culture, from its Yoruba and Kikongo roots to its modernized, hybrid forms. This in itself posed a challenge for the DIP, given the official preference for Catholicism (over other Christian religions) and Kardecist spiritism over traditional Afro-diasporic religious practices, such as *umbanda*.[32] The plan was then to shoot "Jangadeiros" in Technicolor, so as to complete a multiregional portrait of Brazil, one that would trace various pathways from the impoverished, yet starkly beautiful beaches of Fortaleza, the cobbled, postcolonial streets of Ouro Preto, and the vibrant hillsides of Rio de Janeiro to the center of modern prosperity, where a quest for social justice could be joined to an affirmation of cultural continuity in the face of modernization. It was the "ubiquity" of *this* vision, concretized in Welles's shooting itinerary and screenplay drafts, and bringing the voices, the resilient bodies of the oppressed in center frame, that met with such opprobrium from RKO and sectors of the DIP.

TOWARD AN "ANATOMY OF SAMBA":
SINFÔNIA DOS TAMBURINS, RIO TENNIS CLUBE,
PRAÇA ONZE, PANAMÉRICA E FOLGA NÊGO

With the branching out of the Brazilian itinerary, and Welles's transition from international celebrity into participant observer, deep transformations occurred within the work in progress that, realized within the text, would likely have enhanced audience engagement for millions of Brazilians, even as they went against the grain of officially authorized documentary practice. The first, and most obvious, was the conversion of Carnaval from tourist spectacle into an authentic depiction of ritual activity, with scenes linking neighborhood gatherings to performances at the city center. By the end of March 1942, Welles and his two film crews had gathered enough material to make a straightforward documentary of the Carnaval celebration and Easter, its Lenten complement. Yet rather than print and edit this footage as a travelogue that would have been suggestive of a dichotomy between colonial "tradition" (Ouro Preto) and pluralistic "modernity" (Rio de Janeiro), Welles wanted this part of his film to feature a collaborative reenactment that would spark awareness both of the social significance of Carnaval in releasing accumulated tensions arising from the persistence of centuries-old class and race inequality and of the perennial centrality of musical performance to the formation of urban, ethnic, and national identity, a theme that Welles had wished to explore by focusing on Louis Armstrong's career in "The Story of Jazz."

Welles planned to order the events in a manner that respected the unfolding of the ritual, reflecting the diverse ways in which Carnaval was experienced by the denizens of greater Rio de Janeiro. In addition to the rituals of the Catholic calendar writ large, Welles would incorporate other ritualistic elements stemming from the syncretic *umbanda* and *candomblé*, ranging from a statue of São Jorge (Saint George) on the set of the samba school practice to religious practitioners performing in traditional regalia, thereby ensuring the realism of the cinematic portrayal of Rio Carnaval.[33] It was music, more than visual spectacle that was the driving force for this episode, and the variations of music Welles recorded reflected the diversity in Brazilian urban society in 1942.

In contrast to Walt Disney's *Saludos Amigos* (1942), which featured the animated parrot Zé Carioca singing the mass hit "Aquarela do Brasil" (Ary Barroso), Welles's "Carnaval" sequences would be built around the number two seasonal hit "Adeus Praça Onze" (Herivelto Martins and Sebastião de Souza Prata) and local samba jam sessions in addition to the number one hit "Saudades da Amélia" (Ataulpho Alves and Mario Lago) and the romantic standard "Carinhoso" (Pixinguinha).[34] These selections, bearing specific associations with national and urban history and space, and chosen in consultation with Brazilian advisers, reflect Welles's efforts to inscribe a "lived topography" of greater Rio. The alternation between these musical themes had the effect of exposing, rather than effacing, differences within urban and national society, foregrounding Praça Onze (Square Eleven), a place where samba schools and *batuqueiros* (free-form drummers) would congregate, rather than the European-influenced Teatro Municipal, site of the most prestigious Carnaval ball, or the élite Tennis Clube. Moreover, and significantly, the documentary footage was to be interwoven with reenacted sequences, such as Grande Othelo leading a *banda* in the remote neighborhood of Quintino, a creative departure from the usual practice in fictional wartime propaganda of turning Carnaval into a series of musical numbers.[35]

Tying this amalgam together was a twofold narrative movement through urban space, with Grande Othelo and Herivelto Martins's son Pery serving as links among scenes across the city. The inclusion of Pery, in the role of a lost boy in search of his mother, added psychological tension to the episode as well as an intimation of the broad theme of the "restoration of order" in preparation for renewal, and it would have resonated with the story of the young boy, Chico, in "My Friend Bonito," who tries to save his favorite bull from execution in the ring. Grande Othelo, cast in the allegorical role of "the muse of Carnaval," helped to resignify the spaces of Carnaval as spaces inspired by, and infused with, Afro-Brazilian culture, highlighting its power as an energizing force within national modernity, much like jazz in "The Jazz Story" (the first of the North American episodes). Neither RKO executives nor, evidently, the OIAA, were receptive to the attention to Afro-diasporic integration coupled with inter-American unity, and they failed to see any meaningful narrative patterns in the midst of "tropical chaos," yet such an integration is precisely what Meltzer, Welles, Martins, and Othelo had in mind when they developed the blueprints for "Carnaval."[36]

Fittingly, the urban itineraries of Othelo and Pery finally meet not on the modern boulevard of Cinelândia nor the traffic circle near Teatro Municipal, but in Praça Onze, soon to be razed to make way for Avenida Getúlio Vargas, named after the Brazilian President. From this standpoint, the narrative arc of "Carnaval" can be read as a tale of collective loss (we see the forlorn Pery with Othelo, alone and adrift after leading crowds into musical "battle") and recovery through the inscription of popular celebration within a new transnational space of cultural exchange in which Afro-Brazilian and *caboclo* identities and rhythms are to be as valued as Euro-Brazilian forms of culture, favored by the Vargas regime. The episode ends not with the calendar-bound end of Carnaval, but with a flourishing return to Cassino da Urca, where, past a "big neon sign" and "expensive cars jamming the entrance," one finds a "big crowd in masquerade," dancing to "Saudades da Amélia" sung by the Mexican bolero star Chucho Martínez Gil "in serapi [sic]." Of this sequence, Welles writes, "Each time we cut back to the Urca—from other Carnaval locations—things should be getting hotter—to finish on the climax of 'Carnaval Finale,'" specially composed for the film and featuring US bandmaster Ray Ventura and his orchestra. Inside the Urca Grill, we find that the "center glass-paneled platform is still up and now Otello [sic] is entertaining... Otello will decide which specialty he will do."[37] Othelo is paired with the mainstream vocalist Linda Batista, followed by popular singer Francisco Alves, a *choro* (ragtime number), and a performance of the northeastern *machiche*. Welles thus creates a musical mosaic within the transnational space of the Cassino, overlaid with a larger, moving mosaic of Carnaval venues across the city, recapping the sites visited in the microitineraries.

Performance itself, then, covering a spectrum from spontaneous, unrehearsed revelry to polished club and theatrical presentations, functioned both as a mechanism for narrative continuity linking different spaces and modes of representation, and a vehicle for cultural symbolism, a concept that would reemerge in hybrid integrated musicals such as Otto Preminger's *Carmen Jones* (1954) and Marcel Camus's *Black Orpheus* (1959), albeit with diminished intercultural content. Beyond the immediate transcultural effects of music and performance, the juxtaposition of the two primary narrative grids, the ritual and the quest, both of which imply movement in time and across space, formed the foundation for a hybrid aesthetic that could lead to a more locally responsive form of modernity and broadly based democratic process than what was being offered under the Estado Nóvo. In Praça Onze, Othelo joins his allegorical quest—to reach beyond the *favela* to Praça Onze, and then the national stage—to that of little Pery; once Othelo reaches the Cassino da Urca (the very location where Carmen Miranda was "discovered" by Broadway impresario Lee Shubert three years earlier), his own quest for recognition can finally be joined to that of the *jangadeiros*. Othelo is embraced by a sophisticated international (albeit largely Brazilian, and by extension hemispheric) audience; the *jangadeiros* are received by the Brazilian president.

These narrative grids are also present in "My Friend Bonito," where the quotidian rhythms of bull raising and post-Lenten ritual of the "Blessing of the Animals" are joined to the quest of a poor, rural *mestizo* citizen (Chico) to be heard and granted a pardon for his bull at the center of national power. Within the larger discursive structure of the multipart film, these grids serve an important complementary role within Welles's proposal for Good Neighbor representation: that ritual (or local cultural tradition) be respected without cordoning it off from the modern democratic process, which, if vigorously embraced, could succeed in deflecting the advance of the Axis powers in the Southern Hemisphere.

THE CONSEQUENCES OF CHANGING ITINERARIES

As I hope I have shown, *It's All True* was not so much a film "about Brazil," as it was a film that placed communities (within and beyond Latin America) in conversation with one another, so as to launch a process of mutual transformation and understanding. Emblematic of this concept is the use of fictional reenactment to extend the itinerary and narrative of the *jangadeiros*' arrival in Rio into the space of the Carnaval celebration. While the latest script describes the incorporation of the *jangada* São Pedro into the general street parade in city center, there is also photographic evidence of the four smartly dressed *jangadeiros* on

Figure 4.4. *Jangadeiros* on the set of "Carnaval." Source: Richard Wilson-Orson Welles Papers, University of Michigan Library (Special Collections Library).

the set of the Carnaval reenactment, as shown in this still of the Praça Onze sequence (fig. 4.4). Also effective is the use of Herivelto Martins's composition, *Ave Maria no Morro* (*Ave Maria on the Hill*, adapted from Franz Schubert) to introduce the audience to the *favela* where samba practice will begin (*Sinfônia dos Tamburins*), thereby uplifting, rather than exoticizing or ghettoizing that community.[38] Finally, Welles brings Northeast Brazilian musical culture (the *forró* and the *frevo*) into the spotlight of the nightclub and into the visual foreground in an exterior shot against a picturesque Rio landscape as in a production still (with the Pão de Açucar looming boldly in the background).[39] Welles thus

utilizes Carnaval, a ritual metaphor for democracy, to focus our attention on the potential for transculturation (following Ramos's definition)
within Brazilian society.

Welles's portrayal of the places of Carnaval and its ritual aftermath
in the Easter celebration would undoubtedly have been familiar and
acceptable to Afro-diasporic and Catholic viewers alike, even in the
United States. But the allegedly "indiscriminate intermingling" of races
and social classes in the public spaces of *It's All True*; his filming of impoverished sites and subjects in Technicolor; his use of precious screen
time and space to show nonprofessional performers; and the derisive
vocal reaction of the Brazilian sociopolitical elite prompted RKO (and
eventually the OIAA) to begin withdrawing their support for the film
in May 1942.[40] Perhaps more than his break from conventional film style
and his deviation from the script and plan envisioned by the film's public
and private sponsors, Welles's rapid embrace of Latin American—here,
Brazilian—frameworks of sociality and ethnic interaction, his attention
to vernacular musical and dance forms, as well as mass culture, and his
exploration, through Praça Onze, of the consequences for Brazilians of
US-propelled modernization, prompted suspicion and opposition by
studio and government officials, leading to censure and a withdrawal of
the support required to complete the film. More than gestures of disap-
proval, these were, in effect, acts of destruction. In his essay film *O Signo
do Caos* (2005), the fourth of a series on Welles in Brazil, Brazilian filmmaker Rogério Sganzerla dramatizes Welles's troubles with the regime
of Getúlio Vargas by showing members of the DIP and metropolitan
police previewing, then packing and dumping cans of the film into the
Atlantic Ocean, a powerful figurative rendering of the fate of *It's All True*.

In conceptualizing Welles's approach in making this film and
what energized the opposition to his redirection of the official plan, it
is useful to refer to Claude Lévi-Strauss's dichotomy of the "raw" (or
"crude") and the "cooked."[41] Welles understood the need for a "raw"
vision that would allow the process of culture making to unfold and
the biases of standard camera setups to unravel. Rather than yield a
fully "cooked" set of episodes (propaganda) or a film that was too "raw"
to serve the purposes of popular education and transnational recognition, Welles sought a balance between these poles, by planning to

record a soundtrack back in Hollywood featuring dialogue and narration by the principal performers—Jesús Vásquez and Domingo Soler ("My Friend Bonito"), Grande Othelo (the muse of "Carnaval"), and Francisca Moreira da Silva (the young bride) and surviving *jangadeiros* (in "Jangadeiros"). The sense of place, ritual and habitual activity, and spontaneity rendered by the silent images could thus be joined to clearly intelligible dialogue and an expertly mixed musical soundtrack, which, among other things, would allow sound bridges to link urban segments in a complex pattern of call and response. That Welles was not able to finalize these plans once he found his production itinerary cut short (both in Mexico and Brazil) and support for the project's completion withdrawn does not diminish the importance and impact of his effort or the mapping of this modern-artisanal hybrid aesthetic suited to the cultural practices represented in the film.

Among the casualties of RKO's abandonment of Welles and Mercury in mid-1942 was Welles's ability to make good on plans for the Cassino da Urca finale as well as maintain continuity in shooting techniques for the third episode, "Jangadeiros," which he had started shooting in Technicolor on location in Rio in March 1942 parallel to the staged scenes for "Carnaval." In contrast to the previous two episodes, the Northeastern shoot for "Jangadeiros" was carried out with a skeleton crew involving Welles's closest Mercury collaborators, a Rio-based cameraman, George Fanto, his assistant and equipment (a silent Mitchell 35mm camera and sound-on-disk recording equipment) dispatched from Cinédia Studio, and a local *cearense* photographer, Chico Albuquerque. Shot in black-and-white on the beach without electricity, the northeastern scenes featured an improvised love story that, while it did not overshadow the drama of the *jangadeiros'* heroic journey to Rio de Janeiro by raft, helped to fill the void left by the untimely death of *jangadeiro* leader Jacaré on May 19, 1942.[42] While this institutionally "orphaned" episode marked a shift away from industrial-scale filmmaking compared to "My Friend Bonito" and especially "Carnaval," it should be noted that Welles had already experimented with location shooting utilizing nonprofessional actors during Carnaval. In his pursuit of the hidden Carnaval, Welles began to use an 8mm camera (fig. 4.5), with which he was able to shoot at close range, deep in the crowds, a strategy that would be re-

Figure 4.5. Orson Welles shooting with an 8mm camera on location during Carnaval in Rio de Janeiro. Source: Richard Wilson-Orson Welles Papers, University of Michigan Library (Special Collections Library).

peated with the use of an Eyemo camera to shoot fishing scenes from the *jangadas* themselves in Fortaleza. Striving for spontaneity and authenticity, he also engaged local community members to perform in staged scenes at Cinédia ("Sinfonia dos Tamburins" and "Adeus, Praça Onze" sequences), an effort that would be repeated throughout "Jangadeiros."

Welles had far-reaching ambitions for his project, and spoke of laying the basis for what Mette Hjort might refer to as "affinitive transnationalism," such that, in addition to "returning the footage" to Latin America with a finished product on the screen, the United States could help Brazil develop its own film industry through technology transfer, much along the lines of US investment in Mexico's film industry during this same period.[43] The termination of Welles's contract at RKO affected his ability to realize this goal, but even without resulting in a completed film, the project did yield some of the transcultural effects he envisioned. His presence was galvanizing and memorable to the communities featured in the film, while the social and aesthetic vectors traced by his itineraries contributed to the renewal of Latin American cinema and, in particular, can be palpably detected in the northeastern films of Glauber Rocha (*Barravento*, 1962) and Nelson Pereira dos Santos (*Rio 40 Graus*, 1954, *Rio Zona Norte*, 1958) during the Brazilian Cinema Nôvo.

It's All True has also had an impact on world cinema outside of Brazil. A new type of interregional and hemispheric dialogue emerged through the production of *It's All True* that pointed in several directions: to the productive role to be played by Afro-diasporic culture in shaping modern popular music and performative circuits, from jazz to samba to mambo and salsa (featured in the Brazilian musical comedy or *chanchada* and the Mexican *cabaretera*); and to the role of self-reflexive ethnography and place-based scene construction in generating a new type of socially-engaged cinema.[44] Here, one might trace links between *Redes*, directed by Fred Zinnemann (Mexico, 1936), and "Jangadeiros"; and between "Carnaval" and two films directed by Nelson Pereira dos Santos: *Rio, 40 Graus* (Brazil, 1955), and *Rio, Zona Norte* (Brazil, 1958), the latter starring Grande Othelo. The shooting methods of *It's All True* arguably helped pave the way for experiments in *cinema vérité* such as *Les Racquetteurs*, directed by Michel Brault and Gilles Groux (Québec, Canada, 1958), and hybrid musical performance, such as *Orfeu Negro* and especially the play *Orfeu da Conceição* (1954), written and directed by Vinicius de Moraes.

ESSAY AND PLACE IN WELLES'S LATER WORKS

It's All True resonates not only throughout world cinema but also, concomitantly, in Welles's subsequent work. Instead of treating *It's All True* as a satellite project that formed an exception in Welles's cinematic practice (because it was part documentary, a government-sponsored project, and it involved processes of transculturation), we should consider it as a formative moment in his early film career, and try to identify its influence in terms of both shooting strategy and ethos on his later projects. Even though it remained unfinished, a certain amount of ambiguity, of incompletion would have been retained *even in the completed work* as an essay film, especially involving the relationship between documentary and fictional modes of representation. This is a mode that, as Jonathan Rosenbaum has insightfully argued, Welles would cultivate not only in radio, but also in his later film and television work, notably in *F for Fake* (1973) and *Filming Othello* (1981).[45] Indeed, we might find within the essay format an additional source of tension between *It's All True* as the exploratory enterprise it became and the official plan for it as part of the Good Neighbor mission. As Robert Stam has noted, "One of the salient characteristics of the essay, from Montaigne to Adorno, is the *freedom of invention*, which makes possible an indulgence in a digressive aesthetic in which concerns that are superficially peripheral to the topic come into the foreground."[46] Once completed, *It's All True* (as projected) would have likely reflected the process of the discovery and importance of place to cross-cultural representation, with peripheral places taking on foundational significance with respect to the national cultural process as they had in the progressive cinema of the New Deal. It is important to recognize how, with few exceptions, a keen attentiveness to place reoccurs within the *mise-en-scène* and semantics of later projects by Welles, such as *The Stranger* (1945), *Lady from Shanghai* (1948), as well as films produced while in self-imposed exile in Europe, including *Return to Glennascaul* (with Hilton Edwards as the director of record, 1949), *Othello* (1952), which was partially shot by George Fanto, the Hungarian-born cinematographer who filmed "Jangadeiros" on location in Ceará, *Don Quijote* (1957–69), *Chimes at Midnight* (1965), and *The Other Side of the Wind* (1970–76). What distinguishes these latter projects is that place is less the primary referent or destination of the narrative than the audiovisual incubator for a representation that, even after postproduction, retains its organicity, its texture.

CONCLUSION

While it may seem paradoxical that a project that was designed to serve US and Brazilian national interests became a platform for transnational authorship as well as intercultural and social critique, this is precisely what Welles's changes of itinerary during the production of *It's All True* accomplished. Even though the film was not completed by Welles, the effects of these changes opened up new possibilities for ethnic and social representation within both the Brazilian and US contexts and they were fueled in powerful ways by Welles's abiding interest in the essay form (allowing the blending of documentary and fiction, each mode leading back to place as a site of meaning making) and a periodic return to an improvisational engagement with lived topography in his subsequent film projects, including those shot in the United States. It is my hope that these relationships can be pursued in future Welles scholarship, and that additional evidence of Welles's accomplishments in *It's All True* can be brought to light through further preservation of the elements, filmed more than seventy-five years ago, especially given how central it is to Welles's work and his legacy.

CATHERINE L. BENAMOU is associate professor of Film and Media Studies, Chicano-Latino Studies, Latin American Studies, and Visual Studies at the University of California–Irvine. She is author of *It's All True: Orson Welles's Pan-American Odyssey* and was associate producer and senior researcher for the film, *It's All True: Based on an Unfinished Film by Orson Welles.*

NOTES

I wish to thank the editors of this volume, James Gilmore and Sidney Gottlieb, as well as an anonymous reader for the Indiana University Press for their helpful suggestions regarding the structure of this essay.

1. The statements regarding the war appear in Ross R. Hastings to Mr. Charles W. Koerner, Inter-Department Communication, April 27, 1942, RKO General Archives, 1–3, quoted in Catherine L. Benamou, *It's All True: Orson Welles's Pan-American Odyssey* (Berkeley: University of California Press, 2007), 253. According to documents consulted by both Joseph McBride and myself, RKO inflated the actual expenditures made by Welles and Mercury Productions on *It's All True*, stating the film was over budget, and failed to acknowledge openly that Welles had estimated the production would cost between $850,000 and $1 million to produce, with $300,000 guaranteed by the OIAA in the event the film incurred losses following its theatrical release. In August 1943, the overall cost, including overhead, was $832,347; as late as February 1949, the net costs, including overhead, were listed as $875,502.09, still under the top original estimate; see Joseph McBride, *What Ever Happened to Orson Welles? A Portrait of an Independent Career* (Lexington: University Press of Kentucky, 2006), 74; and Benamou, *It's All True*, 252, respectively.

2. Lynn Shores to Dr. Alfredo Pessôa, Departamento de Imprensa e Propaganda, April 11, 1942, Orson Welles Manuscripts, Lilly Library, Indiana University, Bloomington, Indiana, 1; and William Gordon to Mr. C. W. [Charles] Koerner, RKO Radio Pictures, Inc., July 9, 1942, RKO General Archive, quoted in Benamou,

It's All True: Orson Welles's Pan-American Odyssey, 237–38. For further observations on RKO's response to Welles's handling of Afro-Brazilian culture and documentary subjects, see Robert P. Stam, *Tropical Multiculturalism: A Comparative History of Race in Brazilian Cinema and Culture* (Durham, NC: Duke University Press, 2004), 107–32. For a discussion of how the indeterminate structure of the film along with a sketch and synopsis, the approach used by Welles (rather than following a preapproved shooting script) might have factored into RKO's decision to withdraw support from the production, see Benamou, *It's All True*, 231–35.

3. Until recently, this footage was available at the Paramount Pictures footage library, and appears in the TV documentary, "The Orson Welles Story," produced by Leslie Megahey and Alan Yentob, *Arena*, BBC, 1982.

4. The 1986 trailer, *Four Men on a Raft*, was coproduced by Richard Wilson and Fred Chandler, and sponsored by the American Film Institute; 1993 version was directed by Richard Wilson, Myron Meisel, and Bill Krohn, and produced by Les Films Balenciaga and Paramount Pictures. The surviving film elements reside in a vault at UCLA Film and Television; other materials may be found in the Orson Welles Manuscripts Collection at Lilly Library, the Orson Welles Archive in the Special Collections Library, University of Michigan, and the Cinemateca Brasileira in São Paulo, Brazil.

5. For an excellent summary of this period in Latin American cinema, see Paulo Antônio Paranaguá, "Of Periodizations and Paradigms: The Fifties in Comparative Perspective," *Nuevo Texto Crítico*, no. 21–22 (January–December 1998): 37–43.

6. In cultural and artistic texts, simple *hybridity* is "the juxtaposition of, and intercutting between, different forms of cultural expression, styles, settings, or moods"; see Benamou, *It's All True*, 184.

7. See Mette Hjort, "On the Plurality of Cinematic Transnationalism," in *World Cinemas, Transnational Perspectives*, ed. Nataša Ďuričová and Kathleen Newman (New York: Routledge, 2010), 20–24.

8. Bakhtin notes that "No utterance in general can be atrributed to the speaker exclusively; it is the product of the interaction of the interlocutors, and broadly speaking, the product of the whole complex social situation in which it has occurred"; cited in Tzevetan Todorov, *Mikhail Bakhtin: The Dialogical Principle*, trans. Wlad Godzich (Minneapolis: University of Minnesota Press, 1985), 30.

9. See Fernando Ortiz, *Cuban Counterpoint: Tobacco and Sugar*, trans. Harriet de Onís (New York: Knopf, 1947).

10. See David Frye, "Introduction," in Ángel Rama, *Writing Across Cultures: Narrative Transculturation in Latin America* (Durham, NC: Duke University Press, 2012), xii–xiv, and David MacDougall, *Transcultural Cinema* (Princeton, NJ: Princeton University Press, 1998), 259–62.

11. MacDougall, *Transcultural Cinema*, 261.

12. For further discussion of "lived topography," see Gary Backhaus, "Introduction," in *Lived Topographies and Their Mediational Forces*, ed. Gary Backhaus and John Murungi (Lanham, MD: Lexington Books, 2005), xiii.

13. Based on a 2005 inventory at the UCLA Film and Television Archive, there are 16,793 feet of "My Friend Bonito" in nitrate positive, coupled with 75,145 feet of nitrate negative, of which 8,000 feet have been preserved; for "Jangadeiros" there are 13,978 feet of nitrate positive, along with 63,950 feet of nitrate negative of which 35,950 feet have been preserved.

14. For more on this point, see Benamou, *It's All True*, 190–92, 215–18.

15. Sebastião Bernardes de Souza Prata, *aka* "Grande Othelo," interview by author, 8mm videotape recording, Rio de Janeiro, Brazil, 30 August, 1989.

16. In a previous publication, I include three maps portraying five separate textual itineraries linked to *It's All True*; see Catherine L. Benamou, "Retrieving Orson Welles's Suspended Inter-American Film, *It's All True*," *Nuevo Texto Crítico*, no. 21–22 (January–December, 1998): 257–58, 260.

17. Gatinha Angora in *Ciné-Radio-Jornal*, quoted in Stam, *Tropical Multiculturalism*, 129.

18. For more on the *jangadeiros'* raid or expedition, see Benamou, *It's All True*, 36–39.

19. For an excellent overview of the OIAA's cultural activities, especially those involving media production and distribution, see Gisela Cramer and Ursula Prutsch, "Nelson A. Rockefeller's Office of Inter-American Affairs and the Quest for Pan-American Unity: An Introductory Essay," in *¡Américas Unidas! Nelson A. Rockefeller's Office of Inter-American Affairs (1940–46)*, ed. Gisela Cramer and Ursula Prutsch (Madrid: Iberoamericana, 2012), 15–51.

20. Interestingly, Welles's proposed portrayal of Mexico in a previous project that he planned but never filmed, *The Way to Santiago* (alternately titled *Mexican Melodrama*), which went into development in spring 1941, met with criticism from both the Mexican government and RKO executives. See, for example, Alejandro Buelna, Jr., Jefe del Departamento de Turismo, Mexico, to William Gordon [RKO], letter of May 13, 1942, 1–2, Richard Wilson-Orson Welles Papers, Special Collections Library, University of Michigan, Ann Arbor, MI.

21. "The Orson Welles Story," *Arena*. In addition to a sixteen-member Technicolor camera and sound crew, RKO dispatched a three-member black-and-white second unit (which was directed on location by Mercury collaborators Richard Wilson and Robert Meltzer) as safety backup until test reels of the Technicolor footage could be developed.

22. For information on the other (unproduced) North American episodes, see Benamou, *It's All True*, 70–79, 119–29.

23. For more on the importance of radio to the OIAA's propaganda efforts in Brazil, see Cramer and Prutsch, "Nelson A. Rockefeller's Office of Inter-American Affairs in Brazil," 264–65.

24. This footage is available at the National Archive in Washington, DC.

25. On the nuanced parameters of "soft power" in OIAA program implementation, see Cramer and Prutsch, "Nelson A. Rockefeller's Office of Inter-American Affairs," 24–28.

26. Orson Welles, "Synopsis of IT'S ALL TRUE," n.d., page 3, microfilm roll 7, "Welles Collection," RKO General Archives, Richard Wilson-Orson Welles Papers; all capitals in original.

27. For more on the thematics and social orientation of OIAA films shot in Latin America, see Pennee Bender, " 'There's Only One America Now:' The OIAA Film Programs in the United States," in Cramer and Prutsch, *¡Américas Unidas!*, 77–105.

28. "Representational machine" is Ricardo D. Salvatore's term, applied by Cramer and Prutsch to the OIAA's media-related initiatives; see Cramer and Prutsch, "Nelson A. Rockefeller's Office of Inter-American Affairs," 28, 47n33. On the concern for expanding the consumer market, see Antonio Pedro Tota, "Seductive Imperialism: The Americanization of Brazil during World War II," in *Brazilian Perspectives on the United States: Advancing U.S. Studies in Brazil*, ed. Paulo Sotero and Daniel Budny (Washington, D.C.: Woodrow Wilson International Center for Scholars; Brazilian Embassy in Washington, 2007), 35–36.

29. See my "Dual-Engined Diplomacy: Walt Disney, Orson Welles, and Pan-American Film Policy during World War II," in Cramer and Prutsch, *¡Américas Unidas!*, 107–41, for some of the distinctions between Welles's and Disney's approaches to representing Latin American culture and society, specifically in relation to the articulation of "folk culture" with national identity.

30. Vinícius de Moraes, *O Cinema do Meus Olhos*, ed. Carlos Augusto Calil (São Paulo: Companhia das Letras, 1991), 65.

31. For a useful discussion of US cinematic misrepresentations of Brazil during the Good Neighbor era, see Adrián Pérez Melgosa, *Cinema and Inter-American Relations, Tracking Transnational Affect* (New York: Routledge, 2012), 13–41, 48–64.

32. In fact, for periods of time under Getúlio Vargas's *Estado Nôvo*, the open practice of Afro-Brazilian religion was outlawed; based on documents located in (police chief) Filinto Müller Papers, CHP, SIDS II-1, Centro de Pesquisa e Documentação de História Contemporânea (CPDOC), Setor de Documentação, Fundação Getúlio Vargas, Rio de Janeiro., Brazil.

33. Interview by author with Herivelto Martins, audiotape recording, Rio de Janeiro, January 4, 1991. The controversy over RKO's refusal to issue payment for these regalia has been amply recounted by Welles himself in the television series *Orson Welles' Sketch Book* (1955) and elsewhere.

34. For more on the types of samba music found during Carnaval, see Benamou, *It's All True*, 101.

35. This is visible in a few shots of the final montage of Technicolor footage in *It's All True: Based on an Unfinished Film by Orson Welles*, directed by Bill Krohn, Myron Meisel, Orson Welles, Richard Wilson, and Norman Foster (1993, Hollywood, CA: Paramount Pictures, 1994). Othelo identified the scene in an inteview the author conducted with Sebastião de Souza Prata, August 1989, Rio de Janeiro, Brazil.

36. On the OIAA's trepidation regarding support for African American activists and Hispanic victims of discrimination at home, see Cramer and Prutsch, "Nelson A. Rockefeller's Office of Inter-American Affairs and the Quest for Pan-American

Unity," 29, 48n40. Ironically, according to Tota, racial segregation in the United States was a major target of criticism among the Brazilian intelligentsia prior to Welles's arrival. See "Seductive Imperialism," 30 and 44n20.

37. "Casino Urca," screenplay fragment, March 23, 1942, Orson Welles-Oja Kodar Papers, Special Collections Library, University of Michigan, Ann Arbor, MI.

38. Herivelto Martins, interview by author, audiotape recording, Rio de Janeiro, January 4, 1991.

39. They still can be found in the Richard Wilson-Orson Welles Papers, Mavericks and Makers Archive, Special Collections Library, University of Michigan, Ann Arbor, MI.

40. For some of the negative responses in the local Rio press, see Stam, *Tropical Multiculturalism*, 128–29.

41. Claude Lévi-Strauss, *Le cru et le cuit* (Paris: Plon, 1964).

42. For details of the accident, see Benamou, *It's All True*, 51–54, 307–309.

43. Hjort, "On the Plurality of Cinematic Transnationalism," 17–18.

44. See, for example, George E. Marcus and Michael M. J. Fischer, *Anthropology as Cultural Critique: An Experimental Moment in the Human Sciences*, 2nd ed. (Chicago: University of Chicago Press, 1996). Also relevant to an understanding of Welles's approach are Dell Hymes, "Introduction: Toward Ethnographies of Communication," *American Anthropologist* 66, no. 6 (1964): 1–34, and Victor Segalen, *Essay on Exoticism: An Aesthetics of Diversity*, trans. and ed. Yaël Rachel Schlick (Durham, NC: Duke University Press, 2002).

45. Jonathan Rosenbaum, "Orson Welles's Essay Films and Documentary Fictions," in *Discovering Orson Welles* (Berkeley: University of California Press, 2007), 129–45.

46. Robert Stam, "Do filme-ensaio ao *mockumentary*," in *O Ensaio no Cinema*, ed. Francisco Elinaldo Teixeira (São Paulo: Hucitec Editora, 2015), 123 (my translation).

5

ORSON WELLES AS JOURNALIST
The *New York Post* Columns

SIDNEY GOTTLIEB

Orson Welles was full of . . . words. We have naturally gravitated to those he spoke and filmed, but need to pay more attention to those he wrote—and in fact, Welles's writings may very well be the last remaining unexplored continent of what Jonathan Rosenbaum, setting a research and creative agenda for decades, called the "invisible Welles."[1]

My focus in this essay on Welles as a journalist, and specifically as a daily columnist, is part of a broader effort to restore attention to how seriously Welles took himself as a writer and how much of value he wrote. A close examination of his writings clearly identifies many of his lifelong themes and concerns, as an artist, thinker, and engaged citizen; heightens our awareness of the dynamic interplay of image, orality, and literacy throughout his works; and highlights a kind of reflexivity Welles is not often credited with: an abiding interest in the pivotal role of media, especially in matters of power and knowledge.[2]

There has, in fact, been some substantial attention to Welles as a journalist, which provides a solid basis for the further work that this otherwise somewhat neglected subject requires. James Naremore got there first and got it right. But while his fine comments on a few of Welles's *New York Post* columns are a model of illustrating how these pieces are centrally and significantly (rather than marginally) Wellesian, his interests

lie elsewhere—his book is primarily on the cinema of Orson Welles—
and his comments are all too brief.[3] Simon Callow, on the other hand,
writes a detailed and enormously informative chapter on "Actor Turns
Columnist," but he is often impatient with and not particularly tolerant
of the unevenness of the columns, and to my mind, he lets the commercial failure of the endeavor color his evaluation of its importance.[4] Callow is, in general, an unparalleled appreciator when Welles is at his best,
but is often stern with anything less, and his overview of Welles as a journalist presents an image of a nobly ambitious and resourceful man out
of his element, missing more than hitting. In my essay, I aim to expand
on Naremore, whose sympathetic close readings of several columns are
a model of how to approach these pieces, and to not so much correct as
reorient Callow, emphasizing that the numerous "hits" of Welles's *Post*
columns are palpable ones indeed.

Unlike Charles Foster Kane, Orson Welles never actually ran a
newspaper, but he shared with Kane a boyish glee about the prospect
of being involved in newspaper work, a deep sense of the power and
responsibilities of newspapers, and a commitment to the function of
newspapers in the modern age as antiestablishment, agitational, and educational—along with an increasing awareness that mainstream newspapers in America were none of the above. He had some early experience
as a teenager, writing a column for his hometown paper, and evidently
wrote for a Dublin "sporting and society paper" while traveling in Ireland in 1931–32. But some years later, he turned to the task in a more
dedicated way. No longer an adolescent eager to get free tickets to the
theater and read his words in print, in the early 1940s, Welles approached
writing for a newspaper as an opportunity to be a forceful voice for democracy. He elaborated and publicized his thoughts on the importance
of news writers on a number of occasions, perhaps the earliest and most
important of which was his speech to the Overseas Press Club on November 2, 1943, printed in full two days later in Elsa Maxwell's *New York
Post* column. Prefaced by an admission to Maxwell that while theater
is fun, "working for the cause of human liberty against reactionism and
retrogression is the most serious job I can do today," Welles, again like
Kane, offered what was virtually his Declaration of Principles, a challenge to himself as well as to his audience.[5] In his text he questions and

ultimately discards some of the key components of conventional—and, in fact, typically conservative—journalistic ethics and procedures, and redefines the role of a democratic and progressive press. Such a press should not be an "objective" recorder of contemporary events, an old and outmoded conception of reporting, but an active force in the fight against domestic and worldwide fascism. Welles clearly believed that the principles of first-person singular at the core of his radio work also constituted good journalism. He had a great deal of respect for the "new sort of correspondent who's taken dictation accurately and at high speed from history itself," but what makes this kind of news so valuable and educational is that it is advocacy journalism of the highest order. Tolerance is an important part of democracy, of course, but brings with it the danger that "our Free Press is sometimes and in some places in the hands of freedom's enemies." According to Welles, if we are ever to achieve the four freedoms that Roosevelt outlined in a key speech to Congress in 1941—freedom of expression and worship, and freedom from want and fear—the press must contribute to the fight against "the freedom to take away freedom" by actively "upholding the enormous notion of man's equality." Welles did not endorse neutrality, which he associated with the isolationists who have obstructed the war effort and promised to obstruct the establishment of a just peace, and warned his audience that "your neutrality aids and sustains the enemy." Reporters must be part of a broadly partisan effort: "Putting the truth on the offensive is your job." Anything less than that is a capitulation to the status quo, dangerous at a time when democracy—"economic as well as political," Welles reminds us: "Neither has reality without the other"—is not so much a fully achieved reality as a goal that must be strenuously pursued.

Less than two years later, he had the opportunity to put his ideas into practice when he was invited to write a daily column for the *New York Post*, a prospect that he described in words that seem to echo Kane's stunning and unexpected admission to Thatcher that "I think it would be fun to run a newspaper." In a guest column written for Leonard Lyons's usual slot in the *Post*, Welles confessed that, for him, "printer's ink," like "the smell of grease-paint once savored is not easy to live without" (December 1, 1944). Writing an occasional column "changed the course of my life. I found again the fun of writing for the newspaper." "Once a year isn't enough," he said, so "I'm starting my own column." The managers of the newspaper expected to capitalize on Welles's status as a star of stage, screen, and radio, and the announcement of the column emphasized that it would be "instructive, entertaining, mirth provoking—and always absorbing reading" (*Post*, January 19, 1945, back page). But Welles's own comments in an interview printed in that same announcement should have alerted the editors and the *Post* readers to expect something a bit different: as he explained in a later letter to Hall, he wanted to be more like Dorothy Thompson, a serious political commentator, than like Elsa Maxwell, primarily a chronicler of the world of entertainment and social events. Describing his column as "his most important role," Welles proclaimed his belief that "if I can stir the people to debate and think about our problems, we'll find a way out" of the current "supreme crisis of civilization" (January 19, 1945, back page). If his earlier work in theater can be summed up by the phrase "Everybody's Shakespeare," perhaps this period in his life can be captured by the phrase "Everybody's Politics," which he nearly adopts: "You see," he said, "I am convinced everybody should be interested in politics. If we, the Americans, lose interest, then the democratic way of life is doomed. Let's not forget that the disaster of America in the 1920s was that everybody left the practice of politics to the professionals."

In his newspaper columns, as in his work in theater, film, and radio, Welles attempted to reconcile, if not synthesize, showmanship and serious political commentary, and adapt an essentially commercial entertainment medium to the cause of progressive social action.[6] The style and structure of these columns is quirky and in some ways problematic, but effective, filled with authentically Wellesian dramatic leaps, startling collocations, shifting frames, voices, and subjects of attention. The miscellaneous quality of Welles's columns is often part of a "radical stylization" that he praised so highly in one of his most important columns (May 25, 1945), mixing newsy and gossipy banter, homespun wisdom and advice, serious commentary, and exhortation with modernist maneuvers meant to disorient, provoke, dazzle, and amuse. The column of February 2, for example, moves in quick cuts through a bewildering assortment of images and impressions: an announcement of Ground Hog Day and the birthday of odd couples like Heifetz and Dickens, James Joyce and Nell

Gwynn; a dictionary definition of embalming followed by the identification of an influential politician trying "to revitalize the Republican Party" as a licensed embalmer; an extended critique of Margaret Webster's Shakespearean productions as too competent, unimaginative, and successful; an ironic anecdote about a British statesman whose titles of "Ambassador" and "Lord" don't entirely cloak his past associations with fascism; and a final comment that "Cracks in dishes can be concealed by boiling in sweet milk," simultaneously a whimsical bit of irrelevancy and homespun surrealism and a haunting gnomic pronouncement. Here, and throughout the columns, Welles tips his hat to Ben Franklin and other conventional almanac writers, but follows more in the path of Picasso and Eisenstein and, I would argue, the experimental theatrical Living Newspaper in framing a journalistic art of dynamic collage and montage.[7]

Although working in a print medium, Welles integrated and adapted oral dimensions in his columns, and showed himself to be a master of not only the booming basso that he is usually associated with but also the vocal versatility that he prided himself on. Characteristically, a not altogether pleasing grandiosity and stylistic excess run through his editorializing, commenting, and general ruminating. The theatrical—and sometimes royal—"we" that he adopts can sound affected and grating, as when he describes his friendship with John Barrymore: "We loved the man this side of idolatry. . . . We knew Jack since we were five. He was our foster uncle and our foster brother . . . And so we're prejudiced" (February 1, 1945). Some of his humor is smug or sophomoric, as in his dramatization of an imaginary conference of fascists that tediously fills up two columns (May 22 and 24, 1945). The attempt to do justice to the seriousness and urgency of the issues he presents occasionally leads him to overload irony upon irony, drama upon melodrama, and his relentless hatred of fascism at times becomes somewhat shrill, as when, in the course of arguing for justifiably severe punishment for war criminals, he approves of a French plan to use 50,000 captured Germans to clean up land mines and booby traps, "figuring that 35,000 men will be killed on the job and they might as well be Nazis" (May 28, 1945), an eminently rational but nonetheless startling "modest proposal." But there is much more to the columns than self-announcing brass and thunder, and even those qualities that, taken by themselves, seem regrettable often serve to effectively counterpoint other critical elements, underscoring Welles's ability to impersonate many characters, change tones instantly, and create dramatic effects with understatement, comic deflations, pauses, and whispers as well as noisy rhetorical flourishes. A variety of voices weave in and out of the columns: he is playfully self-deprecating as well as self-promoting, and alongside boldness and bravado, he voices humility and nervous concern, requisites for those dark days when the end of the war seemed near but not assured.

Welles not only uses many tones for his own voice, but allows a variety of characters to speak in his columns: sometimes through him but many times for themselves as he presents portraits of decency, courage, satiric humor, intelligence, and justifiable complaint and worry. He shares his platform with well-known writers, entertainers, and politicians (essayist George Ade, Frank Sinatra, President Roosevelt, and Henry Wallace, for example), but also with lesser-known Latin American progressives defending their revolutions (February 26 and 28, 1945), an anonymous "lady tourist from Weehawken" who corners and criticizes a Hollywood mogul (September 11, 1945), the head of the American Veterans Committee delegation at the San Francisco conference (April 26, 1945), and various incarnations of John Q. Public, who, Welles insists, must speak for himself in any true democracy (April 24, 1945).

Even when Welles turns to the high rhetorical mode with which most people associate him, it is with full recognition that the most important stop even on a baroque organ is the aptly named *vox humana*. Behind his oft-repeated "we" is an aspiration toward and believably authentic, deep feeling of companionship and community: with the soldiers, victims of war and fascism, and the underprivileged in all nations, whose causes and rights he articulates and champions, and with the readers he addresses as compatriots in experiencing what he memorably calls "the sorrow of freedom" (March 2, 1945). The "rhetoric of democracy," based on "love of the truth" and "the life of the spirit" (November 6, 1945), that animates his journalistic version of *Why We Fight* (directed by Frank Capra et al., 1942–45) is not an oxymoron but a vital necessity, part of a critical effort to define, dramatize, and sustain the worldwide struggle for freedom, equality, and justice.

Welles was shrewdly aware of the importance of mass media in this struggle, not only during but also after the war, when the contours of the peacetime settlement might be greatly influenced by a public consciousness to a large extent shaped by the media. Accordingly, he did as much as he could in a positive way to seize the media for what he conceived of as progressive and democratic purposes. He used his columns to provide information and commentaries otherwise missing in more conservative outlets and outline and reinforce what is in many ways a radical agenda, that is, one true to the principles and aims of a country founded on a revolution against tyranny and presumably committed to democracy and an end to racism, oppression, and inequality of opportunity. And even his format contributes substantively, as he creates an almanac commemorating and celebrating an unconventional set of characters and events to broaden the education and experience of his audience: for example, he dismisses St. Valentine's Day in a quick phrase, but writes a whole column on the exuberant but chaste and religious spirit of Carnival (February 13, 1945), one of many lessons that one America can learn from the other. And the cumulative effect of continual brief notices of such things as the anniversaries of the suppression of the *Chicago Times* (February 8, 1945), the death of African American poet Paul Dunbar (February 9, 1945), and the sentencing of a suffragette "to two months' imprisonment for window-breaking" (March 2, 1945)—an exemplary bit of rebellion—is a significant rewriting of our national calendar.

Alongside demonstrating how progressive media could function, Welles used his columns to mount an ongoing critique of the false rhetoric, antidemocratic tendencies, and improperly used manipulative power of mainstream media, particularly the press, but also radio and film. One of his basic premises is that the media are often dominated by and primarily serve the special interests of conservatives, whose control over the flow of information and the shape of received wisdom dangerously amplifies their negativism and political shortsightedness. Misinformation and disinformation abound, and not only in some of the relatively small-circulation German-language newspapers in America that are, according to Welles, for all intents and purposes, in the hands of the fascists (see February 8, 1945), but in the enormously influential publications of William Randolph Hearst, Eleanor Patterson, Robert McCormick,

Henry Luce, and others like them, which continually confuse readers about our "allies" in order to move more quickly to what they mistakenly consider the real business at hand—conciliation with postwar Germany as a necessary "bulwark against Bolshevism." One of Welles's recurrent topics is spreading the news about the antidemocratic aspects of contemporary newspapers (and media in general). Ironically, Welles notes that Colonel McCormick's editorial and political position, expressed in his *Chicago Tribune*, is accurately and approvingly described in Nazi broadcasts as "anti-Roosevelt, anti-British, anti-Bolshevik and anti-Semitic" (March 8, 1945); and a statement attributed to Clare Boothe Luce, perhaps illustrating not only her own political philosophy but a guiding principle at this time of the Luce communications empire, asserts that "the Administration can give people either social security or freedom, but not both" (March 8, 1945), a common rationale and defense of fascism to this day, and in the very least a troubling capitulation to realpolitik and invitation to authoritarian control. Everywhere present in these columns is the implicit or sometimes explicit affirmation that contributing to the walk toward, not away from, freedom is a fundamental responsibility of journalism, one that is not always satisfactorily fulfilled by the newspapers of the day.

Welles was particularly alert to what Walter Lippmann described as the cinema-like power of media to put "pictures in our heads" that might substitute for or distort our more accurate direct perceptions of the world, and he gives numerous examples, like the following, of the complicity of the media in making and keeping us uninformed, frightened, and provincial: "A man who runs a newspaper warns his defenseless readers against everything alien, everything foreign, which seems to mean everything outside of Chicago, Ill." (April 17, 1945).[8] Cartoon-like journalism is, unfortunately, often the norm: "We start publishing funny pictures in the papers belittling England, denouncing Russia or giving the impression that Uncle Sam is always the goat" (April 18, 1945). As a result, he warns, Russia becomes our irreconcilable enemy, and the hopes for a United Nations are dashed.

Welles's recurrent reference point for his critique of mass media is foreign policy, but he is also deeply concerned about domestic issues. He repeatedly focuses on perhaps our foremost "moral dilemma": the routinely unacknowledged "bitter truths" and "acid facts" of racism (April 4, 1945). The reality of American racism is ever present: in "the noose around a Negro's neck in Alabama" and "memories of a place called Sleepy Lagoon," the site of anti-Hispanic prosecutions that Welles had protested in a pamphlet in 1943 (April 4, 1945);[9] the quotas that, even when expanded, would allow only one hundred immigrants per year from India to become naturalized citizens (March 19, 1945); the demeaning stereotypes enacted as popular radio entertainment by Jack Benny's sidekick, Eddie "Rochester" Anderson, that "perpetuate a dangerous myth" about the real behavior of black people, and the more damning fact that even on a goodwill tour benefiting the troops "Rochester" would have had to sleep in segregated quarters and would not, like Mr. Benny, be invited to or allowed in "the officer's mess for dinner" (June 4, 1945). As part of a necessary corrective to racism, Welles highly recommends what he calls the "pictures" in the album provided by Richard Wright's *Black Boy*. All art has, to some extent, a journalistic function, and good journalism calls our attention to good art. The powerful story of Wright's "life in the moral jungles and deserts of the South" is told in such a way that it may chasten sanctimonious racists and liberals who claim to "understand the Negro," and also reinforce that "the Negro isn't somebody to be studied, he's somebody to be saved"—not in any paternalistic way but by putting into practice the ideals of freedom, equal opportunity, and justice that are so often advertised as the American way (March 2, 1945). Welles longs for the day when these most time-honored and yet revolutionary goals will be achieved, and he catches a brief glimpse of what that day will be like in an issue of the magazine *The American Home*. He calls attention to a picture promoting war bonds with a "run-of-the-mill lay-out" showing two newlyweds "in their bright little home, the poses perfectly traditional. But the young wife and her husband are Negroes" (May 11, 1945). What Welles finds particularly promising about this is the ordinariness of it all, which is as it should be: it is not, he says, "a discussion of Negro housing" or a well-intentioned but ultimately patronizing bit of inclusiveness, but simply a picture of an American home. When such items become "the rule, not the exception," media and society will have achieved a long-overdue transformation, and "such columns as this will be superfluous."

The other domestic issue that captured Welles's attention was labor, a broad term that includes related subjects like strikes, price ceilings, working conditions, business profits, unemployment, union activities, wages, employee benefits and rights, and governmental legislation regulating the economy. Welles was unquestionably pro-labor. He did not always endorse union strategies, positions, and specific demands: he supported the right to strike, for example, but criticized certain applications of this right, whether in Detroit (October 2, 1945) or Hollywood (October 23, 1945), and considered some no-strike pledges to be a valuable contribution to the war effort (February 14, 1945). But he recognized that labor constituted the largest sector of the country, a majority whose interests and voice should be (but were not at the present time sufficiently) central in the news and in the major policy-making decisions in business and government.

Characteristically, one of his most frequent points of entry into discussions of labor-related topics was his insistence that the debate was clouded by media bias and misrepresentations, some of which his columns could counteract. He repeatedly reminds his audience of the framing power of mass media, often used to create distorted impressions—for example, in the news, "It's always labor trouble, never management trouble" (October 2, 1945)—and he made an effort to give his readers at least "a part of labor's point of view, because you don't get to hear it very often."

Welles warns that there are indeed "darker motives" behind conventional media operations: habitual "exaggeration by the press and radio is part of a plot with more scope and a longer range" (September 25, 1945) to which we need to be alerted. But his remarkably comprehensive critique is based not on a knee-jerk and unsubstantiated conspiracy theory but careful analysis of media ownership, content, editorial principles, routines, and manipulative and distracting techniques, and much supporting evidence confirming that there is indeed a well-entrenched, highly organized media support system favoring corporate and political interests that are certainly not always identical or even reconcilable with more fair, just, and democratic public interests. He repeatedly emphasizes the threat of continuing economic consolidation and concentrated ownership of the media. In one column, for example, he notes that "in all the brave new world, the most important single power is communications. It's not surprising, then, that radio, the press and the movies are a big concern of big interests" (February 27, 1945), who, in effect, corner the market. Not surprisingly, he noted, the new medium of television was following the same path of historical development and would soon be "sewn up" by the "Me-Only Boys . . . unless we stop them." "That sort of ownership" and control not only "makes independent productions so perilously close to the impossible" but also turns what should be vehicles of information and arenas of public debate and responsible editorializing into special interest domains dominated by public relations ("the fine art of making yourself attractive to a free press" [May 4, 1945], Welles notes sarcastically), advertising (which amounts to a materialistic and exploitational appropriation of the "American way of life" [March 1, 1945]), and distractions: Welles meditates sadly on the fact that during the dark days of Dunkirk, Hearst "filled his allotted space with a dissertation on the behavior of a puppy dog, and the probable future of Miss Shirley Temple" (October 23, 1945). His overriding worry is that media are ultimately not functioning as, to use Marshall McLuhan's hopeful term, extensions of mankind: the "miracles of our modern communication systems" have shrunk the world, but, "What if the people in it shrink to match?" (May 9, 1945). Unless our communications systems are used for the exchange of "the common man's ideas," the people "will feel more and more like poor fish caught in a network," and the cry will go up: "Readers of the world unite! You have nothing to lose but your newspaper chains!"

With grim commentary like this featured regularly in the columns, it is no surprise that Welles's editor wanted him to turn more to such topics as film, art, theater, literature, and the world of entertainment. He did so, but in a way that was critical and provocative rather than chatty, always aiming to democratize and inform rather than amuse and distract. He focuses his attention almost exclusively on what might be called the middle-brow and the popular realms that largely constitute what Michael Denning calls "the cultural front" and that particularly lend themselves to a serious inquiry into the role of art in society; the lure of the slick, the superficial, the commercial, and the reactionary or politically suspect; and the many pressures on artists who tried to live up to the high personal and public responsibilities of their art.[10]

Comments on films and the world of film—including audiences as well as filmmakers, producers, and studios—weave in and out of the columns regularly, as part of his effort to offer a deep structural analysis of how bad Hollywood is and why it isn't better. In the midst of repeated examinations of the monopolistic practices and arrogance of power of large industries in general, Welles's criticism of Hollywood as not only a big business but a poorly run business at that (see February 27, 1945) takes on added resonance. Hollywood is, he suggests, a profit-driven factory of strikes as well as dreams, out of touch with its audiences as well as its workers, and doomed to continuing mediocrity, if not worse, because it is, alone among big businesses, unwilling to invest even minimal amounts in a long-range plan for research and product enhancement by supporting "a laboratory for experiment" (March 16, 1945). Studios are lorded over by executives like the not-entirely fictitious "Bey of Beverly Hills" (September 11, 1945), who is at best a cinematic simpleton, political know-nothing, and poor businessman—all interrelated deficiencies. "Look at his movies and you'll see what I mean" is Welles's withering comment, but uttered with no sense of triumph, knowing that such men are custodians of a natural resource too precious to be squandered. The few films that Welles praises in his columns are not typical Hollywood productions—like *When Strangers Marry*, a "B minus picture" that's "A 'plus' entertainment," which he prefers to "slick" productions like *Double Indemnity* and *Laura* (January 25, 1945)—and sometimes not Hollywood productions at all. The film he examines in greatest detail is the first part of Eisenstein's *Ivan the Terrible* (May 25, 1945), which as Naremore points out, Welles uses as a weapon in his continuing critique of Hollywood and as a complex model of "radical stylization" useful in his own filmmaking practice and understanding of himself as a progressive artist.[11]

For all his attention to film form, Welles was also very concerned with the substance of films and their far-reaching influence. He was troubled by the overall mind-numbing and misdirecting effects of conventional films, which can take sometimes bizarre forms. In one of his most fascinating columns, he describes a performance of the Philharmonic Orchestra of Los Angeles where the conductor, Toscanini, was suddenly joined on stage by an "unscheduled ballerina" who danced around "in perfect tempo" until she was "cornered in the string section" and led away (April 23, 1945). Despite Toscanini's response—"one of the most whole-hearted double-takes Hollywood has ever been privileged to see"—there is something fundamentally natural and unsurprising about such occurrences in our Hollywood-inspired world. Welles sees the ballerina as simply enacting a scenario portrayed in many films, and he gives a quick shot-by-shot treatment of her imaginary triumph as she fulfills the movie-manufactured fantasy of winning over the conductor, the crowd, and the "fine clean-looking young man waiting for her in the wings." Welles's conclusion is blunt and haunting: "I do believe that Hollywood's to blame. I think the young lady is the victim of a movie."

The fact that conventional films tend to create many such "victims" rather than enlightened citizens is a serious matter for Welles. "Movies are a greater power than the atom bomb," he notes, but the few films he names that release this power beneficially are ones beyond the confines of Hollywood's limited "artistic freedom" (September 11, 1945). He has high praise for the impressive war films made by Hollywood directors (presumably like Frank Capra, John Ford, John Huston, and George Stevens) who "have produced better pictures in uniform than you [Hollywood executives] ever let them make on your lot." And he devotes an entire column to praising the documentary newsreels capturing the "hideous sights" of the concentration camps, the "horror" of today (May 7, 1945), which at least temporarily turn "your local movie palaces" into sources of essential information. "No, you must not miss the newsreels," Welles advises, even as he was working on his own film, *The Stranger,* which included concentration camp footage, and his message is that filmmakers must use the full resources of an art that has enormous social as well as aesthetic power and responsibility, captured in a wonderful concluding pun (even if it may be a fortuitous typo) referring to the essence of cinema as "the real of celluloid."

He sums up his thoughts on the failure of the film medium to fulfill its high mission and vast potential in his final column, a meditation set in the context of the prospect of atomic annihilation but focusing on the even "more terrible" threat to the "life of the spirit" posed by the "civilization of ad-men" who give us "many mansions" of "cardboard" instead of the Chartres cathedral we need (November 6, 1945). He wanders lost in a "strange territory" looking out at the "low horizons of Hollywood," a description that takes on allegorical overtones as he goes on to blame the movies for giving the public only false shrines that, "like the sham church in Sam Goldwyn's backyard, won't keep the rain off a man's head." Ironically, the particular spire he looks at is part of the set for his current production, *The Stranger*. Much to his credit, Welles rarely exempted himself from his critique of the medium and the system, and repeatedly acknowledged and analyzed, although sometimes subtly and indirectly, his own limitations, entrapment, and even his complicity. This reflexive honesty, coupled with and integrally related to his passionate commitment to building a new, much-improved cinema—vital to building and sustaining a new, much improved society, he insists—is a large part of what makes his famous statement "I love movies. But don't get me wrong. I hate Hollywood" not a glib and dismissive witticism but a memorable summation of one of the key subtexts animating his newspaper columns.

It is worth noting that Welles's comments in his columns on other arts are also valuable and harmonize with his analysis of media in general and film in particular. His occasional book reviews call for a far-reaching readjustment and expansion of literary taste and values. Deep sympathy for and support of the Popular Front's emphasis on an alliance of people of all persuasions against fascism did not blind him to the inadequacies of some ostensibly "democratic" fables, and he was concerned that John Hersey's well-intentioned best seller *A Bell for Adano*, praising the "essential goodness" of people and illustrating how "fascism corrupts and cripples," may prompt readers to oversimplify complex political and social issues in a dangerously sentimental and self-serving way (February 16, 1945). Now more than ever, we need to face up to harsh truths, even about the inadequacies of some "democracies": as mentioned earlier, he reserves his highest praise for Richard Wright's *Black Boy*, an extremely challenging and caustic autobiographical tale that forces us to face up to certain realities—specifically, deeply rooted and extensive racism and its poisonous effects—about life in the United States that we might otherwise comfortably avoid.

At the same time, in his reviews, Welles is by no means incapable of lightness and celebration: he spends much of his first effort as a guest columnist filling in for Leonard Lyons, one of the regular *Post* columnists, describing his fascination for Edgar Wallace's enormously popular cliff-hangers and life led "in the best tradition of Phineas Fogg" (February 10, 1943), a tradition Welles himself not much later tried to revive in a spectacular stage production of Jules Verne's *Around the World in 80 Days*; he writes approvingly of Samuel Hopkins Adams's biography capturing the vivacity and good humor of Alexander Woollcott (June 6, 1945), not the only one of Welles's acquaintances to make an appearance in the columns, and also a figure, according to Callow, of singular power, prestige, and celebrity for Welles;[12] and he is thoroughly enraptured by the Whitmanesque exuberance of George R. Stewart's *Names on the Land*, a catalog of linguistic diversity that embodies our history and reminds us of "all the races that have made America" (September 18, 1945). Whitmanesque is indeed an apt description of much that Welles admired, embodied, and espoused, and one of his major efforts throughout the *Post* columns, as seen even in these brief book reviews, was to be an appreciator and architect of democratic vistas and energies and all varieties of the democratic spirit.[13]

His comments on theater in the columns are sporadic, but contribute to his overall effort to call attention to the intimate relationship between art and democracy. Predictably, he is distressed by the prospect of a theater that is thoroughly "respectable," and he chastises Margaret Webster for taming and domesticating Shakespeare (February 2, 1945) and the actor Henry Irving for accepting, for himself and the entire profession, a Knighthood, a misstep in an art that must always maintain a social but also antiestablishment component: "Up to that time no player had bothered his head very much about being a gentleman, but after that a lot of players never bothered about anything else" (February 6, 1945). Theater is afflicted from inside and outside, as Welles further elaborates in his column titled "The Actor's Role in Society" (October 23, 1945): by actors who abdicate their independence and vanguard status (we would do well to remember, Welles suggests, the origin of drama in the spontaneous and self-expressive "huge shouts" and "mighty mugs" of a performer, which then generate a play, a crowd, and a playhouse), and by society at large, which is not living up to its responsibility to provide institutional support ("We need a repertory theatre. We need a lot of them and we need them quick") and a "living audience." The inevitable result is that "the art of acting is deathly sick with the wasting disease of disuse," and his real concern is that this is a social disease: the real risk is to the body politic.

He also, needless to say, takes theater personally, evident in his repeated comments on John Barrymore (in columns of January 24, February 6, and February 15, 1945), occasioned in part by a new biography of the actor by Gene Fowler. The book troubles Welles deeply because despite its length it never manages to get to the heart of Barrymore's genius, which Welles suggests is wrapped up in the fact that he "was the greatest Hamlet since Edwin Booth" (February 15, 1945), a curse wrapped in a compliment because Welles is describing not so much a role Barrymore played as a character he embodied, one for whom "the good life is about to be the death of him" (February 6, 1945). Barrymore was "the living symbol of the living theatre" (January 24, 1945) in everything that he did: ironically, not only in his inimitable acting triumphs on stage (inimitable, as it turns out, even for Barrymore himself) but in the increasing theatricality of his life, much of which was spent playing an alcoholic depressive, bent on "destroying himself as publicly and entertainingly as possible" (February 15, 1945). Welles mentions briefly the dangers of anyone attempting to play Barrymore in a screen adaptation of his life: "The luckless player who tries it is committing suicide" (January 24, 1945), and he says that he himself refused the role when a "myopic producer went so far as to offer it to me." But he seems haunted by the likelihood that he would end up playing Barrymore in his own life. In the shadows of Welles's intimate knowledge and immoderate love of Barrymore is his deep identification with him. "Jack's tragedy," he tells us, was that his greatest success came early, in an "inspired performance" of Hamlet that was devastatingly brilliant: it was "the best thing Jack ever did, and it killed him ... The rest of his life was anti-climax" (February 15, 1945). Welles might just as well have been talking about himself. Perhaps he was. Welles's fate was not nearly as grim as Barrymore's, but unquestionably part of what afflicted and animated him was a prolonged and intense struggle with the many stresses of creativity, celebrity, ambition, early achievement, and, as he ascribed to Barrymore, hatred of "the responsibility of his own genius" (February 15, 1945). All this is an important dimension of Welles's life that simply can't be fathomed if we misrepresent it by some trivialized and dismissive notion of his "fear of success" or "inability to complete."

Finally, Welles's comments on well-known filmmakers and actors are nicely complemented by columns on pictorial art that are among his most important and revealing. His two-column discussion of the great "muralists, orators in paint for Mexico's revolutions" (March 6 and 7, 1945), José Orozco, Diego Rivera, and David Siqueiros, begins with a cautionary tale about the dangers of governmental censorship but moves quickly to praise and, equally important, distinguish their respective approaches to forging a revolutionary and democratic art. It is difficult to miss the kinship he feels with them as he examines artists dedicated to a "rich and provocative" progressive art but struggling with mundane materials, limited expressive forms, external pressures and inconsistent support, their own often complex and compromised motives, and the threat of either selling out or becoming disillusioned.

Welles gets a lot of inspiration from another progressive artist he devotes one of his last columns to—Bill Mauldin (September 4, 1945). For Welles, the art of the future—and the useful art of today—includes what some people rather condescendingly refer to as the low-brow, or even the no-brow. Mauldin's Willie and Joe cartoons hang in foxholes, not museums, and this insulates them from being coopted by collectors or Army generals and deflected from their mission of truth telling. Mauldin is unquestionably "an artist, the genuine article": because of his perennial enthusiasm for and skill at his work, resolute hatred of "what's phony," his antiauthoritarian critique of the "vices of brass-hattery," and incorrigible concern for the interests of the "dogfaces," which is to say, the majority of people in the modern world. If Welles's admiration of Mauldin as an eminently worthy artist and model of the critical challenge of, to paraphrase Godard, "how to make art politically" seems surprising, we need to adjust our understanding of what is essentially Wellesian—an adjustment that can be aided enormously by a close attention to such authentic and revealing Wellesian texts as his *New York Post* columns.

Perhaps this is the right note on which to end my overview of this stage of Welles activities as a journalist, emphasizing one last time the multiple dimensions and ambitions of these writings. He wanted his *New York Post* columns to be popular and entertaining as well as serious, provocative, and educational, and wanted to both support himself and adapt an essentially corporate commercial medium to the cause of innovative and progressive social action and artistic expression. Not surprisingly, the response was, to say the least, uneven. A week after the debut of Welles's column, a writer in *Time* magazine described it as a mixture of "excerpts from Welles's favorite reading, the *Farmer's Almanac*; handy hints about cooking; cocksure remarks about foreign affairs; and personal chitchat," questioned whether the column would hold either Welles's or the audience's interest for very long, and somewhat snidely assessed his political involvement as that of "a Hollywood highbrow's vocal interest in the world since 1940."[14] John McCarten, in the *New Yorker*, portrayed Welles as a "Dedicated Wunderkind," the title of a jaunty, by no means completely antagonistic but certainly patronizing and trivializing piece that, as Welles objected in one of his columns, "manages to imply that his hatred of Fascism is nothing but a rather silly fad" (January 30, 1945).[15]

Welles protested—"*The New Yorker* ought to be ashamed of itself; it knows as well as you do that anti-Fascism is never silly, even when a movie director or comic paper works in its behalf" (January 30, 1945)— and persisted. The columns were never extremely popular, but they were syndicated and read (by thousands, although not the millions that mass media aim for), and when gathered together, they make up a substantial body of work that not only stands up to but rewards close scrutiny. After reading through this work, even in a brief retrospective article titled "Why Orson Welles Failed as a *Post* Columnist," written to mark the seventieth anniversary of "Orson Welles' Almanac," *Post* writer Lou Lumenick devotes most of his article to intriguing short quotations from the columns that, more than anything, illustrate how unfortunate it is that "few are aware of [Welles's] brief, eccentric career as a political columnist for the *New York Post*."[16] And recently a writer for the *New Yorker* has made amends for John McCarten's dismissive treatment of Welles many years ago by ending a detailed overview of the many achievements that should allow us to speak sympathetically, even reverentially, of "King Orson" by specifically mentioning and praising his newspaper work. The piece concludes: "I wonder whether Welles's journalism has been collected. It should be."[17] It should indeed be collected, read carefully, and integrated into our response to the perennially fascinating and challenging questions posed in inimitable journalese in the context of long overdue praise from the *New Yorker*: "Who, after all, was Orson Welles, and why was he such a big deal?"

SIDNEY GOTTLIEB is professor of Media Studies at Sacred Heart University. His recent publications include volume 21 of the *Hitchcock Annual*, which he coedits with Richard Allen, and the second volume of *Hitchcock on Hitchcock: Selected Writings and Interviews*.

NOTES

1. Jonathan Rosenbaum, "The Invisible Welles: A First Inventory," *Sight and Sound* (Summer 1986): 164–71; reprinted in Jonathan Rosenbaum, *Discovering Orson Welles* (Berkeley: University of California Press, 2007), 67–89.

2. Paul Heyer, in *The Medium and the Magician: Orson Welles, The Radio Years, 1934–1952* (New York: Rowman & Littlefield, 2005), comments insightfully on Welles as a "critical media theorist" (xv), and much of the material that he discusses throughout his book underscores important continuities between Welles's radio and newspaper work.

3. James Naremore, *The Magic World of Orson Welles*, 2nd ed. (Dallas, TX: Southern Methodist University Press, 1989), 111–22.

4. Simon Callow, "Actor Turns Columnist," in *Orson Welles: Hello Americans* (New York: Viking, 2006), 222–51. I am also extremely grateful to Frank Brady for sending me a copy of his unpublished essay, "Orson Welles as Journalist," presented at the American Journalism Historians Association Northeast Regional Conference, March 9, 1996, which contains much information about Welles's relationship with the managing editors of the *Post* and a thoughtful overview of the depth and variety of his columns.

5. Orson Welles, speech to the Overseas Press Club on November 2, 1943, printed in *New York Post*, November 4, 1943. All further quotations from Welles's *New York Post* columns will be cited by date in the text of my essay.

6. What I describe as Welles's attempt in his journalism to reconcile showmanship that had entertainment value and appeal with serious commentary that served important intellectual, educational, and political value parallels and substantively overlaps with what Michael Anderegg persuasively identifies as Welles's career-long effort to master and blend both high and popular art; see *Orson Welles, Shakespeare, and Popular Culture* (New York: Columbia University Press, 1999).

7. Michael Denning, in *The Cultural Front: The Laboring of American Culture in the Twentieth Century* (New York: Verso, 1997), 367–70, briefly discusses the Federal Theatre Project's Living Newspaper, informational and agitational stage

presentations that involved journalists and theater people, as a key part of the "People's Theatre" of the 1930s that is an essential context for Welles's theatrical work at this time.

8. The dangers of relying on "pictures in our heads" rather than "the world outside" are discussed throughout Walter Lippman's still relevant and important book, *Public Opinion* (New York: Harcourt, Brace, 1922).

9. Orson Welles, "Foreword," in *The Sleepy Lagoon Murder Case* (Los Angeles: Sleepy Lagoon Defense Committee, 1943), unnumbered first page.

10. See especially Denning, "The Politics of Magic: Orson Welles's Allegories of Anti-Fascism," in *The Cultural Front*, 362–402.

11. Naremore discusses in detail the Eisenstein column and its relationship to Welles's filmmaking; see *The Magic World of Orson Welles*, 119–23.

12. For brief information on Welles and Woollcott, see Simon Callow, *Orson Welles*, Vol. 1: *The Road to Xanadu* (New York: Viking, 1996), 139–40.

13. One of the epigraphs to Simon Callow's *Orson Welles*, Vol 3: *One Man Band* (New York: Viking, 2015) is from Whitman's *Song of Myself*, and in several places throughout the volume, he makes brief but eye-opening comparisons of Welles and Whitman.

14. *Time*, January 29, 1945, 68.

15. John McCarten, "Dedicated Wunderkind," *New Yorker*, January 27, 1945, 15. Some critics to this day deemphasize or disregard the importance of politics in Welles's life and works, despite direct statements like the following in *Filming The Trial* (1981), which are consistent with comments throughout the *Post* columns: "I am more interested in politics than in anything in the world—much more interested in politics than I am in movies or art or anything. I am absolutely fascinated by politics, and have been all my life. . . . The truth is that every work is a political statement—as opposed to using art to make a political statement, which ends up in rhetoric."

16. Lou Lumenick, "Why Orson Welles Failed as a *Post* Columnist," *New York Post*, January 24, 2015, http://nypost.com/2015/01/24/why-orson-welles-failed-as -a-new-york-post-columnist/.

17. "King Orson," *New Yorker*, June 27, 2013, http://www.newyorker.com/books /page-turner/king-orson. At least some of it will be gathered and republished before too long: I include extensive selections from the *New York Post* columns, along with numerous examples of his other writings, in my forthcoming collection, *Welles on Welles: Selected Writings and Interviews*.

6

PROGRESSIVISM AND THE STRUGGLES AGAINST RACISM AND ANTISEMITISM

Welles's Correspondences in 1946

JAMES N. GILMORE

> I appreciate very much your thoughtfulness in sending out the book
> of Mr. Miller's, FOCUS, and I am looking forward to reading it. I
> commend you for your efforts in trying to alleviate the prejudice
> and hate in our country. There is much need for such endeavor.
>
> —Congressman J. W. Trimble,
> Letter to Orson Welles, April 1, 1946

The above letter from Congressman Trimble to Orson Welles is one of thirty similar letters from United States congresspersons located in the "Orson Welles MSS Correspondences" (hereafter called "the Welles Correspondences") of Indiana University's Lilly Library. The letters, dated from April 1 to April 24, 1946, acknowledge or thank Welles for sending the recipient a copy of Arthur Miller's novel *Focus*, which is largely about the experience and festering of antisemitism in America. They pose an interesting provocation to Welles scholars who have made increased use of telegrams, letters, and public speeches to provide a more holistic sense of how Welles participated in public life beyond his much-discussed creative efforts in cinema, radio, and theater. As such, the Welles Correspondences reveal much about the progressive political discourses of social equality in which Welles participated.

This chapter focuses on several examples of Welles engaging—as well as the ways he was engaged by—Jewish communities, humanitarian groups, and sociopolitical issues of equality in the post-World War II moment of 1946. The decision to concentrate on the year 1946 is in no way arbitrary: in 1945–46, Welles directed the film *The Stranger*, wrote a newspaper column for the *New York Post*, delivered a regular fifteen-minute radio broadcast for ABC, and staged a version of Jules Verne's *Around the World in 80 Days* with songs by Cole Porter, in addition to appearing at a variety of events for political associations. This was, putting it simply, a very busy year in Welles's life, wherein his work traversed, seemingly, as many media forms as possible, positioning him as a preeminent public intellectual of the immediate postwar period.

Situating antisemitism as a crucial but often unacknowledged part of Welles's broader political interest in civil rights and social equality, this chapter examines his support for Jewish refugees immediately following World War II as well as his responses to antisemitic discourse in America. Additionally, it argues that in order to understand how Welles approached the task of analyzing and critiquing social injustice, his critique must be traced across his work in a number of different forms of media and communication.

Welles's Correspondences provide an important supplement to existing studies that emphasize the relationships and consistencies across his public works. For example, Welles's private correspondences can help to bolster the ties between, say, his work in radio and his public speeches through tracing how certain social groups approached him, and how he, in return, dialogued with their representatives. The letters sent to Welles during this period reveal some of the ways in which demographics valued his voice (often quite literally, as many progressive groups asked Welles for speeches at rallies, or voice-over work in educational films). The Welles Correspondences expand information about Welles's robust and diverse political activities, housing fan (and hate) mail along with conversations both personal and professional. His progressive ideology—emphasizing civil rights, racial tolerance, and social equality—helped him become a symbol for smaller grassroots groups attempting to combat local racial and cultural discrimination. The Correspondences provide an underutilized means to assess how ideologically progressive individuals and groups with sympathetic social goals approached Welles. These letters, in other words, provide a way to assess how Welles's public voice was received.

In a different context, Eric Smoodin has suggested that audience letters reveal "a more significant understanding of at least one small part of a much larger history of reading, listening, watching, and responding."[1] Emphasizing the act of responding through letter writing highlights Welles's place in American society through asking questions such as: How did Welles discuss and represent the specific conditions of the American political and cultural landscape in which he worked, and how did that work matter to the publics who engaged him? How did letter writing lead to or supplement other forms of civic engagement, such as fundraising, forums, and educational films?

In answering these questions, I take Jonathan Rosenbaum's contention quite seriously that "most ambitious Welles studies have been unresponsive to the wider aspects of culture . . . that Welles himself was engaged with throughout his life," and see it as a call to action for a more sociocultural analysis of Welles and the archival traces he left behind to take center stage.[2] My analysis builds off the work of other scholars, such as James Naremore and Michael Denning, who have done exactly this, often to great effect, with other aspects of Welles's life and career.[3] Continuing to place these ephemera into conversation with the more substantively researched texts and works of Welles's life can only expand, complicate, and deepen the degree to which his contributions to American culture are understood.

In what follows, I include a series of examples of both public and private communications to demonstrate the extent to which Welles engaged issues surrounding antisemitism and racism in 1946. While these varied examples do not encapsulate all of Welles's work in this period, they nevertheless point to the depth and breadth of his commitment to social equality for marginalized groups, including Jewish persons profoundly affected by the Holocaust who sought humanitarian aid, as well as Welles's more familiar efforts to address racism in America.

THE STRANGER, THE BLINDED VETERAN,
AND THE HOLOCAUST

Released in May 1946, *The Stranger* remains a largely undervalued piece of Welles's cinematic oeuvre—not least of which by Welles himself, who supposedly declared it his "worst film."[4] Jonathan Rosenbaum calls *The Stranger* "perhaps the least distinctive and adventurous film he directed—a film made in order to prove he was bankable."[5] Indeed, the persisting narrative surrounding *The Stranger* suggests that Welles agreed to direct the film for producer Sam Spiegel because of both his growing financial constraints as well as his attempt to rebuild his image after the fallout from his second feature film for RKO Studios, *The Magnificent Ambersons* (1942)—as well as the unfinished *It's All True*—that resulted in Welles and the Mercury Productions' ousting from RKO. James Naremore has corroborated this position, suggesting Welles "was lying low, intentionally suppressing his style in order to prove that he, too, could do ordinary good work."[6] Certainly, Welles was in the midst of financial turbulence—his staging of *Around the World* cost him over $300,000 of his own investment—but this focus on stylistic suppression and the reediting of the film in postproduction diverts attention from the real substance and achievement of the film. While the film may not be as aesthetically daring as his productions for RKO, its treatment of Nazism and the Holocaust are nevertheless politically complex.

Joseph McBride, for one, acknowledges that *The Stranger* evokes Welles's antifascist ideology.[7] In it, Welles plays Charles Rankin, a Nazi hiding out as a professor in a small town; Edward G. Robinson plays Mr. Wilson, the FBI agent hunting him down. Robinson, it is worth pointing out, was born "Emmanuel Goldenberg" to a Jewish family in Bucharest, Romania, and immigrated to the United States in the early 1900s. As such, the decision to cast Robinson in the role of Mr. Wilson provides an additional layer of meaning to the film's engagement with Nazism and the Holocaust. Roughly an hour into the film, Mr. Wilson shows Rankin's wife, Mary (Loretta Young), images of the Holocaust in an effort to convince her of her husband's evil. The sequence deserves attention here for its incorporation of documentary footage of concentration camps taken from George Stevens's *Nazi Concentration Camps*

(1945), which was "also being used as evidence during the Nuremberg Trials, which were taking place during filming of *The Stranger*."[8] Much of this footage was also incorporated into the War Department film *Death Mills* (1945), which was circulated both in the United States and Germany to, according to its first intertitle, serve as "a reminder that behind the curtain of Nazi pageants and parades, millions of men, women, and children were tortured to death—the worst mass murder in human history."[9] The period of 1945–46 thus already demonstrates a marked interest in circulating this kind of footage through a number of different channels and to a number of different audiences for pedagogic value.

Wilson sets up a portable 16mm film projector to show Mary the sequence. The first shot of the footage is a pile of dead bodies, followed by a cut to an alarmed Mary who proclaims, "Why Mr. Wilson, I haven't so much as seen a Nazi!" There is then a cut back to a shot of an empty gas chamber, with Mr. Wilson narrating its use: "The candidates were first given hot showers so that their pores would be open, and the gas would act that much more quickly." Wilson then approaches the screen to discuss a projected image of a mass grave. In a subsequent close-up, Mary asks, "Why do you want me to look at these horrors?" to which Wilson replies, "It's all a product of one mind." That singularly nefarious mind turns out, of course, to be Mary's husband. As Wilson goes on to talk about genocide, footage of an emaciated and praying concentration camp survivor is shown. Throughout the sequence, the clicking of the 16mm projector persists on the soundtrack, and the projected images bounce light off the characters' faces. This sequence operates as a sort of bolded exclamation point about the effect fascism has had on human bodies, and the ways in which Nazism provided a means to commit genocide against other human begins. Apart from "merely" showing this footage to many filmgoers who might not otherwise have seen it, the editing pattern of the sequence introduces a layer of reflexive shock. It displays both the footage itself as well as Mary's increasingly horrified reaction; much like Mary, the spectator is asked to watch images of atrocity they might not have otherwise encountered at the time.

While much of the film's suspense comes from its generic cat-and-mouse structure, *The Stranger* nevertheless incorporates a strong political shock in this sequence. The film circulates this footage as part of a broader effort to raise consciousness regarding the Holocaust in the period immediately following World War II. This is a shock that is not necessarily designed to evoke thrills, but rather a disruptive and disorienting shock. For Jennifer L. Barker, *The Stranger* serves as "a model for how to accurately represent, in film, the complex historical, political, and psychological matrix of a nation's relation to social justice and the enormity of genocide."[10] *The Stranger* is an attempt to raise consciousness not only about the Holocaust in and of itself, but more precisely about what the space of concentration camps looked like and what sorts of actions occurred there. It is a film that develops a form of useful disruptiveness, using the ostensibly "safe" structures of a Hollywood genre film in order to argue for the need to view images of the Holocaust. Cinema becomes one way to begin a longer processing of historical trauma. R. Barton Palmer has connected the film's depiction of fascism to Welles's newspaper columns at the time, using these as discursive links to demonstrate the consistency of Welles's ideology across media forms.[11]

Welles's radio programs of the time also incorporated arguments about the inequalities of racism in America. These have been well documented through repeated invocation of the Isaac Woodard incident, which commanded significant attention on Welles's radio show beginning in July 1946. Woodard was a black veteran who was severely beaten and blinded by two police officers in South Carolina. Welles, on his radio show, read an affidavit from the NAACP and made a plea to "root out the officer responsible." As the case developed, Woodard "became the major focus of the show . . . and his case more generally became a *cause celebre*," and a symbol for the progressive notions of tolerance Welles attempted to instill in his American listeners at the time.[12] His radio show was subsequently terminated before the officer was tried—and acquitted—for beating Woodard.[13]

The first broadcast about Woodard, on July 28, contains a number of arguments characteristic of Welles's radio performances. He declared: "The officer of the law who blinded the young Negro boy in the affidavit has not been named, the boy saw him while he could still see, but of course he had no way of knowing what particular policeman it was who brought the justice of Dachau . . . to Aiken, South Carolina. It was just another white man with a stick who wanted to teach a Negro boy a lesson, to show a Negro boy where he belonged. In the darkness."[14] This comparison of Dachau and Aiken also invites a further comparison between the Holocaust and American racial oppression. This demonstrates Welles not only connecting global issues of oppression, but also using the recent specter of the Holocaust as a way to interpret domestic problems of racism. Just as Welles had been incorporating the problem of fascism into his theatrical work and his public lectures for years prior to *The Stranger*—notably in his 1937 staging of *Julius Caesar*, where the costumes and set designs drew from Nazi Germany—he had also discussed racism in earlier published essays, including "Race Hate Must Be Outlawed" (1944). Written against the backdrop of World War II, and making continuous note of how American men and women were dying overseas to defeat tyranny, Welles wrote: "There is no room in the American century for Jim Crow. The times urge new militancy upon the democratic attitude. Tomorrow's democracy discriminates against discrimination; its charter won't include the freedom to end freedom."[15] Here Welles again uses a kind of relational style of argumentation that ties warfare abroad to racism at home. Welles is thinking, in other words, about the relationships between different forms of violence, power, and intolerance that betray notions of democracy and percolate into institutions.

Taken together, *The Stranger* and the Isaac Woodard broadcast reveal Welles's ability to utilize the social capacities of each medium with which he engaged. In *The Stranger*, for instance, the screening of the documentary images is disruptive. Their framing begs for them to be looked at, while the accompanying dialogue explains the images in a matter-of-fact language. Radio, however, emphasizes the dynamic possibilities of voice, and not only through Welles's characteristically passionate vocals. Radio demonstrates Welles's capacity to link myriad social issues into a global web of oppression, marginalization, and bodily disfiguration. In suggesting that Welles relates and conflates various issues of antisemitism, racism, and warfare, I do not mean to suggest that he treats them as identical. By juxtaposing various forms of discrimination and violence, Welles crafts a form of argument and address that seems designed to force his listeners, spectators, and readers to consider echoes across spaces and practices. In other words, this is a "conflation" that does not detract from any particular instance of intolerance or violence, but rather aims to achieve a form of amplification.

THE *FOCUS* LETTER AND CORRESPONDENCE AS SOCIAL ACTION

While Welles scholars have substantially quoted the radio broadcasts to demonstrate his commitment to progressive social equality, many materials that did not circulate publicly expand and deepen the purview of his commitments and actions. This section returns to the letter that served as an epigraph for this chapter, a response to Welles's undated letter sent to at least thirty congresspersons with copies of the novel *Focus*. This letter helps further frame his position regarding marginalization and discrimination of minority groups, extending and clarifying the commitments traceable in his films, radio broadcasts, and newspaper columns. His juxtaposition of racism and antisemitism—echoing the juxtaposition of Aiken and Dachau—continues to amplify the attentions he placed on widespread forms of discrimination. He writes:

> Dear Representative:
>
> This nation was founded on the principle of equality and freedom for all men, regardless of race or national origin. Through the years, Americans have fought many battles to keep this heritage inviolate. The nation grew through these struggles, and the word "American" took on an added meaning through them. Not all men have always cared to decently respect the precepts of our founding fathers. Some of our fellow-countrymen, even some of our statesmen and legislators, have paid only a disinterested lip-service to racial equality.
>
> But at least they paid lip-service, and the country was not presented daily with the sorry spectacle of a Representative on the floor of the Congress of the United States, making complete mockery of his office and his fellow Congressmen with vicious, crude, and debasing attacks on any American minority group.
>
> As a fellow Representative of the gentleman from Mississippi, you probably shudder with disgust at the exhibition. You probably wonder: "What shall I say about it? Is it MY affair?"
>
> A young American boy, Arthur Miller, has recently written a wonderful novel about the cancer of race hate, and how it suddenly and strangely comes home to roost with a man who has always done the hating, and now is hated and attacked himself. The book is called FOCUS—I'm taking the liberty of sending you a copy with this letter, because I'd like you to read it, and see for yourself a potent example of just where "doing nothing and saying nothing" can eventually end up.

The attacks in the House ARE your affair. Attacks on any minority group for merely being a minority group, are the affair of anyone with a decent respect for the memory of the thousands of American boys who died in the fight for a better and freer world, and a better and freer America. It is particularly your affair because of the trust you hold for the people you serve. Who is better qualified than you to speak out for your people now against demagoguery, slander, race hatred, and real un-Americanism?

Sincerely,
Orson Welles[16]

Throughout this letter, Welles makes explicitly political pleas for congressmen to take an active stand on the floor of the House, especially regarding the House Un-American Activities Committee, which at this time was commonly called the Wood-Rankin Committee, after Representative John S. Wood of Georgia and Representative John Rankin of Mississippi. While it is unclear what incident in particular Welles references in this letter, or even what led him to decide to write it, the letters surrounding it in the archives offer some potential clues. In February 1946, several groups contacted Welles for his support against the House Un-American Activities Committee (HUAC). Two February 5 letters—one from the Society for Ethical Culture in the city of New York and the other from the Joint Anti-Fascist Refugee Committee—asked for Welles to support the creation of a group designed to bolster the committee's efforts to counter HUAC interrogations. Both groups existed largely to help Spanish Republican refugees who were living in exile from Franco's regime.

Dr. Edward K. Barsky, an American surgeon, wrote to Welles on behalf of the Joint Anti-Fascist Refugee Committee, of which he served as head. In his letter, he detailed the testimony of a "Miss Bryan," who had appeared before the House Un-American Activities Committee and "was not allowed to consult with counsel in the hearings. She was not allowed to make any statement whatsoever regarding the activities of the Joint Anti-Fascist Refugee Committee, although she was entirely prepared to do so." Barsky goes on to detail the development of a group to help safeguard the Joint Anti-Fascist Refugee Committee against legal expenses, and asks Welles to join.

The reply letters indicate that Welles sent his own letter to both representatives and senators, to both Republicans and Democrats, and to

members who spanned a number of committees across the Congress.[17]
Welles does not discuss the particularities of the attacks in the House,
choosing instead to use sweeping rhetoric tied to American ideals—
particularly, how he defines the word "American" as synonymous with
freedom and equality. Including copies of Miller's novel particularizes
this otherwise general call to action. *Focus* revolves around a man named
Newman who harbors a number of prejudices against different races and
cultures, including Jewish people. A new pair of glasses makes Newman
appear Jewish, and so he is repeatedly targeted and attacked by members
of his community for his appearance, even as he attempts to maintain his
own antisemitic stance. The novel thus skewers the ignorance of prejudice, calling for a more humanist social acceptance of other, seemingly
different persons and ethnic groups. The *Focus* letter thus shows Welles
turning more of his attention to specifically antisemitic concerns, while
maintaining his wider focus on tolerance and equality.

While most of the replies to this letter are vague variations of form
letters thanking Welles and promising to find time to read the book, a
comparatively late letter dated April 24 from Matthew M. Neely, Democratic representative from West Virginia, took a much more personal
tone, and included copies of a speech Neely gave entitled "The Rights
of the Jews to Palestine and the Conduct of Britain Which Has Made
It Impossible for the Possessors of Those Rights to Enjoy Them." In
his letter to Welles, Neely states, "May I not invite your attention to the
marked parts of the enclosure which I hope will tend to convince you
that your views concerning those who attack American minorities are
fully shared by the under-signed, who will never cease to be grateful to
you" for a speech Welles had made years earlier in Neely's home state.[18]

Many civic and political groups sent Welles letters imploring his
services as a public figure. There are letters in the Correspondences from,
among other groups representing various humanitarian and progressive causes, the American Committee for Yugoslav Relief, the Indian
National Congress, the Victory Clothing Collection, a luncheon club
formed by a woman in Sacramento, and the National Committee to
Abolish the Poll Tax—all in the first half of January 1946. Similar letters
were sent with regular frequency across 1946.[19] They ask for Welles's
voice, his physical presence at rallies, and other forms of commitment.

For example, on February 8, Nathan Sinai—who identified himself as a professor of public health who had just returned from the International Health Conference—wanted to find ways to use educational film to teach viewers about international health issues. He began his letter by writing, "I am writing you because I have been impressed by your contributions to the screen and your comments on current events. Rather than follow the usual devious approach via someone-who-knows-someone-who-knows-Orson-Welles, I am choosing this direct method."[20] While it is unclear whether or not Welles replied, the possibility of grabbing his attention via letter seems enough for Professor Sinai. Further, it is precisely because Welles's progressive ideology was familiar to Sinai that he felt encouraged to reach out for assistance. Other requests for appearances similarly tapped into Welles's liberalism, such as a letter from Albina Brinton on behalf of the National Committee to Abolish the Poll Tax, which wished to honor Welles at its 1946 "Festival for Freedom." She writes at the end of her letter: "Immediate repeal of the poll tax will allow the white supremacy in Congress, faced by a new electorate of ten million, will be forced [sic] to retreat in their poisonous racist campaign. Your many activities in [sic] behalf of the peoples [sic] cause have won the admiration and respect of the progressive people throughout this country."[21]

Some asked Welles to take more institutional or formal steps toward sociopolitical change. On February 6, John Anson Ford wrote Welles to suggest he run for office: "It's easy for a man of skill like yourself to *talk about* government. But why not accept the challenge and go into the field of *doing.* You should run for the U.S. Senate . . . I think it is a serious challenge that you cannot dismiss without the strongest of reasons."[22] Ford was, evidently, not the only person to suggest that Welles enter the political arena in a more official capacity. In a March 2 letter, Welles wrote to Lloyd F. Saunders that he was "deeply honored by your interest in me as a possible Congressional candidate. Regret commitments make it impossible to consider entering active political life this year."[23] Implicitly, Welles saw the work he was doing across media as a form of politics (or, at least, a form of critique).

Beyond organizations looking to bring Welles's image and voice to support their various causes, many letters directly address Welles's radio program, either in the form of fan mail, hate mail, or further political commentary. One of the most interesting items is from a seventeen-year-old girl named Marla Cantor, who, in January, penned a lengthy and impassioned letter to Welles about intolerance. She writes:

> I am a normal high-school girl with the same high hopes and aspirations of young people just like me. But there is something that has always blocked my path as it has blocked the path of civilization ever since the beginning of time: Intolerance! It has always been there, in school, at parties and gatherings, in new friendships: People seem to forget that tolerance might even be called the root of life.... Why can't people realize that your religion or color does not count as much as what type [of] person you are and the good you do for your fellow man! ... Why can't people learn this, Mr. Welles, why can't they begin to understand that thing which men, both great and small, have been trying to teach for ages? ... Well, Mr. Welles, I've said what was on my mind and now I'm asking you to talk further on the subject of Tolerance! Oh, I know right now that talks and lectures are constantly being given on the subject, but I feel that every extra one will help people to understand a little better. Somehow I feel that you can make them understand because you have made *me* understand many other things![24]

Miss Cantor's letter, of which this is only a small excerpt, is exceptional in relation to the rest of the correspondences surveyed, in both its length and candor. Her emphasis on the act of talking in and of itself is crucial, and demonstrates the sort of validation and encouragement that Welles received from his admirers.

In addition to supportive responses, there are also letters sent to ABC decrying Welles's radio program. A listener named Louise suggested "that you change your name American Broadcasting Co. to Moscow Broadcasting Co. or Communist Broadcasting Co. because of the types of programs you sponsor ... a disgrace to the name American."[25] Other letter writers took offense at the very mention of "sordid" stories of racial violence and discrimination. As one anonymous postcard writer puts it: "I think I could name ten favorable examples for every sordid one you dramatize. There may be places in the country that need such recitals but certainly the West Coast is not one of them."[26] If Welles developed a rhetoric that juxtaposed parallels of discrimination across different spaces, this listener did not see the value, suggesting a more locally specific, "positive" approach to race-related stories that seems largely incongruous with the liberalism Welles espoused.

A letter from W. L. Cook on February 8 to ABC regarding Welles's attack on the politics of an unnamed senator includes a rejoinder to Welles's socially progressive ideology: "Nor will that kind of slanderous abuse lessen the prejudice which exists against negroes and Jews. When the Jew voluntarily places himself in the same category with the negro his strategy is definitely not good."[27] Cook's retort attacks Welles's strategy of juxtaposing social and racial issues, but it does not consider the benefits of this rhetorical style for drawing necessary comparisons between forms of discrimination. If anything, this "hate mail" demonstrates a negative way in which Welles's rhetoric can be interpreted, where juxtaposition becomes a way of weakening the specificities of particular instances of discrimination, rather than calling attention to parallels, similarities, and larger relationships.

These samples represent a cross section of letters directly pertaining to Welles's social and political work. While certainly there are many letters about business proceedings or scheduling that paint a picture of Welles's daily life and his interactions with his associates, these letters demonstrate an equally interesting vein of engagement. The responses and interactions, in other words, demonstrate how Welles's political action entailed not only the mass communication of radio broadcasts, but also the personal communication of letter writing.

BATTLE FOR SURVIVAL

One other example from the Correspondences is useful for understanding how humanitarian groups valued Welles's politics: his voice-over work for a short documentary, *Battle for Survival*, produced by United Jewish Appeal. Writing on February 13, 1946, William Rosenwald, the group's national chairman, addressed Welles "in the name of 1,400,000 Jews who remain alive in Europe but still face [the] spectre of mass death," and went on to write, "We appeal to you who have given such splendid expression to American ideals of humanity and freedom to lend your great talents to our historic cause. May we count on you to narrate a new 15 minute film that will be utilized for stimulating Jewish communities throughout country[?]"[28]

Welles had provided his voice for other documentaries, such as *Tanks* (1942). *Tanks* was produced by the Office of Emergency Management and distributed by the War Activities Committee of the Motion Picture Industry, and was used to promote the United States' development of the M-3 Stuart Tanks for the war effort. It is also worth noting that Welles's unfinished documentary about Brazil, *It's All True*, began as part of the United States' Good Neighbor Policy with Latin America during World War II, and was in part initiated by the Office of the Co-ordinator of Latin American Affairs. *Tanks* and *It's All True* thus serve as important precursors for this sort of documentary-based "service work," where Welles utilized his voice and cinematic prowess for national service and promotion. In the case of *Battle for Survival*, that service was not directly for his government, but rather for groups that were actively pursuing humanitarian aid in line with Welles's liberal commitments.

Welles responded to Rosenwald the next day: "I shall be happy to narrate your film. If you will send me the script and let me know all the details, I will work it into my schedule."[29] There are a number of instances in the Correspondences where Welles declines events and requests because of his hectic schedule (or, at least, that is the reason he provides), and so this immediate willingness to accommodate the group is telling. On April 29, the United Jewish Appeal sent another letter to Welles's office, enclosing a small lobby card for the film that featured Welles's face as part of the advertising campaign for *Battle for Survival*. The letter states, in part, "You have undoubtedly seen the press clippings resulting from the above releases and literature. The mat[te] of Mr. Welles was used extensively in the weekly Anglo-Jewish press throughout the country. We are very grateful to Mr. Welles for his generous service to our cause."[30] Here, Welles's face is just as important as his voice for lending the documentary credibility; his involvement in the film was a crucial selling point, lending it potentially artistic and political merit.

The film itself is largely a promotional piece for the efforts of the United Jewish Appeal, editing together speeches and testaments from members and supporters while discussing how to raise money to help Jewish refugees. Welles was, evidently, considered a very important part of this production. His narration received first billing above both the writer and the editor of the documentary. The opening minutes of the film mix Welles's poetic voice-over reading with footage of refugees and concentration camps, ultimately culminating in the question, "What of our obligation?" Welles's voice-over begins as follows: "Once, long ago, these feet were shoed. Once, long ago, they turned home toward evening, toward shelter and warmth . . . to firesides, synagogues, light, and laughter, and prayers. These are the remnants of a people, let them represent the one and a half million European Jews incredibly alive, hardly a fraction more alive than when their six million brothers were starved and burned to death. Look homeward, wanderers."[31] Beneath this voiceover are images of refugees constantly moving, many in tattered clothes and some with large packs strapped across their backs. These images are certainly designed to elicit sympathy, but they also generate the same sort of affect—although perhaps less shocking—as present in the concentration camp sequence in *The Stranger*. Although Welles did not edit this film or even write the narration, *Battle for Survival* is nevertheless consonant with the sort of work he was doing throughout 1946. While it is perhaps a bit more direct in its calls to help fund a particular organization, Welles's voice continues to perform a consciousness-raising function through a different mode of filmmaking.

The voice-overs in *Battle for Survival* echo the concerns, arguments, and efforts illustrated in the other examples throughout this chapter. Again, Welles is only narrating the film; it is neither his writing nor his direction. Yet the film's use of concentration camp footage mirrors that of *The Stranger*; its invocation for viewers to realize "our obligation" to others fits with the sentiments of Welles's radio broadcasts in support of Isaac Woodard as a marginalized victim of violence, and its call to help the global Jewish community resonates with the *Focus* letter's plea to take seriously "the cancer of race hate."[32] *Battle for Survival* demonstrates, then, how United Jewish Appeal valued Welles's voice in ways consonant with the political ideals he advocated in his public addresses, his media productions, and his private correspondences. The documentary and its related correspondences also show Welles's willingness to help groups concentrating on oppression, human rights abuse, and humanitarian relief. As with his letter writing, this constitutes a form of political action.

CONCLUSION

One of Welles's friends and collaborators, Dominique Antoine—herself a Jew and an uncredited producer on *F for Fake* (1973)—described her relationship with Welles in a 1998 interview for *Positif*: "One day—and I am sure he was utterly sincere—he told me: 'Dominique, I would have loved to have the Jewish intelligence!'—'Now now, Orson, please stop. You are an intelligence from the Renaissance. You are totally European.'—'Yes, but I am not Jewish.'"[33] If this chapter has sought to make anything clear, it is that Welles's empathy with the Jewish people informed a number of his professional and personal actions following World War II. It additionally helped fuel his argumentative style of the period, which sought to juxtapose and explore relationships between different forms of injustice and racial violence. Antoine's brief recollection reveals that this empathy was not short-lived, and remained with him throughout his life, beyond the particular political circumstances of the mid-1940s.

The patterns and propositions that emerge in the personal act of letter writing—especially those sent to Welles seeking some form of political validation in the form of physical appearance, signatures, mentions on the radio, or other voice work—clarify some of the ways Welles mattered to different individuals and groups. These people each saw in Welles a genuine opportunity to bolster their cause through a prominent, sympathetic cultural figure who regularly participated in political action and argument. Orson Welles's voice came to signify, in the years immediately following the war, a progressive commitment to social equality that directly addressed antisemitism and racial discrimination.

Throughout this period—and certainly throughout much of his life—Orson Welles was a passionate progressive activist, one who was sought and desired by a number of groups for various ends. Critiques of antisemitism were a central part of this attack on intolerance, and support for Jewish communities was part of his broader social progressive politics. Using the Correspondences to help position Welles in the social, cultural, and political context of the postwar period can help bring more nuanced understandings of his cultural value for progressive groups struggling to have their own causes validated and received on a national or international level. These letters offer expansive ways of conceiving the place, status, and function of Orson Welles in American political and cultural life.

JAMES N. GILMORE is associate instructor in the Media School at Indiana University. He is coeditor of *Superhero Synergies: Comic Book Characters Go Digital.*

NOTES

I would like to thank Gregory A. Waller for his support and feedback on the development of my research and especially, on an earlier draft, and also thank the staff of the Lilly Library for their assistance.

1. Eric Smoodin, *Regarding Frank Capra: Audience, Celebrity, and American Film Studies, 1930–1960* (Durham, NC: Duke University Press, 2005), 22.

2. Jonathan Rosenbaum, *Discovering Orson Welles* (Berkeley: University of California Press, 2007), 8.

3. James Naremore, *The Magic World of Orson Welles*, 2nd ed. (Dallas, TX: Southern Methodist University Press, 1989), and Michael Denning, *The Cultural Front: The Laboring of American Culture in the Twentieth Century* (New York: Verso, 1997).

4. R. Barton Palmer, "The Politics of Genre in Welles' *The Stranger,*" *Film Criticism* 11, no. 1–2 (1987), 31–42.

5. Rosenbaum, *Discovering Orson Welles,* 270.

6. Naremore, *The Magic World of Orson Welles,* 125. Naremore, however, does spend considerable time discussing a *planned* version of *The Stranger* that is much more cinematically and thematically complex than the released version of the film. Like *The Magnificent Ambersons* before it, the film was evidently truncated and changed considerably during postproduction.

7. Joseph McBride, *What Ever Happened to Orson Welles?* (Lexington: University Press of Kentucky, 2006).

8. Jennifer L. Barker, "Documenting the Holocaust in Orson Welles's *The Stranger,*" in *Film & Genocide,* ed. Kristi Wilson and Tomas F. Crowder-Taraborrelli (Madison: University of Wisconsin Press, 2012), 45–67, 58.

9. *Death Mills* has been included as a special feature on DVD editions of *The Stranger,* further tying these two together.

10. Barker, "Documenting the Holocaust in Orson Welles's *The Stranger,*" 64.

11. Palmer, "The Politics of Genre in Welles' *The Stranger.*" See also Sidney Gottlieb's essay in this volume, which details the antifascist arguments of Welles's newspaper columns.

12. Rosenbaum, *Discovering Orson Welles,* 9.

13. For a more detailed recounting of the Isaac Woodard broadcasts, see Simon Callow, *Orson Welles,* Vol. 2: *Hello Americans* (London: Jonathan Cape, 2006),

323–42. See also Craig S. Simpson, "Presenting Orson Welles: An Exhibition Challenge," in this volume, for a discussion of the Woodard incident.

14. Transcribed from a recording of the broadcast.

15. Orson Welles, "Race Hate Must be Outlawed," *Free World*, July 1944, available at *wellesnet*, accessed March 16, 2016, http://www.wellesnet.com/orson-welles-says-race-hate-must-be-outlawed/.

16. Orson Welles to Congress, Undated, Welles MSS Correspondences, Lilly Library, Indiana University, box 4.

17. The congressmen who sent Welles reply letters are: Homer E. Capehart (R-IN), Homer Ferguson (R-MI), Theodore Francis Green (D-RI), Charles A. Halleck (R-IN), Carl A. Hatch (D-NM), Robert K. Henry (D-WI), Warren G. Magnuson (D-WA), Louis C. Rabaut (D-MI), John J. Riley (D-SC), J. W. Trimble (D-AK), Wallace H. White (R-ME), Antonio M. Fernandez (D-NM), Joseph F. Guffey (D-PA), Harold C. Hagen (R-MN), Franck R. Havenner (D-CA), Karl M. Lecompte (R-IA), Emmet O'Neal (D-AL), Chapman Revercomb (R-WV), Frank L. Sundstrom (R-NJ), James M. Tunnell (D-DE), Brien McMahon (D-CT), W. Lee O'Daniel (D-TX), Forrest C. Donnell (R-MO), Ross Rizley (R-OK), Henry M. Jackson (D-WA), Ernest W. McFarland (D-AZ), Matthew M. Neely (D-WV).

18. Matthew M. Neely to Orson Welles, April 24, 1946, Welles MSS Correspondences, Lilly Library, Indiana University, box 4.

19. These letters are dated as follows: The American Committee for Yugoslov Relief to Orson Welles, January 4, 1946; Indian National Congress to Orson Welles, January 5, 1946; Nelson A. Rockefeller to Orson Welles (on behalf of Victory Clothing Collection), January 7, 1946; Albina Brinton to Orson Welles (on behalf of the National Committee to Abolish the Poll Tax), January 16, 1946; Sam O'Neal to Orson Welles (on behalf of *The Democrat*), January 16, 1946; Chicago Independent Citizens Committee to Orson Welles, January 22, 1946. Welles MSS Correspondences, Lilly Library, Indiana University, box 4.

20. Nathan Sinai to Orson Welles, February 8, 1946, Welles MSS Correspondences, Lilly Library, Indiana University, box 4.

21. Albina Brinton to Orson Welles, January 16, 1946, Welles MSS Correspondences, Lilly Library, Indiana University, box 4.

22. John Anson Ford to Orson Welles, February 6, 1946, Welles MSS Correspondences, Lilly Library, Indiana University, emphasis in original, box 4.

23. Orson Welles to Lloyd F. Saunders, March 2, 1946, Welles MSS Correspondences, Lilly Library, Indiana University, box 4.

24. Marla Cantor to Orson Welles, January 28, 1946, Welles MSS Correspondences, Lilly Library, Indiana University, box 4.

25. Louise [last name illegible] to ABC, March 6, 1946, Welles MSS Correspondences, Lilly Library, Indiana University, box 4.

26. Anonymous letter to ABC, March 23, 1946, Welles MSS Correspondences, Lilly Library, Indiana University, box 4.

27. W.L. Cook to ABC, February 7, 1946, Welles MSS Correspondences, Lilly Library, Indiana University, box 4.

28. William Rosenwald to Orson Welles (on behalf of United Jewish Appeal), February 13, 1946, Welles MSS Correspondences, Lilly Library, Indiana University, box 4.

29. Orson Welles to National Chairman of United Jewish Appeal, February 14, 1946, Welles MSS Correspondence, Lilly Library, Indiana University, box 4.

30. Samuel R. Kan to Orson Welles (on behalf of United Jewish Appeal), April 29, 1946, Welles MSS Correspondence, Lilly Library, Indiana University, box 4.

31. *Battle for Survival*, narrated by Orson Welles (Los Angeles: RKO Pathe, 1946), *YouTube*, 00:00:36–00:01:11 [time stamp location of quote], accessed August 4, 2017, https://www.youtube.com/watch?v=LlkhGehvYAU.

32. Welles addressed social and moral obligations in some of his earlier writings, as well. See, for example, "Moral Indebtedness," *Free World* 6, no. 4 (October 1943), 375–76.

33. Jean-Pierre Bethomé, "Deux portes ouvertes dans le labyrinth," interview with Dominique Antoine, *Positif* no. 449–450 (July–August 1998), 20. I am indebted to François Thomas for providing a translation of this article.

7

MULTIMEDIA MAGIC IN *AROUND THE WORLD*

Orson Welles's Film-and-Theater Hybrid

VINCENT LONGO

In his two essays titled "Theatre and Film" published in 1951, André Bazin asserts how Orson Welles's film adaptation of *Macbeth* (1948) challenged the aesthetic boundaries between film and theater. Welles, however, was not only blurring the two media in his films. As Bazin also mentions, albeit briefly, Welles accomplished comparable feats in his theatrical work: "The fact that aristocrats had seats on the stage in the seventeenth century does not deny the existence of the apron, it confirms it by means of a kind of privileged violation, the same as when in our day Orson Welles on Broadway scatters actors about the hall to fire shots on the audience: he isn't reducing the apron to nothing, he's crossing to the other side of it. The rules of the game are also made to be broken, and we expect some players to cheat."[1] Bazin describes how Welles diverged from theatrical conventions that distance the audience from the action on stage by crossing over the stage's physical barrier in order to forcefully immerse the audience in the action of the play. The above passage, however, appears to be more than just a generalization describing Welles's theatrical work as a whole. The production Bazin seems to be referring to, which involved different encroachments across the footlights of the theater and countless prop guns being fired in all directions, is Welles's Broadway musical

Around the World (1946).[2] One of the most remarkable encroachments involved a "Slide for Life" over the audience, where an acrobat walked on a tight rope from the stage to a balcony over the audience, then slid backward back to the stage. Several cities banned Welles from having it performed during the show in fear that the acrobat "might fall and demolish some of the people in the seats below."[3] The revolvers Bazin mentioned included one wielded by a robber who threatened the audience as if they were bank patrons and another fired at a larger-than-life plaster eagle (which carried the lead actor in the air) and subsequently showered its feathers onto the audience and crashed to the stage.[4] In the unabridged transcription of the interviews that Peter Bogdanovich turned into *This is Orson Welles*, Welles proclaimed *Around the World* his "masterpiece . . . in any form."[5]

Bazin did not see *Around the World*, and it is unclear exactly how he learned the details of the production—though it is easy to speculate that Welles could have told him; or Jean Cocteau, who worked with Bazin on his book about Welles, may have learned the details from Welles himself. In his profile of Welles published in Bazin's book, Cocteau charged Bazin with the responsibility of discussing *Around the World*'s importance to Welles's body of work: "I leave Bazin the task of speaking to you in detail of a multiple of work which is not limited to cinematography, in which journalism, the Martian practical joke, the stage productions of *Julius Caesar* and *Around the World in 80 Days* [sic] have an important place."[6] In his book, however, Bazin only mentioned *Around the World* briefly, using it to reaffirm that Welles "had never in fact lost touch with Broadway," and finished by mentioning the production's extravagant budget and Michael Todd's subsequent film production.[7] It is clear, however, that Bazin was aware of *Around the World*, and he seems to cite the production as an example of Welles's tendency to diverge from the conventions of a medium.

Throughout his "Theatre and Film" essays, Bazin declared that Welles, along with Laurence Olivier, William Wyler, and Cocteau, created an "aesthetic problem of a special kind." This "problem" was the result of Welles's emerging approach to adapting theatrical works into film.[8] Welles's 1948 adaptation of *Macbeth*, according to Bazin, did not conform to the stereotyped filming of a stage performance with a single static shot, nor did his adaptation fit the common model of fidelity, in which the play's aesthetics and conventions are mediated by—or translated into—cinema's specific language. As Bazin noted, before this aesthetic evolution, most directors' principal concern "was to camouflage the model's theatrical origin, to adapt it, to dissolve it in the cinema."[9] In contrast, Bazin—breaking the ostensibly core assumption of medium specificity shared by modernist film theorists—saw the films of Welles and a few other directors as aimed at highlighting their theatrical basis (i.e., its aesthetics and conventions), a feat they accomplished by using the camera to capture the perspective of an interested theater viewer, who had a "pair of magic opera glasses and a flying seat."[10] Bazin called this phenomenon "aesthetic limbo" [*limbes esthétiques*].[11] As a result, films like *Macbeth*, according to Bazin, "are no longer subjects that one 'adapts'; they are plays staged using cinema."[12]

Welles's *Around the World* was, in an even more literal sense, a play "staged using cinema." It included five original film sequences that Welles shot and integrated into the performances. Consigned by scholars to a mere footnote in the director's career, or at best as a financial disaster and a misstep that led him to direct his subsequent film *The Lady from Shanghai* (1947), with *Around the World*, Welles accomplished much more than just violating theatrical conventions. By looking at surviving archival material, most of which has gone unexamined for decades, it becomes clear that *Around the World* combined theater and cinema to create stunning effects that pushed the already blurry boundaries between both media. Typically categorized as a stage musical, *Around the World* is, perhaps, better described as a multimedia production because of the ways in which Welles blended film and theater together in illusionistic combinations. Though he had previously attempted to integrate a similar combination of media into *Too Much Johnson* (1938)—a feat he ultimately achieved in his vaudeville act *The Green Goddess* (1939)—Welles never intended for the film sequences and live performance in those productions to directly interact. In contrast, in *Around the World's* most magical displays of stagecraft and multimedia Welles had the actors on stage interact with characters and images in the projected films and seamlessly staged the transitions between film sequences and live theater. Welles even made the live action onstage "cinematic," by creating an illusion that the film sequences were being projected, not onto the screen, but onto the entire stage.

This essay supplies one of the first accurate and detailed descriptions of the five missing silent film sequences for *Around the World* and their context within the action onstage. Afterward, by putting this production the context of Welles's interest in hybrid magic and European avant-garde theater, I will demonstrate that *Around the World* provides persuasive evidence that Welles blended media and stretched aesthetic conventions not just within a single medium, but across cinema, radio, and theater. This intermedial approach characterizes much of his work from 1938 to 1950 and can be seen most clearly in the hybrid works he created, beginning with *Too Much Johnson* and leading to *The Unthinking Lobster* (1950). These observations apply to more than Welles's hybrid productions. Rick Altman has effectively argued that Welles extended a radio style sound aesthetic into *Citizen Kane* (1941), and, as noted above, Bazin grounds his theoretical concept of aesthetic limbo in part in Welles's ability to emulate theatrical spectatorship cinematographically.[13] What makes *Around the World* unique, however, is that Welles foregrounded and materialized this creative process in the dramatic form of actual magic tricks, ones that collapsed conventional distinctions between cinema and live performance.

A BRIEF INTRODUCTION TO A GIANT EXTRAVAGANZA

Produced in the summer of 1946 under the reinstated Mercury Productions banner and with artistic autonomy, *Around the World* was based loosely on Jules Verne's novel *Around the World in 80 Days*. The show began on a one-month "tryout tour," traveling from Boston, to New Haven, and then to Philadelphia, before playing on Broadway for two months. Surviving scripts of the production reveal that, like Verne's novel, the musical follows the aristocratic Englishman Phileas Fogg and his sidekick Passepartout (or Pat) as they travel around the world to win a wager—all while being pursued by Inspector Fix and saving the Hindu princess Mrs. Aouda from being burned alive.[14] Welles's version, however, adds several new characters and ancillary narratives, including changing Inspector Fix, a misguided deputy of Scotland Yard, to

"Dick Fix," a private investigator who wears a new local disguise in every international location he visits. Welles also has Dick Fix frame Fogg for robbing a bank that he himself robbed through an accomplice and adds the Irish nursemaid Molly as a love interest for Pat. In addition, Welles turns Verne's somewhat critical view of the 1873 British Empire into explicitly anti-imperialist satire.

Around the World was not merely a musical comedy, but is best described using the analogy of a circus, due to its overarching focus on the spectacular and the exotic. Around the World included huge dance numbers, a full-length Chinese magic show, a lantern slide travelogue lecture, and an actual Japanese circus act. As Welles himself explained: "Around the World is made up of very old stuff—things that have enchanted me from the time I saw them under canvas, in a one ring circus, in the theater, or a carnival. It's like hanging around the toy display at a department store around Christmas time. Or going out and buying out a whole toy store. There's a train wreck, an attack by Indians, a circus, old fashioned movies, low comedy, and a score by Cole Porter."[15] Around the World also had the structure of a vaudeville show. The production consisted of performances by a "Chinese" magician (played by Welles himself), dance troupes, and acrobats; it had multiple musical numbers, projected silent movies, and for a short time included an illustrated song, during which projected colored lantern slides accompanied and embellished a vocal performance. All of these sequences were staple vaudeville acts. In Around the World, however, Welles linked all of the "vaudeville performances" together within a single cohesive narrative. For example, magic tricks were used for several different narrative purposes. Spies in Suez perform the "Indian Rope trick" in an attempt to delay Fogg long enough to capture him. While in Hong Kong, Dick Fix separates Pat from his group by knocking him out, drugging him with opium, and then shanghaiing him onto a ship bound for Japan. Instead of working as a crew member on the ship, Pat becomes a clown in the Oka-Saka circus and acts as an assistant in Fu San's magic show, which concludes the circus number and the first act. At the end of the magic show, Fu San hoists his assistant inside a large bag into the air with the supposed intention of making him disappear. However, Fu San then reveals himself to be Dick Fix in disguise and proclaims his intentions to murder Pat. Fix then pulls out a pistol, aims it at the hanging bag and fires. After the gunshot, however, it is revealed that the magic trick had accidentally worked and had transported Pat into the audience, where he was somehow watching the show the whole time.

In essence, even calling the show an extravaganza may understate the production's sheer excess of and emphasis on spectacle. In early drafts, Welles subverted the importance of narrative tension altogether by calling the show *Around the World: A Wager Won*, which eliminated any possible mystery about the play's conclusion. In addition, although a production's curtain call is usually reserved for the actors, Welles emphasized the importance of spectacle by bringing the mechanical eagle, a toy train, and a larger-than-life papier-mâché elephant onstage alongside the actors during the final bow.

"OLD-TIME MOVIES THAT FLICKER AND JUMP"

It goes without saying that there is one intrinsic problem with analyzing *Around the World*'s film sequences: they have disappeared without a trace. One frame and a single on-set production photo depicting the shooting of the "Hong Kong" sequence are the only visual evidence known to survive.[16] This makes analysis of the actual cinematography, mise-en-scène, and editing conjectural, if not impossible. However, by scrutinizing three versions of the script, the shot list for the film sequences with notes from the script supervisor, the film editor's cutting script, and published critical reviews, it is possible to reconstruct the missing film sequences and how Welles integrated them into the play.[17] It is important to stress, however, that there is no single version of any of the film sequences. In fact, in addition to the several versions that have material traces, Welles likely scripted and staged more versions than we will ever know about. True to his approach to theater directing, Welles constantly tweaked the film sequences during *Around the World*'s theatrical run in a constant search for the perfect length or the loudest laughs. In fact, hybrid sequences—at least in the interconnected manner Welles devised them—demand this unconventional, theatrical-like process of changing an already publicly released film sequence. Since the film segments and onstage action were carefully coordinated, any major change to the live performance—such as an actor change or staging—required reediting. Surviving material sheds light on film sequences during many stages of their conception and existence, including both Welles's abandoned ideas for hybrid techniques and the two ways he actually used them during *Around the World*'s tour. In the early script drafts, Welles proposed to use a scrim (a theatrical screen that becomes transparent when lights only illuminate an area behind it) for a movie screen in order to transpose entire scenes from the film directly onto the stage.[18] As staged on Broadway, however, Welles created constant interactions between the film and the stage, so that what happens on the stage appears to affect what happens in the film, and vice versa. All of these techniques blended film and theater together to create striking moments of spectacle while complicating traditional ideas of time and space. Instead of erroneously declaring a definitive version of the *Around the World*'s hybrid sequences, by treating their many versions and conceptions together as one whole—as one normally does the many performances of a single stage production—the various versions supply us with an unprecedented glimpse into Welles's belief in the confluence of cinema and theater aesthetics, and the dazzling effects they can create only when combined.

Welles shot the film sequences to echo the aesthetic and style of silent American comedies. The five silent black-and-white film sequences for *Around the World* resembled what Welles called "old-time movies that flicker and jump" (Draft Script, Welles MSS, Lilly Library, box 7, 2; subsequent scripts referred to parenthetically throughout this chapter are from the same source). Consistent with this silent-movie aesthetic, the films used at least one iris-in, which began the first film sequence (and the play), as well as intertitles for opening title credits, short bits of dialogue, the names of some locations, and to introduce and give a quick profile of various characters and the actor who played them. When Fogg first appears in a film sequence, an intertitle reads, "Phileas Fogg, a Bachelor of Considerable Means and Exact Habits . . . Arthur Margetson" (Cutting Script, 1). A live orchestra accompanied the silent films by playing music and providing selected sound effects, including the sound of gas escaping into a room. Welles was very fond of silent films in general, as Matthew Solomon aptly describes in his chapter in this volume, and commonly praised the form in interviews.[19] In 1939, he told the *Los Angeles Times*, "Radio, for instance, in my opinion, does not bear the same relation to television that the silent films did to the talking pictures. It would be well, incidentally, if we had some silent films from time to time. That form was great in itself."[20] His affection for (and familiarity with) silent films extended to the area of set design. For one scene, Welles specifically noted in the script that one set shown in an *Around the World* film was "a typical Vitagraph movie set of a London street" (Draft Script, 3). Welles also later claimed that all thirty-eight sets for *Around the World* were based on the films of Georges Méliès, though there is no proof of this in the production documents.[21]

The film sequences used a comedic style that mimicked the silent films of Mack Sennett and Charlie Chaplin. Like those Welles planned to use in his theatrical production of *Too Much Johnson*, which he publicized on flyers as being in the Mack Sennett tradition, the sequences in *Around the World* utilized slapstick conventions.[22] These include Keystone Kop chase scenes performed with English bobbies that were characterized by Sennett's chaotic physical comedy. Welles also briefly mentions Chaplin in the script, noting that several characters should waddle jerkily "ala [sic] Essanay," the studio that produced many of Chaplin's short films (Draft Script, 4). The styles of Sennett, Méliès, and Chaplin embodied the antique and anachronistic appearance Welles wanted in *Around the World*. As Welles later noted, "the silent pictures always look as though they happened in a world earlier than they did when they were shot. They all derive from the nineteenth century."[23]

With the assistance of a cameraman named B. Kelley and the entire cast of the production, Welles began shooting the film sequences during rehearsals for *Around the World* on April 15, 1946 (eleven days before the scheduled opening night).[24] With one exception, each was shot on the corresponding set of the play so that the locations and settings appeared roughly the same on stage and screen. Welles shot the film sequences quickly, never taking more than four takes of a particular shot and several times, only a single take.[25] The film shoot yielded five sequences edited together by Irving Lerner, a documentary filmmaker who had just left the Office of War Information to direct New York University's Education Film Institute.[26] The sequences totaled less than fifteen minutes in duration and were projected on a movie screen near the back of the stage that could be removed as needed.[27] When in place, the screen was sometimes set in between the stage curtains.

MULTIMEDIA MAGIC

Like the rest of the production, Welles's ideas and plans for the film sequences and their integration into the live performance continually changed throughout preproduction and during the tryout tour. In the early stages of planning, Welles proposed two film sequences that he later abandoned before shooting. In the early draft, all of the film sequences would have been projected onto a scrim movie screen. One sequence, while Fogg and his crew travel from California to the East Coast, would have featured a series of shots from the point of view of a passenger on a train that is steaming out of control through the Rocky Mountains. These shots were to be sped up and include "wild curves, [and] ghastly twists and turns," accompanied by intense chase music (Draft Script, 145). This thrilling phantom ride film anticipates the roller coaster sequence in *This is Cinerama* (1952). More pertinently, the sequence looks back to Hale's Tours. A fixture of storefront theaters and amusement parks during the first decade of the 1900s, Hale's Tours included motion pictures filmed from the point of view of a traveling train projected inside a mechanical "train" theater which both looked like the interior of a passenger car and vibrated and moved to further create the sensory illusion of a locomotive. Echoing a title like those used in Hale's Tour productions (e.g., *The Hold Up of the Rocky Mountain Express* (1906) and *Trip Through the Black Hills* (1906)), Welles planned to project this film sequence following the scene entitled "On Board a Train Somewhere on the Rocky Mountains" (Draft Script, 135). Also similar to Hale Tour's films, this scene featured the characters in an open train car and created some of its effects by using a giant treadmill.[28]

Though the train sequence would not have combined film and theater in the same scene, another one of Welles's early ideas involved conversations between characters on stage and characters on film, even integrating a live actor into the film itself. This scene (unnamed in surviving documents—I call it "Fogg's Market Price") would have opened with the intertitle, "IN LONDON THE BETTING ON PHILEAS FOGG HAS REACHED A FEVERISH PITCH," and several shots of members of Fogg's whist club and a variety of Londoners betting and negotiating with bookies on the odds that Fogg will make it around the world within eighty days. From the right side of the stage, a newsboy enters shouting the headline of the *London Times*, "FOGG A BANK ROBBER." This news causes the "market price" on Fogg shown in the film sequence to spiral downward. Two whist club members then join the newsboy onstage and one buys a paper. After reading the article, the two leave, declaring that Fogg has no chance of winning the bet. The film cuts to a shot of a "broker's blackboard" as a hand draws an immense zero around the word "Fogg" to indicate his odds of winning. The film continues with a freeze-frame of the large zero, when suddenly Fogg's real face appears in the middle of the large zero when lights from behind the scrim illuminate only the actor's face, who physically stands behind the screen. Shortly after, the film fades out, the scrim rises, and Fogg is not there. Rather, behind the scrim is the set for "The Peak of Bald Mountain," and the production transitions to the scene in which Fogg is offered as a sacrifice to the giant eagle by Native Americans (Draft Script, 157).

In "Fogg's Market Price," Welles utilized many of the hybrid techniques he would eventually use to create dramatic effects. The scene begins with the actions of the actors onstage creating the illusion that they are able to directly affect both the characters and the market prices on the screen. Both the newsboy's headline and the whist club members' remarks about Fogg appear to cause the market prices to fall. Fogg's physical appearance on the screen while the film continues further blurs the line between film and theater. Fogg is physically onstage, hidden behind the screen, but, because lights from behind the scrim illuminate his face, Fogg's head appears to be within the projected film. Depending on how this would have been presented, it is possible that the actual Fogg would have appeared to be a superimposition within the film sequence. In this way, an actor who was physically present on the stage would have "magically" appeared to be in the film itself. More pertinently, Welles would have used a hybrid technique to create an effect often credited as characteristic of and specific to cinema. As noted before, Welles never shot either the point-of-view thrill ride film or "Fogg's Market Price," but the latter instance of "what could have been" supplies an important glimpse of how Welles believed that the combination of film and theater could create otherwise unattainable effects. At the same time, it also demonstrates his belief that the aesthetic distinctions separating the two media were not impenetrable lines, but rather permeable ones.

Each of the five scenes that Welles ended up including in *Around the World*'s tour also combined film sequences and live performance in a variety of ways. To quickly summarize, some sequences, like "A Storm at Sea" and "Hong Kong Den," used film to supply exposition for a subsequent scene on stage. "A Storm at Sea," the only film sequence that was not shot on an actual set of the play, opens act 2 and serves to move the narrative of *Around the World* from Japan to California and features the characters floundering to stay on their ship while huge waves overtake them. "Hong Kong Den" captures the initial sights of Fogg's group as they wander the "evil" streets of Hong Kong. This film features the most nefarious actions and characters in the production, including belligerent violent sailors, "sing-song girls in an opium den," stabbings, and torture. As indicated by the intertitle, "To be continued," in the final frames, the "Hong Kong Den" film sequence was used to set up the following "Street of Evil Repute in Hong Kong" scene on stage, in which Pat is knocked unconscious, drugged with opium, and shanghaied onto a ship bound for Japan, where Dick Fix tries to murder him. By the time this occurs on stage, these subsequent violent actions do not come as a surprise, given the savage characterization of Hong Kong in the earlier film sequence (Cutting Script, 7).

Unlike how he planned to stage *Too Much Johnson*, where the film sequences were to begin the production and then play sequentially after (and never simultaneously with) each act of live performance, in three of the sequences in *Around the World*, "Fogg's Flatt," "The Bank," and "Hyde Park," Welles integrated film sequences with action on stage. In "Fogg's Flatt," Welles used a flashbox (a metal box placed in front of a screen that, when detonated, creates an explosive flash with smoke and light) to mimic the physical and shocking experience of a real explosion. Like the techniques proposed in "Fogg's Market Price," the later scenes, "The Bank" and "Hyde Park," blended film and theater together intricately and extensively. When the show began its tryout tour in Boston, Welles staged the transition from both film sequences (discussed in detail below) to their onstage action by transposing the last frame of the sequence directly onto the stage. Each scene began by projecting the film sequences on a large scrim screen, which would have needed to cover much of the height and width of the proscenium. Just before the film sequence ends, Welles cuts to a long shot of the scene. The sequences fade out, just as a change of lighting makes the scrim transparent, revealing the actors and set in the exact same positions and proportions as the final frame of the film—only now in the "living" color of live performance. Before the crew removes it a few moments later, the audience watches the action onstage behind the scrim screen. At least in theory, this transposition effect creates the illusion that the black-and-white film suddenly dissolves into color film onscreen, with the audience unaware that the live performance had begun until the crew removed the screen. This effect resembles the dissolve in *Citizen Kane* where the still photograph of the *Chronicle* newspaper staff, seen through a window, "comes to life" in the shot that follows. Unlike a photograph, however, both film and theater display movement, which means the transformation could not be achieved by contrasting stasis with dynamism. Instead, the sensation of "coming to life" in *Around the World* is created by the transformation of the black-and-white film sequence into the color of the stage.

Unfortunately, the transition did not work as planned. Before he even shot the film sequences, Welles suspected that a scrim screen would be a "problem," though he supplied no specific details about his trepidation.[29] As soon as the show opened in Boston, Welles's fears were realized. Like the other technical issues that plagued the production, the complex rigging and stagecraft needed for the "cinematic-like 'dissolve,'" coupled with the transposition proved logistically impractical and, according to first-hand testimony, did not create a smooth enough transition for Welles's liking.[30] Though he may have abandoned these techniques earlier, Welles likely changed his approach to creating multimedia magic when the show moved to Philadelphia. While at the Philadelphia Opera House, Welles addressed the many critical concerns and technical issues by drastically adjusting the play, cutting the script by 120 pages, adding himself as a revamped villain, and inserting his magic act at the end of the circus number.[31] Some of these changes directly affected the film sequences. Replacing the actor who played Dick Fix, for example, caused Welles to reedit the sequences to remove any shots showing the previous actor, Alan Reed, as the private investigator and not Welles.

To resolve its technical problems, Welles abandoned the scrim screen altogether. Instead, both "The Bank" and "Hyde Park" sequences involve conversations between characters on stage and characters on film through the use of intertitles, and use stage "portals" (small upstage openings on either side of the stage that were separate from the main part of the stage) to figuratively transport characters between media. *Around the World* began with the movie screen in front of a backdrop downstage which depicted the exterior of the bank on a London street. "The Bank" film sequence opens to the interior of Mr. Fogg's local London bank where, much to the dismay of the banker, Fogg withdraws his entire fortune, fearing that it will be stolen by a bank robber who has been relentlessly stealing from London banks. Toward the end of scene, the ominous silhouette of a pistol-wielding bank robber appears on one of the glass doors of the bank. While other bank patrons cower, the unsuspecting Fogg, shown in a close-up, continues counting his money. Suddenly, the onscreen bank robber smashes through the glass door, causing a matching sound of glass breaking behind the London drop. While the bank patrons continue cowering onscreen, the lower left portal onstage opens to reveal the bank robber stepping through the actual broken glass door (fig. 7.1). The bank robber makes his way to the middle of the stage and, even though he is physically in front of the London drop and not inside the bank, he speaks and acts as if he is in the bank shown onscreen. The bank robber threatens the onscreen patrons to surrender, and they comply. To further scare them, the onstage robber fires his gun into the air, which appears to break a glass chandelier onscreen, shown in a subsequent close-up as it shatters, with pieces falling on Fogg's head, who nevertheless continues unflinchingly counting his money. Pointing specifically to Fogg onscreen, the robber commands him not to move and then exits the stage. Suddenly a police inspector (not Dick Fix) runs onstage and asks the head banker onscreen where the source of the disturbance is, to which the banker responds, "THE BANK!" with his reply shown as an intertitle (Cutting Script, 3). The film sequence then ends, and the London drop is taken offstage, revealing the physical interior of

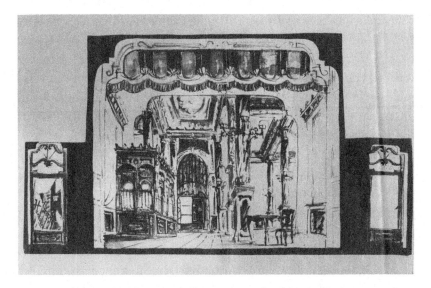

Figure 7.1. "The Bank" set. Designed by Robert Davison. The portals, featured to the left and right of the proscenium, were completely hidden before opening (as pictured) to reveal the glass windows and the robber. From set designs for *Around the World*, Welles MSS, oversize 9, Lilly Library.

the bank as the bank robber leaves carrying moneybags. The inspector, slightly embarrassed by the obvious answer to his question, enters the bank to try to stop the robber, but he escapes. Just then Dick Fix runs on the scene to try to cover up for his friend and accomplice, the bank robber.

The effects of this scene are undoubtedly as confusing as they are sophisticated in manipulating time and space. In this scene, Welles uses film to bypass the theater's physical limitations. At the beginning of the scene, there is only a single unified time and space presented onscreen. However, after the robber enters the stage, the time and space presented onscreen and onstage appear congruent. The side portal of the stage becomes a figurative portal that allows the robber to transport from the separate world of film (and the bank) to the physical stage outside the bank. The characters onstage also interact with characters onscreen. At the same time, however, the stage and the film are spatially and temporally disconnected. The robber and later the inspector interact with the characters onscreen as if they are in the bank, shooting the chandelier and directly speaking with the patrons, even though they are located onstage in front of the London drop and not in the bank set. The robber was still confined to the physical space of the theater and logically did not exist in the same time as the film. When the London drop is taken offstage at the end of the sequence, Welles reveals that what was seen in the film ostensibly exists on the other side of the curtain, not outside of the theater.

The Hyde Park scene uses portals similarly, but also gives the stage itself a film aesthetic. With the lights slightly dimmed, the stage is dressed again with the London drop and a single bush is placed stage right. The film opens on the Hyde Park set. In the film, the bank robber runs from a group of bobbies and hides behind the bush onscreen (placed in the same location as the bush onstage in front of the London drop). Meanwhile onscreen, Molly enters Hyde Park pushing a baby carriage. As she does this onscreen, Molly physically appears onstage just as an onscreen intertitle introduces her as "Molly, An Honest Nursemaid from The Auld Sod . . . Julie Warren" (Cutting Script, 4). When the onscreen Molly stops the carriage and goes to smell a branch on the bush, the onstage Molly matches her action with the bush onstage. Onscreen, Molly then catches the attention of Pat, also onscreen, lying in the grass nearby. As he pursues her onscreen, Pat physically appears onstage as an onscreen intertitle introduces him as "'Pat' Passepartout, a Lackadaisical Yankee . . . Larry Laurence" (Cutting Script, 4). Suddenly, the robber physically darts from stage left into the stage right portal, and then reappears in the film. The robber onscreen then moves from behind the bush to behind Molly's baby carriage. In an act of desperation, he reaches into the carriage and hides the money inside. As this happens, Molly and Pat also watch the actions of the robber (and possibly themselves) onscreen suspecting a kidnapping or robbery has taken place. In a fit of anger, Pat (followed closely by Molly) rush through the lower right portal. Now appearing onscreen, Pat instigates a slapstick fight with the robber. Suddenly, the film ends and the London drop is removed, revealing Pat and the robber fighting onstage on the Hyde Park set. At the same time, a lobsterscope (a fixture that goes over a stage light and has a spinning disc with holes in it to create a strobe-like effect) covers the stage in a flickering light, which continues until Pat chases the robber offstage.[32]

As in the bank scene, there is an ambiguous fusion of time and space, but also a quasi-cinematic flickering light at the end of the scene that blurs the distinction between stage and screen. At the beginning of the scene, the world onscreen mirrors the world onstage: when Molly and Pat appear on the film, they likewise emerge onto the stage, with both embodiments of the characters and the actors who play them introduced by an intertitle. This mirror effect indicates that the actions are identical, but shown in two different media, an effect analogous to a live broadcast onscreen of action onstage. This challenges the audience to simultaneously experience the action occurring both in two-dimensional cinematic space and three-dimensional theatrical space. But the space is still very much theatrical, since cinema is not used to extend the performance outside the theater's physical limitations (e.g., into an actual park). At the same time, the onscreen world is separate from the stage: after first being shown onscreen, the characters run through the lower right portal before appearing in the film. Pat and Molly watch the robber hide the money in the film, but dash through the portal to fight him onscreen. At the end of the scene, the stage "becomes" the film through the use of the lobsterscope. Like the film sequences in *Around the World*, which were shot specifically to flicker and jump, Welles uses the lobsterscope to create the look of a projected film onstage. This effect is especially potent because it occurs just as the film itself ends, when the actors onstage are on the same set where Welles had shot the Hyde Park sequence during rehearsals. This creates the illusion that the film is still being projected, not onto the screen, but onto the entire stage, making the live action and the space within the proscenium "cinematic."

REINVENTING THE MAGIC TRICK

In order to properly analyze the intended effects of Welles's hybrid sequences, they should be contextualized with precedents created by magicians and European avant-garde theater directors. As I have briefly hinted, these sequences and their complex manipulation of time and space need to be understood as magic tricks. Preceding *Around the World*, Welles directed the little-known film sequence *Magic Trick* in 1945, which he shot for bandleader and aspiring magician Richard Himber to integrate into a "musical comedy magical production" called *Abracadabra*, which Himber wanted Welles to coproduce.[33] *Abracadabra* never materialized, but Himber later used *Magic Trick* in his variety magic show *Himberama* (1953) and on the television show *Tonight!* in 1954.[34] It was also later used by David Copperfield in his 1992 TV special.[35]

When combined correctly with a magician onstage, *Magic Trick* created seemingly unexplainable and impossible connections and interactions between a prerecorded film sequence and a live performance. Onscreen, Welles throws "magical powder" and a deck of cards offscreen, which seamlessly appear onstage, and through conversations in which the onscreen Welles seems to acknowledge every word, mannerism, and fumble of the live audience, Welles is able to correctly select their card from a deck of cards that appears to be physically thrown through the screen. Similar to *Magic Trick*, the presentation of time and space in "The Bank" and "Hyde Park" is ambiguous; obscurity is created by sometimes highlighting conventional treatments of time and space in cinema and theater and other times collapsing their differences completely. Characters onstage used portals to transport themselves into the film sequences and could interact between each medium even though they were connected neither spatially nor temporally to each other. The characters were even onscreen and onstage at the same time, as if presenting an identical instance in two different presentations of space. These actions leave no logical way to understand the exact temporality and spatiality of the scenes. In other words, even without a telltale deck of cards, by seemingly bending the laws of time and space to his will, Welles created magic. As Welles noted in his magician research file, "a theater is, after all—the greatest magic box ever."[36]

Unsurprisingly, despite the plethora of lukewarm reviews from theater critics, magicians heavily praised *Around the World* in their trade journals and in social gatherings.[37] To this audience, however, these magic tricks were not completely novel. In 1907, at the Palace Theater in London, magician Horace Goldin exited an onscreen taxi through a trapdoor in the screen onto the stage and then continued to pay the driver in the film.[38] Similarly, in his later "Film to Life" illusion, Goldin fired a bullet onstage toward a thug onscreen, then, by walking behind the screen, he created the illusion that he appeared in the ongoing film and started a fight with him. Goldin threw the thug so hard that he appeared to fly out of the screen and onto the stage. While Goldin still appeared onscreen, the thug onstage removed his makeup and revealed himself to be a second Goldin.[39] While Welles never cites any reference to Goldin or his illusions, he undoubtedly knew about him. Goldin was well-known among the magic community, and Welles was himself an active member of the Society of American Magicians (SAM).[40]

More important than Goldin's potential influence, Welles's own personal interest in magic plays a crucial role in the construction of his multimedia magic tricks. In addition to his membership in the SAM, Welles was a member of the Deceptive Order of Prestidigitorial Entertainers Society (DOPES).[41] Like all of his fellow members of DOPES, Welles was interested in magic tricks that entertained with comedic effects and witty patter, rather than ones that instilled dark mysticism. At the end of his laughter-filled magic routine from the Mercury Wonder Show in *Follow the Boys* (1944), Welles attempted to hypnotize Marlene Dietrich, only to accidentally hypnotize himself and fall flat on his back. In *Around the World*, Welles replicated the same comedic effect, only in reverse, when Dick Fix's disappearing trick accidentally works and botches his attempted murder of Pat, whom Fix tried to shoot in the hanging bag. Likewise, Welles also created the multimedia magic tricks as the punchline of a joke. Critics for *Variety* and the *Chicago Tribune* found the film scenes to be some of the best parts of the show and "unfailingly funny."[42] Of course, the slapstick style supplied a main source of comedy, but this style of blending film and theater was so improbable and exaggerated for a narrative that it became similarly farcical. Like the impossible connections of space and time created through editing in a Buster Keaton chase scene—or Welles's own chase scenes in *Too Much Johnson*—there is no narrative explanation for having live stage actors interact with the film sequences instead of having the scene simply take place on the set that literally sat behind the London drop, a point he punctuates by using the flicker effect when this fact is revealed.

It was not only magicians who appreciated *Around the World*. After a technically disastrous opening night performance in Boston, where the crew botched many set changes, avant-garde German playwright Bertolt Brecht told Welles that *Around the World* "was the greatest American theater he had ever seen."[43] Though others have tied Brecht's exclamation to his love of burlesque and Welles's circus number in particular, I propose that his admiration may have been based also on Welles's hybrid sequences, which resemble techniques often used in avant-garde European theater during the 1920s.[44] For example, German director Georg Kaiser, whom Brecht cited as an influence on and pioneer of his own style of "epic theater," produced *Side by Side* in 1923.[45] In the production, Kaiser projected credit titles onto a screen as the performers entered the stage, and accompanied the projection with a constant flickering light over the stage to emulate the look of projecting frames of an old film.[46]

Though the techniques resemble Welles's, it is unlikely that Welles knew about this particular Kaiser production. However, Welles knew of the multimedia work of Brecht's contemporary and colleague, Erwin Piscator. In 1940, set designer Mordecai Gorelik published *New Theatres for Old*, a major cultural study of the time that included both an in-depth history of European left-wing theater and a brief survey of contemporary American leftist theater. Whether because of his fervent support for Popular Front politics in general or because Gorelik discussed Welles's productions *The Cradle Will Rock* (1937) and *Caesar* (1938), Welles read the book closely and published a laudatory review (one of his few book reviews) in the February 8, 1941, issue of the *Saturday Review*. In his book, Gorelik details the work of many German avant-garde directors, including Kaiser. He also devotes a large section to describe Piscator's epic theater stagecraft, and specifically focuses on Piscator's multimedia techniques. Like Brecht's work, Piscator's epic theater dealt with contemporary or historical political subjects and always explicitly reflected Marxist ideology on world politics, economics, and class struggle. Piscator strove to produce massive spectacular productions that often used film sequences. Typically, Piscator would simultaneously show archival documentary footage on a scrim screen of important national events during an onstage performance, sometimes edited together in newsreel form, to "shock" and challenge the audience to always remember the sociopolitical contexts that shaped the turmoil he presented on the stage.[47]

In one extraordinary example, Piscator used a scrim movie screen and projected an approaching ship onto the scrim. Once the ship in the film was about to overtake the screen, as if ship was about to run over the camera, the film sequence ended and the scrim opened up to allow an identical ship to pass through the scrim and onto the stage; an image visualized in the final frames of Sergei Eisenstein's *Battleship Potemkin*.[48] In another example, Piscator projected a film showing the lineage of Russian czars. When the film reached its final image, a giant "ghost-like" shadow of Rasputin, the actor playing Rasputin, appeared from behind the stage.[49] In his book *The Political Theater*, Piscator expressed his belief that combining film and theater was not only appropriate for presenting political context, but also for creating the "momentary surprise" by seamlessly changing from film to live performance that "provided a shattering human effect, became art, in fact."[50]

Welles's use of the scrim screen shares an uncanny resemblance to Piscator's. What is more important than tracing influence here, however, is to point out that the illusions created by *Around the World*'s hybrid sequences do not solely rely on conventions of magical performance, but also on an explicitly reflexive aesthetic differentiation and association between media that is formally similar to what concerned the avant-garde. Though the political contexts of these aforementioned multimedia examples underlie their construction and may have attracted him to them in the first place, Welles's primary interest in hybrid techniques, in contrast, seems to lie in their inventive theatrical effects and reflexive analysis. The inventive magical effects created with these hybrid techniques relied as much on manipulating the similarities and distinctions between cinema and theater as they did on altering the relationship between time and space as in other magic tricks. When the projector roared to life showing film sequences in the iconic style of American comedies that "flicker and jump" on the screen, these scenes were immediately recognizable as cinema. Combined with medium-specific techniques like the superimposition and the dissolve, the effect was to emphasize the materiality of cinematic spectacle. However, Welles used these spectatorial assumptions to trick viewers into questioning the very medium they were watching. The construction of these hybrid illusions made it difficult to identify when the live performance began, and when the film stopped. Moreover, it was hard to determine if the supposedly prerecorded film was actually a live broadcast of backstage events or, in the case of the mirror effect, even onstage events. Welles also masked the differences between color film and live actors behind a screen as a means of tricking the audience into believing a "living superimposition" was actually part of the film.[51]

With these hybrid sequences, Welles creates a vanishing act that dematerialized many distinctions between film and theater. He strategically incorporated them to create interesting and dramatically effective spectacle, and also as a vehicle to contemplate the differences and, more often, the similarities between film and theater. They raise (and sometimes answer) provocative aesthetic questions that have tantalized theorists since the origins of cinema. Is cinema nothing more than live performance that flickers and jumps? If one cannot tell the difference between a film sequence and a live performance, can there be any real differences between these respective media? Similar to many modernist avant-garde films in their radical reflexivity, Welles's multimedia illusions hypothesize answers to these questions by first blurring the distinctions between media, only then to differentiate them with a spectacular and dramatic reveal.

VINCENT LONGO is a PhD student in the Department of Screen Arts and Cultures at the University of Michigan. He has used his research in the international Welles archives as the basis for conference presentations on Welles's multimedia theater, and his drawings, paintings, and doodles. He was also the dramaturge for a live multimedia staging of *Too Much Johnson*, which appeared at the Detroit Institute of Arts in 2015.

NOTES

I want to thank Alyssa Longo and Benjamin Strassfeld for their careful and insightful readings of previous versions of this essay, and Phillip Hallman, Film Studies field librarian at the University of Michigan, for his tireless efforts to acquire many of the rich sources that made this final version possible. I am especially indebted to the support of Matthew Solomon, whose guidance continually enriched this project from its inception.

1. André Bazin, "Film and Theatre (2)," in *What is Cinema?*, trans. Timothy Barnard (Montreal: Caboose, 2009), 189. The essay was originally published in 1951.

2. For more detailed production histories and other critical discussions of the play, see Simon Callow, *Orson Welles*, Vol. 2: *Hello Americans* (London: Jonathan Cape, 2006), 303–23; Aleksandra B. Jovićević Tatomirović, *The Theatre of Orson Welles, 1946–1960*, PhD diss., New York University, 1990, 19–81, http://proxy.lib .umich.edu/login?url=http://search.proquest.com/docview/303859700?account id=14667.

3. Elliot Norton, "Welles' Musical Starts to Leave Hub Opera House," *Boston Post*, May 5, 1946, n.p.

4. William Hawkins, "Welles Shoots the Works for Jules Verne," *New York World Telegram*, June 1, 1946, 6; Lewis Nichols, "The Play," *New York Times*, June 1, 1946, 9; Douglas Watt, "Operation Screwball Reaches Town with Fun and Headaches," *Daily News* (New York), May 31, 1946, n.p.; "Dizzy 'World' Mixups Snag N. H. Preem: Welles Adlibs His Way Out of Setbacks," *Variety*, May 15, 1946, 64; Elinor Hughes, "The Screen: 'Around the World,'" *Boston Herald*, April 29, 1946, n.p.

5. Typescript transcription of interview with Orson Welles by Peter Bogdanovich, box 2, folders 7–11, tape 8, side 2, 87–88, Richard Wilson-Orson Welles Papers, Special Collections Library, University of Michigan.

6. Jean Cocteau, "Profile of Orson Welles," 1949, trans. Gilbert Adair, in *Orson Welles: A Critical View*, by André Bazin (New York: Harper & Row, 1978), 32.

7. Bazin, *Orson Welles*, 99.

8. André Bazin, "Film and Theatre (1)," 1951, in *What is Cinema?*, trans. Timothy Barnard (Montreal: Caboose, 2009), 169–70.

9. Bazin, "Film and Theatre (1)," 170.

10. Bazin, "Film and Theatre (1)," 179.

11. Bazin, "Film and Theatre (2)," 203.

12. Bazin, "Film and Theatre (2)," 203.

13. Rick Altman, "Deep-focus Sound: *Citizen Kane* and the Radio Aesthetic," *Quarterly Review of Film and Video* 15, no. 3 (1994): 1–33.

14. *Around the World* (*in 80 Days or A Wager Won*), draft script, undated, Welles MSS, box 7, folder 4, Welles MSS, Lilly Library; *Around the World* final script, undated, Welles MSS, box 7, folder 5, Lilly Library; Nelson Barclift's *Around the World Draft Script*, undated, The Orson Welles Collection, Special Collections Library, University of Michigan; Around the World Script, undated, *2003MT-353. Houghton Library, Harvard University; Around the World Script, undated, ML50.P848, Performing Arts Collection Library of Congress. This essay largely refers to the first two scripts mentioned in this list; I use parenthetical citations in the text of my essay to identify whatever particular script I refer to. A Suttee is a never widely practiced Hindu ritual in which a widow is burned alive with the corpse of her late husband.

15. Orson Welles, Draft Radio Script, *Orson Welles Commentaries*, transcript, ABC, June 16, 1946, Welles MSS, box 7, folder 10, Lilly Library.

16. Al Hirshfeld, "Shenanigans in 'Around the World,'" *New York Times*, May 26, 1946, X1; Al Fenn, *Orson Welles Directs "Around the World*," April 1946, *Life* Photograph Collection.

17. For more information on surviving versions of the script at the Lilly Library and how Welles transformed *Around the World* throughout its run, see Vincent Longo, "Going *Around the World* with Orson Welles: A Multimedia Auteur," Honor's Thesis, University of Michigan, 2014, 22, http://deepblue.lib.umich.edu/handle /2027.42/107756.

18. *Around the World* shot list, April 15, 1946, Welles MSS, box 7, folder 6, Lilly Library; Stage photos, undated, Welles MSS, box 31, folders 10–14, Lilly Library; Irving Lerner, "Cutting Script for the *Around the World* Film Sequences," The Orson Welles Collection.

19. See Matthew Solomon, "Old-Time Movies: Welles and Silent Pictures," in this volume.

20. Edwin Schallert, "Drama Stage and Screen: Welles Sees Television Boon to Dramatic Arts Screen's 'Four-Ways Man Finds Distinct Fields for Films, Radio, Stage and Telecasts,'" *Los Angeles Times*, August 6, 1939.

21. Orson Welles and Peter Bogdanovich, *This Is Orson Welles*, rev. ed., ed. Jonathan Rosenbaum (Cambridge, MA: De Capo Press, 1998), 111. Being a fellow magician and filmmaker, many of Méliès's films also embody cinematic magic tricks.

22. Theatre, *Too Much Johnson* (1938), box 1, Orson Welles-Oja Kodar Papers, Special Collections Library, University of Michigan; Cyrus Durgin, "'Wonder Boy' Welles Having Busy Time in New Grandiose Production," *Boston Daily Globe*, April 29, 1946.

23. Peter Biskind, *My Lunches with Orson: Conversations between Henry Jaglom and Orson Welles* (New York: Metropolitan Books/Henry Holt, 2013), 146.

24. *Around the World* shot list; "Welles Rehearsals Beat Housing Shortage," *Boston Herald*, April 28, 1946, n.p. I have found no other trace of B. Kelley.

25. Welles filmed only fifty-four individual shots in all the scenes combined.

26. "Biography," finding aid, Irving Lerner papers, 1935–78, collection 112. Performing Arts Special Collections, Young Research Library, University of California, Los Angeles. Lerner was also later an editor for Stanley Kubrick and Martin Scorsese.

27. *Around the World* shot list. This is contrary to many other reports. For example, Simon Callow in *Hello Americans* (291) posits that the film sequences lasted more than thirty minutes. However, the total running time of every shot Welles filmed lasted only just over seventeen minutes. In my thesis, I claimed that there were six film sequences in the production. The cutting script clarifies that the "Ext. Whist Club" sequence was actually a scene depicting the exterior of the bank and was edited into "The Bank" sequence.

28. Lauren Rabinovitz, "Hale's Tours," in *Encyclopedia of Early Cinema*, ed. Richard Abel (New York: Routledge, 2005), 293–94. In *Around the World*, the train car moved on and off stage via the treadmill.

29. "Set List" for *Around the World*, undated, Welles MSS, box 7, folder 6, Lilly Library.

30. Bart Whaley, *Orson Welles: The Man Who Was Magic*, www.lybrary.com, 2005, 228, PDF e-book.

31. For information on Welles's many changes to the script of *Around the World*, see Jovićević Tatomirović, *The Theatre of Orson Welles*, 175–93.

32. In the stage directions, Welles calls this a "lobstascope."

33. Sam Zolotow, "Welles Is Sought for 'Abracadabra,'" *New York Times*, May 24, 1944, 24;
"Himber's Full-Scale Run-Through in Order to Cast His Backers," *Variety*, December 11, 1946, 2; Bill Sachs, "Magic," *Billboard*, June 3, 1944, 30.

34. Peter Warlock, "Magic-Go-Round," *The Stage*, August 13, 1953, 7; Paul Ackerman, "Billboard Backstage," *Billboard Backstage*, November 14, 1953, 2; Bill Sachs, "Hocus-Pocus," June 20, 1953, 56; "Unit Review—Himberama," *Variety*, November 18, 1953, 69.

35. "Himberama," *Variety*, November 18, 1953, 18. After Himber died of a heart attack in 1966, the only print of *Magic Trick* stayed in the protection of his wife until the magician David Copperfield purchased the film at an unknown time. Copperfield flipped the film's image so Welles would face stage right and dubbed Welles's voice to say "David" in place of "Dick," and used the film sequence in his own 1992 TV special *The Magic of David Copperfield XIV: Flying—Live the Dream.* Since Welles had died seven years prior to the television special, Copperfield added an extra layer of mysticism to the illusion by supposedly channeling Welles from the grave to perform the trick. The film print continues to reside in Copperfield's private magic memorabilia collection, The International Museum and Library of the Conjuring Arts in Las Vegas, Nevada. I viewed the film by watching Copperfield's magic show on a personally recorded VHS of the broadcast. Though it has not received a commercial rerelease, many parts of Copperfield's special currently exist on YouTube.

36. Research Files of Magicians for Welles's unfinished film *The Magic Show*, uncataloged and undated as of January 2016, Orson Welles-Oja Kodar Papers. For more information on *The Magic Show*, which Welles shot over the course of the 1970s, see, Whaley, *Orson Welles: The Man Who Was Magic*, 419–23, 427–34.

37. John Braun, *The Linking Ring*, August 1946, 6; *The Conjurers' Magazine*, October 1946, 21; Bill Sachs, "Magic," *Billboard*, June 29, 1946, 53; Milbourne Christopher, "One Wizard's Wanderings," *The Linking Ring*, August 1946, 26.

38. Matthew Solomon, "Up-to-Date Magic: Theatrical Conjuring and the Trick Film," *Theatre Journal* 58, no. 4 (December 2006): 595.

39. Gwendolyn Waltz, "Half Real-Half Reel: Alternation Format Stage-and-Screen Hybrids," in *A Companion to Early Cinema*, ed. André Gaudreault, Nicolas Dulac, and Santiago Hidalgo (Malden, MA: Wiley-Blackwell, 2012), 373.

40. Research Files of Magicians for *The Magic Show* (1985); "Soo, Chung Ling," Research Files, box 25, folder 99, Welles MSS, Lilly Library. Goldin is often mentioned

among other great masters of the magic craft, including Robert Houdin, Harry Houdini, Howard Thurston, Alexander and Adelaide Herrmann, and Chung Ling Soo, all of whose careers and illusions Welles meticulously researched throughout his career. For more on Welles's engagement with the magic community, see Whaley, *Orson Welles: The Man Who Was Magic*.

41. Tommy Windsor, "Life Story of George McAthy," *The Linking Ring*, November 1946, 29.

42. John Chapman, "*Around the World* is Grand, Gorgeous and Goofy," *Chicago Sunday Tribune*, June 9, 1946; "*Around the World (in 80 Days)*," *Variety*, May 1, 1946.

43. Welles and Bogdanovich, *This Is Orson Welles*, 112.

44. Whaley, *Orson Welles: The Man Who Was Magic*, 232; James K. Lyon, *Bertolt Brecht in America* (Princeton, NJ: Princeton University Press, 1980), 179.

45. Bertolt Brecht, *Brecht on Art and Politics*, ed. Tom Kuhn and Steve Giles, trans. Laura Bradley, Tom Kuhn, and Steve Giles (London: Methuen, 2003), 72–73; Michael A. Anderegg, *Orson Welles, Shakespeare, and Popular Culture* (New York: Columbia University Press, 1999), 149–52. Anderegg analyzes how Welles's film performances during this period, especially in *The Lady from Shanghai*, drew from Brechtian techniques, insinuating, at the very least, Welles and Brecht shared a variety of artistic sensibilities.

46. Greg Giesekam, *Staging the Screen: The Use of Film and Video in Theatre* (New York: Palgrave Macmillan, 2007), 39–49.

47. Mordecai Gorelik, *New Theatres for Old* (New York: Samuel French, 1940), 428.

48. Giesekam, *Staging the Screen*, 39–49; Gorelik, *New Theatres for Old*, 427–30; Joseph McBride, "*Too Much Johnson*: Recovering Orson Welles's Dream of Early Cinema," *Bright Lights Film Journal*, April 7, 2014; rev. August 24, 2014; accessed February 23, 2017, http://brightlightsfilm.com/too-much-johnson-orson-welles-film-recovering-orson-welless-dream-of-early-cinema/#.V4vHH74rJ8e. As McBride notes, Eisenstein's own multimedia productions may have influenced Welles. Eisenstein's first attempt at filmmaking, *Glumov's Diary*, was created for his montage of attraction style theatrical production, *Enough Simplicity for Every Wise Man* (1923). In his *New York Post* column of May 25, 1945, Welles talks about his admiration for Eisenstein, and in *This is Orson Welles*, he alludes to their extensive correspondence (144). No record exists of these exchanges. However, a letter from Eisenstein to Alexander Korda (which Korda forwarded to Welles) reveals that Eisenstein believed that Welles was "one of the most interesting and promising figures of Western Cinema" and that he "would like to learn more of him in order check up on [his own] intuition"; see Alexander Korda to Orson Welles, Feburary 9, 1944, Welles MSS, box 2, The Lilly Library.

49. Gorelik, *New Theatres for Old*, 419–21.

50. Erwin Piscator, *The Political Theatre: A History 1914–1929*, trans. Hugh Rorrison (New York: Avon, 1978), 97.

51. Welles also ends *Magic Trick* by poking fun at some assumed differences between film and live performance. After first incorrectly guessing the card from the deck his assistant threw toward the screen, the camera dollies back from a close-up on Welles to reveal he is now holding a giant-sized playing card. Just before flipping it over to reveal he knew the correct card all along, Welles proclaims: "You know, it's remarkable, but on the screen some objects enlarge quite unusually."

8

"THE WORST POSSIBLE PARTNERS FOR MOVIE PRODUCTION"

Orson Welles, Louis Dolivet, and the Filmorsa Years (1953–56)

FRANÇOIS THOMAS

In 1953, at the age of thirty-eight, Welles was at a low point in his European film career when he entered a partnership with his friend and political mentor Louis Dolivet, a newcomer to film production, who founded the production company Filmorsa for Welles's benefit (fig. 8.1). Welles was under exclusive contract with Dolivet for three years, from late 1953 to late 1956, so that all of Welles's activities in film, television, and other media were supposed to emanate from Filmorsa. It both allowed the making of *Mr. Arkadin* and was the cause of extreme tensions that lasted until Welles disregarded his contract and went back to the United States in October 1955.

My account of Welles's Filmorsa years is based on the archives that I had access to in Paris in 2004–2005 thanks to Gray Film, the company that took over Filmorsa. Apart from filmmaker Christophe Cognet, who directed a documentary on Welles's unfinished television episode on the Dominici case (the triple murder of British tourists in a French village in 1952) and wrote an article about it, the files had never been used for research before.[1] They contain thousands of documents. Out of sheer luck, the very first box I opened allowed me to understand that

Figure 8.1. Louis Dolivet and Orson Welles.

most of what we thought we knew about the production history and, especially, the editing process of *Mr. Arkadin* was inaccurate, oftentimes wildly so. For instance, we thought that Welles and Dolivet ended their relationship around Christmas 1954 because Dolivet took the editing away from Welles, that the reedit retitled *Confidential Report*, as we know it today, premiered in London in August 1955, and that Dolivet later sued Welles merely for misconduct on and around the set of *Mr. Arkadin*.

Actually, Welles decided to get away from the editing room on his own accord; the two men broke up in July 1955 over the way the advance for a film project by Jacques Becker that Welles was supposed to act in should be spent; the version of *Confidential Report* that opened in London is now lost and the reedit was made several months later; Dolivet's main cause of legal action was Welles's breaches of contract. The Filmorsa documents present a new and different picture of the relationship between Welles and Dolivet. Although their activities in

the United States in the 1940s have been well documented, especially
in Simon Callow's *Orson Welles: Hello Americans*, without this archival
material there was no way to guess that they shared such a close friendship, that the very intensity of that friendship affected their professional
behavior, nor that, to Dolivet at least, *Mr. Arkadin* was only a small item
among grander plans.[2] I have made use of the Filmorsa files in earlier
writings, notably *Orson Welles at Work*, cowritten with Jean-Pierre Berthomé, and it has helped other writers to revise the production history
of *Mr. Arkadin*, but my aim in the present essay is to further define the
Welles-Dolivet relationship and the role of Filmorsa in Welles's career.[3]
Mr. Arkadin is central, but the story involves numerous realized or unrealized film, television, and theater projects.

A PASSIONATE FRIENDSHIP

Born Ludovic Brecher in Transylvania in 1908, seven years Welles's
senior, Dolivet acquired French nationality in 1937. A member of the
Komintern from 1933 to 1938, a founding coordinator of left-wing associations in France, a pacifist and an internationalist opposed to the
German-Soviet Nonaggression Pact, and linked with the French Resis-
tance, he immigrated to the United States in early 1941, where his first
duties were to try and gain support for the underground movements in
occupied Europe.[4] A man of influence noted for his charm, fieriness,
oratorical talent, ability to enter any circle, skill at handling people, and
taste for secrecy, he created the International Free World Association,
an active and influential antifascist organization, in New York in the
summer of 1941. He met Welles in 1943 and soon tried to launch his
new friend's career in politics. For a time, Welles became an editorialist
and political speaker, and in 1945, Dolivet lobbied for him to become
the first secretary-general of the United Nations. After his divorce from
the American heiress Beatrice Straight, Dolivet settled in Paris in 1949.
Welles and he resumed their passionate friendship probably in 1951, and
Dolivet was grateful to Welles for comforting him after his young son's
death by drowning the following year. Dolivet became the head of a
pacifist association, Démocratie combattante, for which he asked Welles
to write a tribute to anticommunist trade union leader Léon Jouhaux,

the latest recipient of the Nobel Peace Prize, in the guise of a dialogue in verse read publicly by Jean-Louis Barrault and Madeleine Renaud in January 1952.[5] Dolivet was the editor of the short-lived monthly journal *Démocratie combattante* and he published three articles by Welles, starting in January 1953.[6] Their relationship blossomed again after Welles's time in Italy came to an end in March 1953. In the summer, the two friends began to record their conversations in order to write a book on sociopolitical issues.

The Filmorsa files include a huge number of letters and telegrams exchanged between Welles and Dolivet. They often wrote lengthy letters, sometimes several on the same day. Many were soul-searching, and make for riveting reading. Dolivet considered Welles his best friend, and quoted Welles as saying as much. For instance, Welles wrote Dolivet, "Please believe that there is never any time in the day or night when you aren't the person I most want to see."[7] In Welles's letters, the comparison with a marriage came up several times in moments of severe conflict. For example, in October of 1954 he wrote: "A real friendship or partnership is like a marriage in many ways, and many of the quarrels are embarrassingly similar."[8] Earlier he had noted that "our kind of partnership was (or I pray *is*) a kind of marriage. That is to say it includes vows—solemn commitments like 'in sickness, or in health.'"[9]

Dolivet and Welles's plans did not merely call for filmmaking. The two friends had grander ambitions, although Dolivet probably believed in them more than Welles did. To Dolivet, Welles was first and foremost a thinker. Several letters from both men mention their "dreams and ideals": that is, to write sociopolitical books together, publish books and magazines, and set up a private foundation. Welles's interest in the latter as a key part of how he could further his commitment to public service is conveyed in a statement quoted in 1946 by his first book-length biographer, Roy Alexander Fowler: "If I really had my way, I would be working in a foundation financed by three or four Marshall Fields on adult education and political science for the purpose of selling the dignity and solemn obligations of democracy. I would have with me a group of people—educators, show folk, Washington people—and we would make movies, recordings, hold public forums, show slides. It would be strictly a non-partisan project."[10]

In 1953, as Dolivet would put it in retrospect, he and Welles planned to produce a few successful films and "work for two years very hard, very economically, so as to make it possible to undertake other financial activities, all of which being aimed at creating the great FOUNDATION for a new humanism which was our main aim."[11] Welles also alluded to those "more vital projects," or those "grand programs we are dreaming," but it is difficult to tell if he was as keen on those plans or if filmmaking was now his priority.[12] One of his options still was to go back to Hollywood after ensuring his financial independence. The Hollywood productions filmed in Europe that he starred in (Gregory Ratoff's *Black Magic*, Henry King's *Prince of Foxes* and Henry Hathaway's *The Black Rose*), as well as the American release of Carol Reed's *The Third Man* and the American syndication of the British radio series *The Lives of Harry Lime* and *Black Museum*, kept Welles's name familiar to the American audience up to 1952, as would some of his later international work. Regardless, beyond *Mr. Arkadin*, Welles expected his new European career to originate from opportunities provided by Filmorsa.

THE FOUNDING OF FILMORSA

Welles completed the original screenplay of *Mr. Arkadin* (entitled *Masquerade* at the time) in March 1953. The plot, in which billionaire Gregory Arkadin hires a petty racketeer to investigate his dubious past life so that he can eliminate undesirable witnesses, was that of a thriller aimed at the popular audience, and Welles counted on an international cast to play the colorful former gangsters who emerge in the course of the investigation. In mid-September 1953, Welles signed an agreement with a Swiss company to be formed by Dolivet, then called Film Inter-Continental. Dolivet was acting for a group of some ten investors, primarily administrators of the most powerful Swiss banks, thanks to his connections from the times he lived in Geneva in the 1930s. He would produce *Masquerade*, which Welles would direct and star in as Arkadin starting around November 1. There would be nearly no time for preproduction, as Welles was to spend three weeks in October in New York, preparing to play the title role in Peter Brook's live television version of *King Lear* to be broadcast on CBS. Because the financial arrangement for *Masquerade* had yet to be completed, Dolivet was all the more ready to postpone the shoot. In early November, Welles paid a visit to Geneva in order to meet his backers for the one and only time.

The company was finally incorporated in December 1953 under the name Filmorsa (or Film Organisation S.A.). For fiscal reasons, it was incorporated in Tangiers, and domiciled in both Tangiers and Geneva. Welles gave his places of residence as Mogador and Paris. His agreement with Film Inter-Continental was transferred to Filmorsa. He and Dolivet invested enough cash to retain 73 percent of the profits. Welles's salaries would be deferred and paid in the form of 20 percent of the total net income of the film in the Western Hemisphere. Welles's expenses would be paid during the whole time of production.

As chief executive officer of Filmorsa, Dolivet managed Welles's professional activities. Dolivet was authorized to negotiate and sign agreements on his partner's behalf. Filmorsa lent Welles's services as an actor for Herbert Wilcox's *Trouble in the Glen* (1954), Sacha Guitry's *Napoléon* (1955), and John Huston's *Moby Dick* (1956). The company contributed to negotiations of the American and British distribution rights of *Othello*, and it faced the legal actions (or threats of action) regarding the professional debts that Welles had incurred in earlier years, mainly on *Othello*.

As for *Mr. Arkadin*, as it was called by then, Dolivet was looking for a European coproduction arrangement, with Welles ready to adapt his screenplay to the chosen country. On January 5, 1954, Dolivet signed a coproduction agreement with Hispano Film, a Spanish company based in Madrid. The agreement covered not only *Mr. Arkadin*, but no less than two other feature films and two TV programs to be directed by Welles in the next fifteen months. Hispano Film would have the exclusive rights to Spain of *Mr. Arkadin*, as well as 20 percent from the gross receipts in Latin America and other Spanish territories and 4 percent of the world receipts. The film would be shot mainly in Spain, both on location and in the Sevilla Films studios in Madrid, with an international cast performing in English. The preproduction was hurried for a shoot that began in late January. Hispano Film soon was in financial trouble and withdrew, so Dolivet found another Spanish coproducer in early February, Cervantes Films, with the same overall arrangement regarding *Mr. Arkadin*. But that coproducer would only back one film and would not have the means to come to Filmorsa's help if additional money was needed. The shooting schedule was ten to twelve weeks, meaning a mid-April wrap at the latest, and the agreed-upon completion date was July 15. But the shooting schedule far more than doubled, and some important scenes were shot as late as September. The budget overran considerably. Dolivet had to raise more money four or five times.

The working methods of Welles and Dolivet were instantly at odds. Welles resented Dolivet's authority and blamed him for his lack of experience in film production, while Dolivet complained about his partner's unreliability and disregard of schedules, commitments, and financial considerations (the files support the accusations of both men). Scenes that involved Akim Tamiroff, Peter Van Eyck, Michael Redgrave, and Grégoire Aslan were shot at top speed. Other than that, the atmosphere on and off the set was one of conflict most of the time. Welles ranted at an "extremely uncooperative crew."[13] Dolivet reproached Welles for what he would later call "the cruelty and the unscrupulousness to the staff, the disorder in planning, the refusal to go through with the adopted programs of work, the refusal to shoot your own scenes."[14] Dolivet often took exception to Welles's reluctance to meet with set designers and set dressers, and "the barrier of fear which you have built around you in your relations with your working crew," and he maintained that every crew member at some time or another threatened to leave.[15]

Despite these difficulties, during the shoot, Welles and Dolivet still believed in their ability to tackle one project after another. On April 1, Filmorsa signed a coproduction agreement with Spanish producers José Luis Duro Alonso de Celada, Ángel Martínez Olcoz, and Alberto Colomina Boti, according to which Welles would direct what probably was his own script of *Paris by Night* (a three-part anthology film about the night life of Paris as seen through the memories of a former Russian prince turned taxi driver), with production to begin in mid-June.

Also in April, as Filmorsa was running out of money, Welles suggested to Dolivet that they should "quickly complete the film in some acceptable form, with the idea of seeing later if added financing could be obtained for a more elaborate version."[16] Nevertheless, the shoot proceeded on location in the South of France and Monte Carlo, came back to Spain, and then transferred to Munich for some twelve days, both on location and in the studio, before coming back to Spain. The principal photography ended around June 24, but several key scenes remained to be entirely or partially shot.

Welles began editing right from the beginning of the shoot, first with a British editor, William Morton, then with an Italian one, Renzo Lucidi, for three weeks. Editing work was also done at LTC, a lab and editorial facility near Paris, for one week, then stopped on May 27 for close to two months. Originally, a fully dubbed version was supposed to be shown in Spain. Yet toward the end of the shoot, Welles filmed two scenes with Spanish actresses Irene López Heredia and Amparo Rivelles speaking their own language in order to allow for a Spanish version to be quickly finished in Madrid, while he would later reshoot those scenes with actresses still to be found for the English-language version. The Spanish version, close to the rough cut that Welles and Lucidi had assembled by the time they left Spain, was virtually completed by August, although it was not released by distributor Chamartín until October of the following year. Another later Spanish version was never released theatrically.[17]

THE SECOND WELLES-FILMORSA AGREEMENT

Dolivet and Welles's cash investment in *Mr. Arkadin* would not be recoupable until they sold the film to foreign distributors, and they needed more money to complete the film, fulfill their obligations toward their backers, and keep themselves afloat. In mid-June 1954, Dolivet outlined three alternatives: either Welles would buy the film back and Dolivet would withdraw as producer without financial compensation (this was his preferred solution), Welles would finally discipline his work and make himself available to the chief technicians when needed, or Dolivet would complete the film without Welles. That last solution would involve bringing in a new director, although Welles would still be expected to perform as an actor and do the postsync. Dolivet would be glad, he said, to continue to serve as Welles's financial adviser and help raise the money for his next projects, but not as his producer: "You need either a tougher producer or none at all."[18]

In order to obtain new investments and loans for *Mr. Arkadin*, on June 26, 1954, Welles signed another, even more binding exclusive contract for work as an actor, writer, performer, and director, and in other capacities outside film and television until December 31, 1956. All sums due by other employers were to be paid directly to Filmorsa. It was more clearly stated that Welles obligated himself to transmit to Filmorsa all offers which he might receive and he could not sign any contract without Filmorsa's consent. Moreover, Welles put up the property of his writings as a collateral to Filmorsa, transferring the ownership of five screenplays he had written from 1951 to 1953 to the company. They included *Noah* (a modern version in which the Flood is caused by an atomic bomb and two rival arks are constructed—Noah's and an American gambling ship); *Operation Cinderella* (about the postwar "occupation" of an ancient Italian village by a Hollywood crew that shoots on location a spectacle in widescreen and 3D); the already mentioned *Paris by Night*; and the little-known projects *Goya* and *Beware of the Greeks*. In return, Filmorsa would pay for Welles's living expenses and other incidentals, such as a secretary and a life and accident insurance policy for the benefit of his daughters. Welles would receive 50 percent of Filmorsa's net profits, more than provided for by the original agreement.

Dolivet continued to look for deals with coproducers. In July, he concluded an agreement with a newly formed, seemingly unstable Spanish group, unnamed in the documents. Welles was slated to begin filming *Operation Cinderella* before October. In August, Dolivet signed a provisional memorandum of agreement with an American intermediary for *Orson Welles' World of Tomorrow*, a series of twenty-six TV shows to be shot in Europe, beginning in October. Welles would narrate all episodes and act in at least six of them. None of these contracts was honored. Dolivet established other, looser connections with producers from various European countries.

EDITING *MR. ARKADIN* AND RELINQUISHING THE FINAL CUT

Editing the English-language version of *Mr. Arkadin* resumed with Lucidi at LTC on July 19. Lucidi worked nonstop during the next eight months, necessitated by the wealth of material shot and Welles's painstaking editing process. During the summer, Welles spent some time in

Venice, then in Montecatini Terme, a spa city in Tuscany, to get some rest upon medical advice. He confided to Dolivet that he felt "stranded in a 'watering place'" and "close to a real crack-up": "*Now I don't have a glimmer of a thought or an idea that's new.* I feel myself shrivelling up inside. I've never been quite like this, quite as low—as truly desperate."[19] In the second half of September, back in shape, Welles shot some material in a studio near Paris, including shots involving Katina Paxinou and Suzanne Flon in the roles played by Spanish actresses in the Spanish versions. Then he filmed exterior location shots in Paris, and completed photographic work on *Mr. Arkadin* with pickup shots on the Riviera in mid-October. When Welles came back in the editing room, Dolivet complained of the endless cutting and recutting. Their relationship further deteriorated.

Welles and Dolivet were unable to break up, or to be firm with each other. Their letters show them torn between their friendship and their business incompatibility. Perpetual reproaches alternated with repeated protestations of friendship. They always wanted to convince each other of their own impeccable rightness and fairness, and each replied to every single argument the other party had brought up. Dolivet constantly explained to Welles how badly he just behaved, because, as he wrote once, "it is vital *that you realize your errors in these matters*."[20] When major differences of recollection about what happened and who should take the blame arose, Dolivet stood on his dignity and suggested that they appear together before a "jury of honor" that would arbitrate between them.

Dolivet could not be a strict father figure, however much he tried. He was never able to assert his authority because his sense of friendship overcame his attempts at setting any limit on Welles's disregard of commitments. In the letter mentioned above delineating the three alternatives for their relationship, he wrote: "Yet, I am more than ever convinced that you are one of the greatest living men, and that your contributions as an artist and a thinker can be of inestimable value to mankind. Your friendship for me is one of the essential elements of my life and whatever you may decide as a result of this letter, I will always in the future, as I have in the past, be ready to help you in any way that is humanly possible."[21] During the editing of *Mr. Arkadin*, in a letter containing a firm ultimatum, Dolivet stated directly, "I am very miserable, but I love you more than ever," and he undermined his purposefulness in his postscript by expressions of his indebtedness to Welles: "In this miserable letter I have not spoken about the wonderful things you did, not only to the picture, but also to me. Life has become again to me worthwhile to be lived."[22] One of Dolivet's mistakes in dealing with Welles was his effort to envision a consistent and predictable guideline that Welles would definitely follow.

On October 27, Dolivet wrote an ultimatum accompanied by a proposed memorandum from Welles and himself to the cutting department, setting out a detailed schedule for the work that remained to be done. The goal was to be ready for final mixing seventeen days later. Welles wrote a twenty-page reply on the same day. He noted that "such ultimatums are very rare in the history of this business" and that "necessity has forced you,—unthinkingly—into a position 'tougher' than the Screen Directors Guild would allow any Hollywood producer to take."[23]

Dolivet's memorandum and Welles's answer show especially well that no common ground could be found by the two partners. On the one hand, Welles denied any hint that his working methods were partly responsible for the delays during the shoot or the postproduction. *"I have at all times been ahead of the work and waiting, quite as impatiently as you, for it to catch up with me,"* he wrote, claiming he had been "waiting month after month for the *chance* to cut the picture."[24] He complained of insufficient equipment and personnel. On the other hand, it was easy for Welles to prove that Dolivet's demands were not realistic. At that time, for instance, the scene in the harbor of Naples and the closing scene were far from finished, and the scene with Katina Paxinou had not yet been even roughly assembled, so that Welles could write in block letters, "I SWEAR TO YOU THAT I COULD SHOOT THE SCENE AGAIN—IN A SINGLE TAKE—AND HAVE IT READY FOR YOU BY YOUR DEADLINE MUCH MORE EASILY THAN I COULD DELIVER A FINAL *CUT* OF THAT SCENE BY DAY AFTER TOMORROW."[25] It is all the more surprising, then, that Welles could claim in the same breath that he was within only a few weeks of being ready for the final mixing.

In January 1955, Welles gave up the final cut of *Mr. Arkadin* on his own accord in order to make peace. He decided to get away from the editing room, and to collaborate with Lucidi from a distance, providing that he would later do a final cleanup and polishing job. Yet he would be unavailable when that opportunity was provided. Lucidi completed his duties on April 9, ten months after the initially agreed-upon date.

During all those harrowing months, despite his differences with Welles over *Mr. Arkadin*, Dolivet still tried to help with his partner's next projects in the hope of further Spanish coproductions. In the fall of 1954, Dolivet took the first steps toward filming *Noah*, so that Welles could begin casting and scheduling, and in January 1955, after Welles stepped down from *Mr. Arkadin*, Dolivet found money to finance some Eastmancolor tests for *Don Quixote*.

ESCAPING THE EXCLUSIVE CONTRACT

Welles could not remain idle until a new Filmorsa project got off the ground. As of March 1955, he disregarded his exclusive contract, mostly to pursue ventures in London. He had developed many unproduced ideas for TV series in the years before. In March 1955, he negotiated by himself a handshake deal with Associated-Rediffusion (hereafter, Associated), a contractor for ITV, the first British commercial TV channel that was going to start broadcasting in September. Welles was to direct and star in a series of "entertainment documentaries," in which he would visit some of the famous places of the world. Called *Around the World with Orson Welles*, the series was to be one of the highlights of the first ITV season. Welles wanted to keep Filmorsa out of this project, but Dolivet soon jumped onboard. In late March, without a formal contract, Welles filmed the first episode in Vienna, provisionally financed by Dolivet, who helped him with the day-to-day operations. On May 3, Dolivet signed an agreement with Associated: twenty-six half-hour documentaries were to be delivered by February 15, 1956. The shooting schedule was four days per episode. Welles and producer Roland Gillett were to have "control of matters of an artistic and editorial nature."[26] Without being the producer, Filmorsa, in addition to providing the services of Welles, would take care of the day-to-day management of the episodes shot outside the United Kingdom. Filmorsa would pay for the expenses, and Associated would pay it back later at the direct cost. Associated would pay for Welles's personal and research expenses. Dolivet would not receive any salary. Associated would hold the rights in the English-speaking countries, Filmorsa in the rest of the world.

To say the least, the TV series was supposed to be a full-time job, involving one hundred shooting days to be spread over nine months, in addition to the research supervision, editing, and traveling. Yet, Welles shot only five more episodes after the Vienna one. In May, he went to Lurs (the village of the Dominici case in the southeast of France), the Basque Country, and Madrid. In July, he went back to the Basque Country and also shot in London. In September, he devoted a couple of days to the Saint-Germain-des-Prés area of Paris. The Lurs shoot was illegal, as the filming permit had been granted for another project on French cuisine as epitomized by a chef in another city, and the French National Center of Cinema immediately warned Filmorsa that the episode could not receive an export visa, hence could not be shown on British TV. In some episodes, part of the shoot was done without Welles. Some episodes were edited in London, others in Paris, often without Welles.

Welles deeply resented what he considered to be Dolivet's meddling with the project, denying Dolivet the right to sign the contract with Associated on his behalf, although Welles had endorsed a number of documents entitling Dolivet to do so. Later, Welles would state that he consented to Filmorsa entering the scheme "only with the firm understanding that it would be transferred to a new company of my own immediately."[27] True, Welles considered establishing new partnerships, and Dolivet welcomed that prospect as a noble way out (he was ready to liquidate Filmorsa after the release of *Mr. Arkadin*), but those partnerships would be either stillborn or short-lived.

American entrepreneur Henry Margolis was Welles's most promising new partner. Margolis coproduced Welles's play *Moby Dick—Rehearsed* in the West End, and there were plans to set up a repertory company. Margolis was not aware that Welles was under exclusive contract elsewhere, and Dolivet refrained from protesting (at various times, both Welles and he explained that they were unwilling to denounce each other to a third party). From the end of May to July 9, 1955, Welles rehearsed and starred in *Moby Dick—Rehearsed*, resuming work on the Associated series after the end of the run. In July, after the play closed, Welles began to shoot a TV adaptation of *Moby Dick—Rehearsed* in London that Margolis optioned, but for which Welles needed extra money.

Welles also entered into a tentative partnership with London-based Harry Saltzman, a theater and television producer soon to become a major film producer, who wanted Welles to direct a series of ninety-minute *Sunday Spectaculars* for American TV. Saltzman first suggested a series of five such *Spectaculars* for NBC in January 1955, then in July he sold the idea to CBS. Welles might shoot the films in Europe, and *Moby Dick—Rehearsed* might be part of the series.

Other commitments were less far-reaching. Welles appeared on the weekly live TV series *Orson Welles' Sketch Book* on BBC from April 24 to May 28. He accepted the role of an arms dealer after the First World War in a film project by Jacques Becker called *Vacances en novembre* ("A Holiday in November") that never materialized. Filmorsa received an advance, using it mostly to reimburse Welles's pressing debts from *Othello* and to pay for some of Welles's personal expenses from the past few months. Then Welles disappeared.

THE INEVITABLE BREAKUP

Dolivet and Welles split up personally in July 1955. Dolivet's exasperation mounted as Welles had consistently stalled him in London, keeping nearly none of their business appointments. They met only briefly in circumstances that prevented them from talking about business. Yet, in order to raise more money, Dolivet had to convince the banks and potential backers that the cooperation between Welles and Filmorsa still existed. And Dolivet was also ready for Welles's new associates to take over *Mr. Arkadin*.

The breakup occurred by cable on July 18, mainly over Welles's insistence about obtaining the advance from Becker for himself. In response to a telegram from Welles, missing from the archives, an indignant Dolivet cabled with forceful irony: "Submit title play be changed from friendship to hypocrisy for public will never believe principal hero despite all talent capable of friendship. Stop. Action shows that for two years he just fooled second hero who is at present for all practical purposes destroyed financially morally and emotionally." Dolivet thought up various scenarios for that "play" of his and concluded: "Matter of taste prefer personally quiet, elegant departure second hero."[28] Dramatic cables and letters followed. Dolivet now began most of his letters with the words "Dear Mr. Welles." On July 19, he wrote that money destroyed their friendship and confessed, "I cried each time at every one of your cables and I felt as if someone had stripped from the walls of a great museum the masterpieces and left ugly holes."[29]

On July 28, ten days after the breakup, Dolivet reiterated his proposal to Welles about what to do with *Mr. Arkadin*:

> You and whatever associates you choose buy away *Arkadin* from Filmorsa by paying back the cash investments and taking over the obligations.... I would in that case renounce any consideration for my personal services and would insist with the investors that they accept this solution. In that case, you and your new group would own the whole picture and you would handle it any way you want. If you like, we could hand you over the whole of Filmorsa. I am sure, Margolis and/or Saltzman would help find such a solution so that you would be completely free and not bound by an exclusivity contract with Filmorsa.[30]

Welles was in no position to take the offer.

Meanwhile, Warner Bros. had agreed to distribute *Mr. Arkadin* worldwide, Spain and North America excepted (Spanish distribution was in other hands, and the North America branch of Warner Bros. was not interested). On August 11, the film opened in London in Welles's absence for a two-week run, in a version unseen since 1962, as Warners supposedly destroyed the print at the end of the seven-year contract. Welles saw it as a mere "selling copy" that he only reluctantly agreed to be shown.[31] It was called *Confidential Report* by then, a title Welles suggested in order to avoid those proposed by the studio.

Dolivet relentlessly continued to ask for a business meeting. Welles arranged meetings in London and Paris, but he never showed up. The only time the two associates met after their breakup was in Paris, where Welles suggested that they postpone the discussion until dinnertime and then left town. Dolivet repeatedly urged Welles to go to London to complete the Associated shows and to Geneva to assuage the backers. Welles regularly announced that he would make the trip to Switzerland, but that never happened. His rationale was that he could not work in such an "unconstructive" atmosphere.

In early August, Welles was in Venice, claiming to be starting an Italian episode of the Associated show that in fact he never began. He also planned, he said, to film Ben Jonson's *Volpone* as a *Sunday Spectacular* in Italy between September 1 and the beginning of October. In several later letters, he explained that his stay was allowing him to finish his own close-ups for *Moby Dick—Rehearsed* (according to him, no sound equipment was currently available in London), shoot his on-screen commentaries for several Associated shows, and get started on *Volpone*. In mid-August, mostly with Margolis's money, he used the facilities of the Fert studio in Turino for one week, apparently only for *Moby Dick—Rehearsed*.

By the end of the summer, Welles had not properly completed any show for Associated. The broadcasting had to begin on September 22, with a show every other week. Associated required Welles's presence in London in order to finish some of the episodes. Actually, Welles spent the end of August and the first half of September 1955 in London, without making himself known. There, he discussed a New York theatrical season with Margolis. During the second half of September, he alternated between Paris, where he began to shoot the Saint-Germain-des-Prés episode, and London. According to Associated, the first show of the series was aired with a live commentary from Welles and the second was "lacking certain essential narration."[32] Welles ceased work on the series around October 2 and spent part of October in Italy where he soon had to be moved to a hospital.

When Welles first hinted at a prospective theatrical season in New York, Dolivet expressed his worry that the Filmorsa investors could sue for breach of contract. On October 13, Dolivet learned of Welles's plans of impending departure to the United States by reading the newspapers. He threatened Welles that he would inform American networks and movie companies of the exclusive contract, but refrained from doing so. He also threatened Welles with legal measures in order to force him to abide by his contracts.

Welles emphatically stated several times that he did not want to argue with Dolivet anymore ("This has been a long letter—I am determined that it shall be the last of its kind"), yet there were more letters.[33] Welles adamantly refused to concede that he was guilty of a breach of contract. His view was that Filmorsa had merely been set up to protect him against personal income taxes and that it could in no way be binding on him or Dolivet. "If I had understood that it would ever be used as an instrument *against* us, I would have studied the contract very carefully before signing it," which Welles said he did without reading.[34] Welles was ready, as he had stated in earlier letters, to abandon all the profits of Filmorsa to Dolivet.

Whatever project Welles would contemplate, he would now invariably find Dolivet and possibly the Swiss investors standing in his way. In late October, Welles escaped from this impasse by boarding a ship to New York, leaving Europe without notice to either Dolivet or Associated. He would stage *King Lear* for Margolis and his partners and remain in the United States for a couple of years.

THE ABANDONED FILMS AND TV SHOWS

During the next eighteen months or so, Welles and Dolivet separately attempted to cope with some of their unfinished projects. The day after Welles landed in New York harbor, he tried another tactic to get around Dolivet: he wrote to one of Filmorsa's Swiss associates, saying he was eager for discussions to begin between them, as he did not know what the claims of the investors were. The response was a suggestion to meet in London so that Welles would also get a chance to finish the Associated shows. Welles did not follow up on this invitation.

Dolivet was left alone to deal with countless legal and financial entanglements with which he would live for years. He had to keep numerous creditors from several countries at bay: coproducer Cervantes Films, the Sevilla Films studios, LTC, Kodak, Lucidi, collaborators of the Associated shows, and others. The negotiations dragged on with most of the above. A good sale of either *Confidential Report* or *Around the World with Orson Welles* to an American distributor or TV network could allow Filmorsa to alleviate its debts, if not to get out of the red. But it was not to happen.

On November 20, 1955, a probably slightly revised version of *Confidential Report* entered general release in England on a double bill with *Tall Man Riding*, a western starring Randolph Scott, directed by Lesley

Selander. Some theater owners put Welles's film on the bottom half. The prints of that second version were also apparently destroyed in 1962.

At the request of Warner Bros., *Confidential Report* was reedited for international release. Dolivet negotiated a new bank loan to do so and hired an unidentified editor, who mostly oversimplified the dramatic structure, although that version remains the most Welles-like surviving version in terms of the picture and sound editing of individual sequences. The new version was completed in February 1956 and internationally released starting in April. In a letter to the Spanish distributor, Dolivet said that he did not believe in the reedit, but that the Warners people preferred it to the former version.[35]

None of the major American TV networks wanted the film. American theatrical distributors insisted on the necessity of recutting and redubbing the first two reels. In November 1956, Dolivet found a Canadian distributor, the Canadian branch of J. Arthur Rank, which ultimately only booked a limited showing in Toronto. The contract was canceled one year later. In 1959, the American distributor M. and A. Alexander took the film for a small sum for a ten-years period for North America. Instead of *Confidential Report*, they were sent another, temporary cut entitled *Mr Arkadin* (without the period). In 1961, they gave up releasing it theatrically and made it available for television. It was ultimately shown in one New York theater in 1962.

Regarding *Around the World with Orson Welles*, Associated threatened legal action against Filmorsa after Welles's departure, as their contract was with the company, not Welles. Dolivet assisted them in preparing to put the unfinished shows on the air. Associated suggested that Filmorsa should send them the filmed material so that they could complete the shows themselves. The Paris episode was nevertheless edited in France. On Associated's instruction, Filmorsa prepared an alternate edit of the Basque show for the United States (the one that features American expatriate writer Lael Wertenbaker). In early November 1955, Welles wrote to Associated and Dolivet that he wanted to resume editing in the United States on his own schedule and he forbade further episodes to be shown in the meantime, but he had no legal ground to do so. Associated replied: "Before two of your programmes appeared you disappeared to the Continent leaving no address, and we now find that you are in New York. In these circumstances we had to do what we can with the material which you have started to shoot, and not finished, in order not to break faith with the public."[36] Associated did not want to discontinue the series before Christmas. They renounced their contract with Filmorsa in January 1956. A settlement was reached the following year, allowing both companies to have a duplicate negative and married print (that is, a positive print with an optical soundtrack) of the episodes held by the other.

The shows were difficult to sell elsewhere, as Welles's on-screen commentaries made it obvious that they were intended for a British audience. In 1959, Dolivet, now the head of Gray Film, prepared a French version of the Madrid episode, with a new commentary and new music from preexisting sources, that was to be released along with a German feature film, as it was then mandatory in France for a full-length film to go with one or several short subjects.

Other projects were shelved. The English footage of *Moby Dick—Rehearsed* fell under the control of Associated, which also received the material shot in Italy, although they considered that the rights belonged to Filmorsa. And Welles abandoned all hope to produce any of his five screenplays, which remained the property of Filmorsa. Dolivet vainly tried to get *Noah* produced with no director yet assigned.

Dolivet and Welles exchanged a few letters up to April 1957. Despite all they went through, their close personal feelings remained. On July 16, 1956, Dolivet wrote to ask Welles if he could help getting an American TV airing of *Confidential Report*, perhaps as part of the series that Welles hoped to develop at the time. Welles's nine-page answer is quite telling about the intensity of their friendship and his regrets over its loss, as the following excerpts show:

> After all, what was between us?—Nothing more than a few differences of opinion on the matter of a movie. Such differences (I've always been convinced), could never justify the break-up of friendship....
>
> If anybody else in the world had attempted such action with a picture of mine, you may be sure I would have fought it tooth and nail.
>
> I could not fight you.
>
> I cannot fight you now....
>
> This is a crazy situation, Louis ... It really is just that—crazy.

You know, I think it's quite seriously possible that our behaviour at one time or another has been rather less than sane. My own memories include a night when you assured me of the absolute certainty that nothing could stop us from coming into a fortune of seven million dollars within a matter of months; and also a morning,—(long before that promised date)—when you stalked into a public bar and shouted at me that you were not going to jail alone—you were going to take me with you.

I can only guess at *your* memories of *my* behaviour.

You evidently think that I went quite berserk as a director in Spain, and it seems to me that as a business man you went berserk in London. . . .

I certainly am faced with an ever-growing mass of evidence to prove my own basic incapacity for a successful life in the film business.

The inescapable conclusion seems to be that no matter how effective we might have been as a team in politics and publishing, we are the worst possible partners for movie production.

Why don't we face that as a fact and let it rest at that?

Does the failure of a partnership have to mean the failure of a friendship?

If it should happen to be quite true that you are a rather inefficient producer and I am an impossible director—what the hell of it? We may regret our failings, but why blame each other for having them?

If you were a drug addict and I were a kleptomaniac, we could still be friends.[37]

FILMORSA VS. ORSON WELLES: THE LAWSUIT

In early 1958, coproducer Cervantes Films sued Welles, Filmorsa, and Warner Bros. in the Supreme Court of the State of New York, protesting (wrongly, it seems) that they had not been informed of the Warner distribution contract and were owed money from the world receipts from *Confidential Report*. Later the same year, Filmorsa's lawyers persuaded Dolivet that the best defense was to enter into litigation against Welles in the same court. There were ultimately four causes of legal action. The first two were that Welles never repaid the debts that Filmorsa discharged in his behalf or the payments from Associated that were sent to him instead of the company. The third claim was that Welles worked for other employers in breach of contract. The fourth claim was that Welles "performed his services in an unskillful and inefficient manner and knowingly neglected and omitted to diligently perform his duties, and further by his omissions and neglects in the performance of his duties prevented the plaintiff from operating in a businesslike and efficient

manner in connection with the production of said motion pictures," so
that Filmorsa's expenses in the production of *Confidential Report* were
greatly increased and the quality of the film was "substantially adversely
affected."[38]

Several years passed before the case reached the point of trial on the
calendar of the Supreme Court. Neither Welles nor Dolivet attended the
pretrial hearing in June 1964. The day after that hearing, Dolivet wrote
his lawyers that he thought the action should be stopped. They maintained their viewpoint, and Dolivet complied with them in order not to
pay their fees without a chance to recoup them from Welles.

On September 2, 1964, six weeks before the shoot of *Chimes at Midnight* for a Spanish producer would begin, Welles wrote from Madrid to
his former partner a two-page letter that read in part:

> Dear Louis,
>
> This is written to a very successful man by one who is close to being a failure. . . .
>
> Frankly, I am desperate. The slightest bad publicity—the vaguest hint of
> trouble in America—will wreck this Spanish picture deal I've been so long put-
> ting together.
>
> At my age—and with all the years of failure behind me—this could well be
> my last real chance. . . .
>
> Louis, if you don't call it off this lawsuit will ruin me.
>
> All begging letters are shameless, and since this is a begging letter, I'm afraid I
> must invoke the name of our old, close friendship. Each of us believes himself to
> have been gravely wronged by the other. Whatever the truth may be, it will not
> be settled in a court of law. The lawyers assure me that if it comes to trial, I'll win.
> I don't know if they're right. I do know that even if I should "win," I would still be
> ruined. The truth is, I'm far more afraid of my lawyers there than I am of you.
>
> I do wish that I were the one who could give proof of the loyalty of an old
> friendship, instead of having to ask for it.[39]

On September 10, upon receiving the letter in New York, Dolivet cabled
a few lines beginning with, "Dear Orson just received your letter will of
course act accordingly and call the whole thing off." The following day,
he wrote Welles at more length in the same spirit and instructed his
lawyers to discontinue the case. The lawyers considered this a serious
mistake and tried to convince him to take advantage of the situation to
clearly settle the matter of the ownership of the abandoned screenplays.

Dolivet by then had become a bona fide film producer. He had produced Jacques Tati's *Mon Oncle* (1958) and Marcel Carné's *Terrain Vague*

(1960), and coproduced Federico Fellini's *La Dolce Vita* (1960) as well as films by Alberto Lattuada, Carlo Lizzani, Mario Monicelli, and Julien Duvivier. In 1979, he contemplated having a hand in the completion of Welles's *The Other Side of the Wind*. Until his death in 1989, he praised Welles as an artist and deplored that he did not become one of the greatest politicians and public figures of his time.

An attempted reconciliation failed in 1982, when Welles came to Paris in order to be decorated by the French government and host the ceremony of the César awards (the French equivalent of the Academy Awards). The day before Welles was decorated, Dolivet wrote him a friendly letter of congratulation and offered to send him all his memorabilia from their years together. Six days later, Dolivet was infuriated when Welles stated that Dolivet had betrayed him. Dolivet again suggested that they appear before a jury of honor. And, as Welles was said to have made defamatory remarks against him, Dolivet threatened to sue. Welles replied that he had been eager to meet with him, but that Dolivet's letter put them further apart than ever. The following days, when he talked to journalists from *Cahiers du cinéma* and *L'Avant-Scène cinéma*, Welles blamed Dolivet, without mentioning him by name, for "brutally" taking away the final cut of *Mr. Arkadin* from him.[40] As for Welles's harsh comments on the reedit in those interviews and elsewhere, it is possible that he only watched the truncated, almost incomprehensible version made by unknown hands in the 1960s that was the most widely circulated one in the United States in his lifetime. In that event, Welles may never have seen Arkadin's Georgian toast on screen.

A TOAST TO FRIENDSHIP

When I compared all the alternate versions of *Mr. Arkadin*, I was puzzled by the fact that the 1956 reedit by Filmorsa added one scene that was to be found in no other version released while Welles was alive, nor in some earlier cuts documented in the archives. The only addition, it was moreover a clumsy one in terms of continuity. I refer to a brief one-shot scene in which Arkadin tells a Georgian story, a dream about finding himself in a graveyard where all the tombstone markings indicate a very short time between birth and death: 1822–26, 1930–34, and so on. A very old man explains the mystery: "Here on our tombstones we do not count the years of a man's life, but rather the length of time he's kept a friend." Thereupon Arkadin proposes a toast, "Let's drink to friendship!" My guess is that putting the scene back in was a personal, reproachful message from Dolivet to Welles, suggesting a tombstone that might read:

Orson Welles

1943–55

FRANÇOIS THOMAS is professor of Film Studies at Université Sorbonne Nouvelle. He coauthored the books *Citizen Kane* and *Orson Welles at Work* with Jean-Pierre Berthomé.

NOTES

Thanks to Véronique Loth and Jacqueline Cirrincione (from Gray Film), who gave me unlimited access to the Filmorsa files. Thanks also to Christophe Cognet, who first mentioned the existence of the files to me, and to Jean-Pierre Berthomé.

1. Christophe Cognet, "Comme un conteur arabe: La Tragédie de Lurs (Orson Welles, 1955, inachevé)," *Vertigo* (July 2004): 79–81.

2. Simon Callow, *Orson Welles*, Vol. 2: *Hello Americans* (London: Jonathan Cape, 2006): 183–86, 223–24. See also Barbara Leaming, *Orson Welles: A Biography* (New York: Viking, 1985): 275–77, 281–82, 393–94, and, on the time period covered in this chapter, Simon Callow, *Orson Welles*, Vol. 3: *One Man Band* (London: Jonathan Cape, 2015): 130–31, 156–58, 381–82.

3. Jean-Pierre Berthomé and François Thomas, *Orson Welles at Work* (London: Phaidon, 2008): 189–97. See also François Thomas, "Mr. Arkadin: A Chronology," booklet to *The Complete Mr. Arkadin a.k.a. Confidential Report* (DVD set, The Criterion Collection, 2006): 26–31, and François Thomas, "Un film d'Orson Welles en cache un autre (2)," *Cinéma 012* (Autumn 2006): 139–57.

4. Books that explore Dolivet's political path include Thierry Wolton, *Le Grand Recrutement* (Paris: Grasset, 1993), 153–58; Pierre Péan, *Vies et Morts de Jean Moulin* (Paris: Fayard, 1998), 69–97, 113–30, 200–5, 210–13, 217–18, 224–25, 286–91, 296–303, 305–34, 341–55, 364–66; Sabine Jansen, *Pierre Cot: Un antifasciste radical* (Paris: Fayard, 2002), 218–19, 359–64; Frédéric Charpier, *Les Valets de la guerre froide* (Paris: François Bourin, 2013), 150–55, 163–65. See also Sabine Jansen, "Louis Dolivet kominternien," *Communisme*, no. 40/41 (June 1995): 117–29.

5. "Dialogue du xxe siècle," French translation by Marcelle Sibon, in *Hommage international à Léon Jouhaux, prix Nobel de la Paix* (Paris: Comité des amis de Léon Jouhaux / Démocratie combattante, 1952): 43–48; abridged version in a different,

anonymous translation, "À Léon Jouhaux," in Maurice Bessy, *Orson Welles* (Paris: Seghers, 1963): 111–14.

6. "La jeunesse décidera," *Démocratie combattante*, no. 1 (January 1953): 20, 59; "Censure: la police secrète du cinéma," *Démocratie combattante*, no. 4 (April–May 1953): 51–53; "Paradoxes en Italie," *Démocratie combattante*, no. 5 (June–July 1953): 12. The first two articles were reprinted under different titles in Maurice Bessy, *Orson Welles* (Paris: Seghers, 1963): 114–18, 100–106. A much-abridged translation of the first article is available in Maurice Bessy, *Orson Welles* (New York, Crown, 1971): 115–16.

7. Welles to Dolivet, undated. All the letters and legal documents that I quote are from the Filmorsa files, identified by date when available and my best guess of a date when such a guess is possible. Italics in the quotations are in the original.

8. Welles to Dolivet, October 27, 1954.

9. Welles to Dolivet, undated (c. August 1954).

10. Roy Alexander Fowler, *Orson Welles* (London: Pendulum, 1946), 94.

11. Dolivet to Welles, October 8, 1955.

12. Welles to Dolivet, October 10, 1955, and October 27, 1954, respectively.

13. Welles to Dolivet, April 21, 1954.

14. Dolivet to Welles, November 12, 1955.

15. Dolivet to Welles, June 14, 1954.

16. Welles to Dolivet, undated (July 1956).

17. I will not go extensively into the details of the six English-language versions and two Spanish versions of *Mr. Arkadin* that were made available to the public at various times under various titles. I summed up their numerous discrepancies, both in terms of general structure and in terms of the editing of individual sequences and the soundtrack, in "Un film d'Orson Welles en cache un autre (2)" (see above, note 3). Earlier attempts to deal with those alternate versions when only four edits were known included articles by Jonathan Rosenbaum, "The Seven *Arkadins*," *Film Comment* 28, no. 1 (January–February 1992): 50–59, later revised several times (last revision posted at http://www.jonathanrosenbaum.net/2010/12/22958), and Tim Lucas, "Will the Real Mr. Arkadin Please Stand Up?," *Video Watchdog*, no. 10 (March–April 1992): 42–60, and "Mr. Arkadin: The Research Continues . . .," *Video Watchdog*, No. 12 (July–August 1992): 26–29. Another useful source on the various versions of *Mr. Arkadin* is Esteve Riambau, *Orson Welles: Una España inmortal* (Valencia: Filmoteca de la Generalitat Valenciana / Filmoteca española, 1993): 75–85.

18. Dolivet to Welles, undated (probably June 16, 1954).

19. Welles to Dolivet, undated (probably September 8, 1954).

20. Dolivet to Welles, undated rough draft (Autumn 1954).

21. Dolivet to Welles, June 14, 1954.

22. Dolivet to Welles, October 27, 1954.

23. Welles to Dolivet, October 27, 1954.

24. Welles to Dolivet, October 27, 1954.

25. Welles to Dolivet, October 27, 1954.

26. "Associated-Rediffusion Limited and Film Organisation Société Anonyme: An Agreement," May 3, 1955.

27. Welles to Dolivet, November 12, 1955.

28. Dolivet to Welles, July 18, 1955.

29. Dolivet to Welles, July 19, 1955.

30. Dolivet to Welles, July 28, 1955.

31. Welles to Dolivet, October 10, 1955.

32. Cecil Lewis, deputy controller of programmes, Associated, to Dolivet, undated (October 1955).

33. Welles to Dolivet, October 10, 1955.

34. Welles to Dolivet, October 10, 1955.

35. Dolivet to José Luis de Navasqués, chief executive officer of Chamartín Films, March 23, 1956.

36. Cecil Lewis to Welles, November 8, 1955.

37. Welles to Dolivet, undated (c. July 1956).

38. Graubard & Moskowitz, attorneys for Filmorsa, undated submissions in the Filmorsa, S.A. vs. Orson Welles case.

39. Welles to Dolivet, September 2, 1964.

40. Alain Bergala and Jean Narboni, "Quatrième entretien," *Cahiers du cinéma*, special issue 12, "Orson Welles" (1982): 67; Claude Beylie, Catherine Schapira and Abraham Segal, "Un conteur d'histoires immortelles," *L'Avant-Scène cinéma*, no. 291–92 (July 1982): 7.

9

PRESENTING ORSON WELLES
An Exhibition Challenge

CRAIG S. SIMPSON

"From the beginning," notes Jonathan Rosenbaum, "Welles scholarship has been undermined by the seductiveness of diverse kinds of journalistic shortcuts, the perceived need to fill in blank spaces in order to offer a coherent picture of the career and oeuvre." The essential instability of Welles's art, he continues, "hasn't prevented critics, journalists, biographers, and scholars . . . [from freezing] the forms and meanings into something comprehensible and finite."[1] Rosenbaum doesn't mention exhibition curators, but filling in blank spaces (and freezing forms in those spaces, however temporarily) is the nature of what we do as exhibitors. Inevitably, then, the objectives of a special collections exhibit—to inform, to entertain, and to highlight materials in a clear, coherent manner—may be at cross-purposes with a life as complex, unpredictable, and disordered as that of Orson Welles.

Notwithstanding, my January–May 2015 exhibition *100 Years of Orson Welles: Master of Stage, Sound, and Screen* attempted to meet these goals via a large display of "Wellesiana" at the Lilly Library. Part of the Indiana University–wide academic conference *Orson Welles: A Centennial Celebration, Symposium, and Exhibition*, the exhibit occupied all eighteen cases in the Lilly's Main Gallery, with 160 items filling twelve regular display cases (58″ × 25½″), two "tall pop-tops" (58″ × 56″), two "small pop-tops" (58″ × 44½″), and two large wall cases (84″ × 44″). Accompanying the physical display was a "media center" featuring footage from Welles's "Voodoo" *Macbeth*, the trailer for *Citizen Kane*, the opening sequence of *Touch of Evil*, and audio excerpts from *The Shadow* and "The War of the Worlds."

Because the Welles Symposium was to be the inaugural conference of Indiana University's new Media School, it was essential that the exhibit cover the arc of Welles's career in the three forms of media most prominently represented in the Welles collection—theater, radio, and film. This left significant gaps concerning his work in television, print journalism, magic, and other areas not well covered in the Lilly's holdings. In other instances, there was simply not enough space for particular items to be included in the exhibition. Yet even with those omissions, it was in many ways more difficult to know what to leave out than what to put in. Not only were the selected materials intended to be more or less evenly divided between "stage," "sound," and "screen," but also well-balanced between Welles's most notable achievements and his lesser-known works—to inform and engage scholars attending the symposium as well as students and casual visitors to the Lilly throughout the semester.

Most scholarship in exhibition theory and practice is restricted to museum studies. A notable exception, and invaluable for its currency, is Jessica Lacher-Feldman's study of exhibition development with special collections and archival materials, a relatively neglected facet of archival work that "allows us to apply historical research methods to collections, to interpret and analyze information and artifacts, and to describe how collections intersect and complement one another."[2] To these interactive qualities, I would add that a key distinction between special collections exhibitions and museum exhibitions is that materials in the former tend to be on display only temporarily and are usually only a fraction of the repository's overall holdings. This means that a special collections exhibition, like *100 Years of Orson Welles*, represents something beyond itself; it serves as an invitation for patrons to explore the larger collection, or to use the displayed materials firsthand after they are returned to their boxes.

An exhibition on Orson Welles should simultaneously emphasize the full scope of his achievements and highlight the different types of materials (what we archivists call *series*) in his collection. These objectives may be more at cross-purposes than is readily apparent. As invaluable as researchers find archival materials, they inevitably discover that rare is the collection that *doesn't* contain gaps in the creator's biography. While the Welles Manuscripts are exceptionally rich in the types of materials that are attractive for an exhibition (e.g., correspondence, photographs, screenplays, artwork, bound transcripts of radio shows), the majority of the material centers on the best-known chapters of Welles's career.

Engaging scholars with an exhibit depends largely on showing them something new and telling them something they don't know, which can be difficult not only when covering relatively familiar terrain but also when using their published works for your own references. Three of the best writers on Welles—James Naremore, Joseph McBride, and Jonathan Rosenbaum—served as program advisors for the symposium. While all three specialize in film studies, their books and essays (which are critical analyses, not biographies) helped to outline not only scope and content for the exhibit but supply the intellectual rigor essential to approach the entirety of Welles's body of work.

Naremore's *The Magic World of Orson Welles*, McBride's *What Ever Happened to Orson Welles?*, and Rosenbaum's *Discovering Orson Welles* belong to the school of Welles's admirers and defenders and part company from the school of scolds, exemplified by David Thomson's *Rosebud* and Charles Higham's *Orson Welles: The Rise and Fall of an American Genius*, which are eager to blame Welles for his failures.[3] Because inaccuracies abound in Welles biographies and critical studies, with facts dismissed as legends and tall tales taken at face value, one of my foremost concerns for the exhibition was providing accurate labeling for the items on display. Naremore, McBride, and Rosenbaum were primary sources for my labels, and pointed the way to a full and fair evaluation of Welles's life and works.

Since my selection of items was determined, at least in part, by the notion of "discovery," one particular essay in Rosenbaum's book offered a useful underlying ideology. Titled "Orson Welles as Ideological Challenge," Rosenbaum outlines in six points how Welles's career went against the conventional wisdom of how movies are made: as (1) an independent artist, and (2) a public intellectual who (3) financed his own work, which (4) often came in unique forms and (5) were frequently incomplete, Welles (6) confounded the notion that great art can be commodified.[4] Rosenbaum emphasizes Welles's late-period career as a movie director, but the seeds of Welles's quest for artistic autonomy were planted when he was a young auteur.

Moreover, "Orson Welles as Ideological Challenge" provided a useful exhibit template for how to *perceive* Welles in the context of American cultural mores. It is a topic I had addressed in previous activities making use of the collection, such as a continuing education class on *The Magnificent Ambersons*. But for that, I only had to know pockets of the Lilly's holdings, rather than the entire breadth and depth. As an exhibition challenge, representing the life of Orson Welles is a daunting one. Gradually, however, strategies emerged, guided by six key principles that enabled the exhibit to take shape.

1. NO ONE COLLECTION CAN EXPLAIN A MAN'S LIFE

Excluding a handful of individually cataloged books and pamphlets, all 160 items came from a dozen collections housed at the Lilly Library, with approximately two-thirds derived from the Orson Welles Manuscripts (or Welles MSS). Acquired in 1978, the Welles MSS were originally the "Mercury Files" of Welles's longtime business associate, Richard Wilson. In a company that thrived on chaos, Wilson was the calm center who organized and maintained its extensive holdings for decades following its dissolution. The collection features over forty cubic feet of materials, including correspondence, screenplays, transcripts of radio broadcasts, photographs, realia (i.e., artifacts), and other rare and unique materials.

Because the bulk of the Welles MSS spans the years 1936–50, drawing exclusively from the collection would cover "stage, sound, and screen" yet would also create a narrowly focused exhibit, one that highlighted primarily the best-known works of Welles's career. It was imperative, then, to incorporate materials from other collections to show the first two decades and last three decades of Welles's life. Additional Lilly collections that provided items included the Welles MSS II, and the papers of, respectively, George Fanto and Peter Bogdanovich.

The Welles MSS II is what is known in the archival profession as an *intentional* or *artificial* collection, in which the items were purchased separately from each other and, unlike the original Welles MSS, have no clear provenance. George Fanto was one of the cinematographers on Welles's *Othello* and *It's All True*, and his collection is small but substantial on both films. Peter Bogdanovich's papers, which contain a voluminous amount of material pertaining to his own career (nearly eight hundred boxes), were especially useful for materials on *The Other Side of the Wind*, the unfinished film that dominated the last fifteen years of Welles's life and which has been in legal and financial limbo in the thirty years since his death. The items belonging to L. Arnold Weissberger (legal records pertaining to *Citizen Kane*), David Bradley (an Orson Welles scrapbook), Rita Hayworth (love letters with watercolor illustrations by Welles), James Naremore (a letter from Charlton Heston regarding the making of *Touch of Evil*), Kenneth Tynan (a journal entry on John Huston, who starred in *The Other Side of the Wind*), and Pauline Kael (her effusive and insightful review of *Chimes at Midnight*, not her damaging and roundly debunked essay "Raising Kane"), among others, were also featured materials on display in the exhibition.

Even if, in some instances, it was only one item, all the aforementioned collections plugged gaps in the historical record of Orson Welles's varied, storied career. "I don't think any word can explain a man's life," the reporter Thompson opines at the end of *Citizen Kane*. By the same token, no one item—or even one collection—can do the same. For the purposes of mounting an exhibition, every piece of the puzzle helps, regardless how many other pieces may be missing in between.

2. THE IMPORTANCE OF BALANCING CHRONOLOGICAL AND THEMATIC ORGANIZATION

An effective exhibition needs a narrative hook—in essence, a compelling story. But *which* story should be told regarding the multifaceted, transcontinental life of Orson Welles? There is the personal Welles, the political Welles, the socially conscious Welles, the expatriate Welles, the unfinished

Welles—and if a planned exhibit were to contain elements of all, how should the items be arranged?

The narrative of many early Welles biographies is a rise-and-fall saga. He was a "Boy Wonder" whose genius was preordained at a young age, a wunderkind who staged the "Voodoo" *Macbeth* and *Julius Caesar* to widespread acclaim, a provocateur who frightened millions with his broadcast of "The War of the Worlds," and finally a genius who made his film debut by directing *Citizen Kane*—"finally" because, according to this narrative, Welles, strictly speaking, did nothing of merit after that. An exhibition that told this tale could showcase only the "greatest hits," such as *Kane*, and would likely end with the "decline" of Welles that began with *The Magnificent Ambersons* and his Latin America documentary *It's All True*.

Thanks to recent scholarship, this simplistic story has been supplanted by a more complex narrative with particular emphasis on Welles's constant, overlapping work. Welles's anonymous voice work on the radio coincided with his meteoric rise in the Federal Theatre. Also overlapping were his whirlwind years in the independent Mercury Theatre, his radio arm *Mercury Theatre on the Air*, and his dramatic arrival in Hollywood via Mercury Productions for RKO Radio Pictures. In a new introduction to the centenary edition of *The Magic World of Orson Welles*, James Naremore focuses on the year 1940–41 as an example of Welles's ceaseless activity:

> In the single year of 1940, for example, he produced, directed, acted in, and supervised scripts for a dozen radio dramas; appeared as a guest on a couple of other radio programs; oversaw the production of a recorded version of *Macbeth* by the Mercury players; toured thirteen cities with a lecture titled "The New Actor"; wrote a screenplay for Dolores del Rio; completed the screenplays for *Smiler with a Knife* and *Mexican Melodrama*; completed the screenplay and principal photography of *Citizen Kane*; sought Richard Wright's approval for the forthcoming Mercury stage production of *Native Son*; and consulted with a dozen US ministers of various faiths regarding his idea for a film about the life of Jesus Christ.[5]

In preparing the exhibition, I considered how to demarcate Welles's concurrent projects in theater, radio, and film. Should the layout unfold chronologically, despite the crosscurrents of his work? And if a thematic

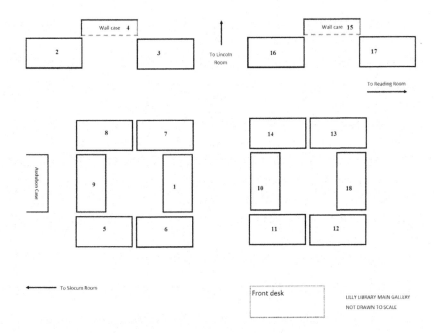

Figure 9.1. *100 Years of Orson Welles: Master of Stage, Sound, and Screen* exhibition, Lilly Library Main Gallery. In-house exhibition design template.

or topical layout rather than chronological, could it be arranged in a way that wasn't confusing for a general audience?

It is useful from a curatorial vantage point to construct a prescribed path through the exhibition. Even if some visitors will navigate an exhibit in no particular order, many will follow the numerical arrangement of the cases. The plan for the exhibit is illustrated in figure 9.1.

The left side of the gallery was devoted to primarily Welles's work in theater and radio:

CASE 1: Orson Welles in Person
CASE 2: The Federal Theatre Project
CASE 3: Mercury Rising
CASE 4: "Boil and Bubble"—Welles and Shakespeare Onstage
CASE 5: On the Air
CASE 6: "The War of the Worlds"
CASE 7: Welles and Politics

CASE 8: Welles and Civil Rights

CASE 9: Experiments in Mixed Media

The large pop-top case 1, which covered Welles's upbringing, education, and extended family, served as an introduction to both the exhibition and its subject. Cases 2–3, 5–6, and 7–8 were designed to complement each other with related topics (respectively: Welles's work in the Federal and Mercury Theatres; his radio career; and his interest in sociopolitical issues). Case 4, the left-side wall case, featured items related to Welles's stage adaptations of William Shakespeare's plays; whereas case 9, a small pop-top, functioned as a transition between Welles's theater work and his film career, the main focus on the right side of the gallery, which included the following:

CASE 10: Sight, Sound, and *Citizen Kane*

CASE 11: Orson in Indiana

CASE 12: Ambassador to Brazil

CASE 13–14: Suckers and Mugs—Welles and Film Noir

CASE 15: "Toil and Trouble"—Welles and Shakespeare Onscreen

CASE 16–17: Unreleased, Unfinished, or Unmade

CASE 18: The "Real Welles"?

Citizen Kane was a logical topic to inhabit the other tall pop-top, occupying a significant place in the exhibition without overwhelming the space. (In an early design, I had *Kane* materials in three separate cases). The film-related cases then followed a pattern similar to the theater/radio cases: cases 11–12 linked *The Magnificent Ambersons* and *It's All True*; cases 13–14 featured materials pertaining to Welles's thrillers *Journey into Fear*, *The Lady from Shanghai*, *The Stranger*, and *Touch of Evil*; and cases 16–17 highlighted his incomplete or fragmented works from his early studio years to his late-period works. Finally, case 18, the second small pop-top, served as an end point to the exhibit by including items that assessed Welles's legacy, such as a heartfelt personal reflection by Jeanette Nolan, who played Lady Macbeth in Welles's 1948 screen adaptation of Shakespeare's tragedy. The result was a clear topical arrangement that also followed a loose chronological progression.

Nevertheless, this arrangement led to a few potential difficulties. For example, case 2: The Federal Theatre Project featured materials on *Horse*

Eats Hat and *Doctor Faustus*; yet the FTP's two most famed productions, the "Voodoo" *Macbeth* and *The Cradle Will Rock*, were in, respectively, case 4 (Welles and Shakespeare) and case 7 (Welles and Politics). Case 3 (Mercury Rising) focused on *The Shoemaker's Holiday* and *Heartbreak House*, both hits, but neither having the impact of *Julius Caesar* (also in case 4). This did not appear to confuse visitors, however; and it freed up space for items regarding Welles's lesser-known works in the Federal and Mercury Theatres.

Technically, *100 Years of Orson Welles* spanned ninety-one years, with the oldest item being Welles's birth certificate (May 16, 1915), and the most recent being a couple of photographs of his birthplace dated 2006. The layout of the exhibition papered over gaps between those items fairly seamlessly, and demonstrated that chronological and thematic approaches can be used in tandem when it comes to representing Orson Welles.

3. THE TENUOUS ROLE OF REGIONALISM

Visitors to the Lilly often ask how we acquired the Welles Manuscripts in the first place. Upon hearing that the collection was purchased, their initial question is invariably followed by a sense of disappointment that Orson Welles was not a born-and-bred Hoosier or an alumnus of IU. Nevertheless, what may be called Welles's "midwesternness" does allow for a general degree of regional identification, and adds yet another layer of complexity to his image as a world citizen.

Case 1: Orson Welles in Person featured a surfeit of materials from Welles's family, education, and the first two of his three marriages, to Virginia Nicolson and Rita Hayworth. (His third and final marriage, to Paola Mori, lasted from 1955–85. The Lilly has no materials on Mori or her daughter with Welles, Beatrice). This case not only introduced the exhibit but also served to humanize its subject with photographs of Welles's wives and children; biographical documents, such as George Orson Welles's birth certificate from Kenosha Hospital, and a 1931 report card from Todd School for Boys. It also included family correspondence, such as a charming letter from Welles's oldest daughter, Christopher, when she was approximately eight years old. Also featured were photographs of Orson as a boy and as a young man, and of his mother Beatrice Ives. (None exist of his father in the Lilly's holdings.)

In addition to photographs of Welles's first two wives, I included photos of his two eldest daughters, Christopher and Rebecca, both in their infancy. Watercolor illustrations by Welles, given to Hayworth, came from a separate collection (the Hayworth MSS) and show Welles's artistic talents along with his morbid sense of humor. One illustration, titled "Another Self-Portrait of Self-Pity," depicts a despondent Orson walking with a cane. Popular with visiting researchers, these items show a private, affectionate, human side to Welles, along with his impressive artistic skill.

Dr. Maurice Bernstein, friend of the Welles family and rumored to be intimate with Orson's mother, became legal guardian to the adolescent Welles following his father's death. Their correspondence—such as a notecard from Bernstein a few days after Welles's fifteenth birthday—often included the nicknames they gave each other: "Pookles" (Orson) and "Dadda" (Bernstein). Welles was performing his first plays at Todd at this time, and in the note, Bernstein writes: "Playing Ceasar [sic] . . . was a wonderful experience for you, and even though you did not get the first prize it was worth doing . . . Some day when you will be in the eyes of the world doing big things as I know you will, you will look back upon this disappointment as having been just a passing experience. We must learn to accept disappointment and profit from it."[6]

Although the "War of the Worlds" exhibition case emphasized both favorable and unfavorable correspondence sent to Welles following the October 30, 1938 "Martian Broadcast" (overwhelmingly pro, as it happens), one of Welles's recollections, transcribed years later, draws an interesting connection between his midwestern upbringing and his methods directing the program. "This was Halloween, remember, and in my middle-western childhood, that was the season for pranks," Welles reflected, which included, at the very least, "dressing up in a sheet and spooking the neighbours with a pumpkin head." He added, "Well, in that notorious broadcast I said 'boo' to several million people over a full network, and the punkin' head was a flying saucer from Mars."[7]

Welles's best-known connection to the Hoosier State was, of course, his adaptation (first as a radio show, then a film) of Indiana native Booth

Tarkington's Pulitzer Prize winning novel, *The Magnificent Ambersons*. Tarkington's tale likely spoke to Welles's sense of nostalgia growing up in the Midwest: both novel and movie conclude around 1915, the year Welles was born. Thus case 11: Orson in Indiana displayed items pertaining to the 1942 film. For context, a first edition of Tarkington's novel was included, opened to a title page illustration by Arthur William Brown. This fit nicely with a letter from Brown to Welles, dated August 19, 1941: "Back in 1917 I had the honor of illustrating Booth Tarkington's THE MAGNIFICENT AMBERSONS," Brown writes. "As you are about to make a picture of it I thought Tark's letter to me at the time might interest you now, as follows." Brown then excerpts Tarkington's description of how the characters should look and dress: "The Ambersons are DuMaurier-like people—Tall, graceful, beautifully dressed—'distinguished' and 'aristocratic.' I have taken liberties and license with the dates of the period covered; George is supposed to have been born about '78 and to reach the age of 25–27 when the story closes, about 1913. The Amberson mansion is a big thing—stone and brick—a big lawn—greenhouses—high ceilings; polished wood; tiger rugs; heavy tall mirrors; Louis XIV chairs and sofas."[8] Rounding out the "Orson in Indiana" case were a publicity still from Welles's original ending to *Ambersons*, in which Eugene Morgan visits Aunt Fanny in her boarding house, the cutting continuity of that ending, and audience comments from the disastrous preview of the film in Pomona, California, on March 18, 1942. While Rosenbaum believes that they were not as negative as RKO made them out to be, they struck me as anything but effusive.[9] Partly, the negative response may have been attributable to the studio's decision to screen a long, dark, challenging film such as *Ambersons* immediately following an upbeat wartime musical, *The Fleet's In*. It's also likely that Welles's period piece was not only alienating to a preview audience of primarily teenagers, but that his critique of industrialization was out of step with the country's buildup toward World War II. Most importantly, the comments added more evidence to the exhibition that the reaction to Welles's art was never indifferent. From Booth Tarkington to the Bard, he could turn any source material, regardless of its time or place, into a provocation.

4. THE SIGNIFICANCE OF SHAKESPEARE

The exhibition emphasized the connection between Orson Welles and William Shakespeare for three reasons. First was the necessity of fore-grounding Welles's adaptations of Shakespeare's works, which are crucial to his output in theater, radio, and film. Secondly, materials related to these works are among the largest—in terms of both quantity and size—in the Welles Manuscripts. Lastly, Welles's "modernized" adaptations of Shakespeare's plays seemed like they might have crossover appeal to undergrads in IU's theater program as well as students familiar with contemporary screen updates, such as Baz Luhrmann's *Romeo & Juliet* (1996), starring Leonardo DiCaprio and Clare Danes.

Welles's adaptations of "Shakespeare Onstage" and "Shakespeare Onscreen"—to use the titles of case 4 (see fig. 9.2) and case 15, respectively—were subjects ideally suited to the pair of wall cases in the Lilly Main Gallery. The largest items in the collection pertain to these topics, most notably the Mercury Theatre poster advertising *The Shoemaker's Holiday* and *Julius Caesar* (*The Shoemaker's Holiday* is not a play by William Shakespeare but rather Thomas Dekker, but I added it to the case with that disclaimer). Along with being one of the most visually striking items in the exhibit, the poster provided another example of Welles's overlapping work, with two successful plays running almost simultaneously in late 1937 and early 1938. At the bottom of the poster reads a blurb from *The New Yorker's* Robert Benchley: "You can't lose no matter which one you hit!"

Other items in the "Welles and Shakespeare Onstage" case were more textual, such as script pages from the "Voodoo" *Macbeth* with Welles's annotations, which are along the lines of, "Voodoo Drums Low," "Smoke Pot," "Thunder Sheet," "Alarm Bell," "Trumpets," and "Raise Hell With Everything." Among the most common items in the Welles MSS, annotated play, radio, and film scripts demonstrate the process of Welles at work in these media.

Correspondence also occupies a substantial part of the Welles MSS, and was represented in the exhibition with letters from fans and peers alike. For example, a February 9, 1937 letter to John Houseman by Hollywood screenwriter Sidney Howard (winner of a posthumous Oscar

Figure 9.2. Case 4: "Welles and Shakespeare Onstage." *100 Years of Orson Welles.* Lilly Library exhibition. Photograph by the author.

three years later for adapting Margaret Mitchell's *Gone with the Wind*), suggests that Houseman and Welles should stage Shakespeare's *Caesar* "in modern dress." Rounding out the case were a *Five Kings* script and a leaf of sheet music by composer Aaron Copland, who wrote the score.

Welles's film adaptations of Shakespeare's plays signal a transition between his Hollywood productions of the 1940s and his independent films in Europe through most of the 1950s and 1960s. Each one different than the other, his three movies based on the Bard's work (two of which he had directed previously onstage) demonstrate the richness and diversity in subject and style of both Welles and the playwright he revered. The distinctiveness of his Shakespeare films, observed Michael Anderegg, "lies in a different direction from the popularizing and sensationalist impulses that lay behind Welles's stage productions."[10]

The materials for Welles's Republic Pictures *Macbeth* (1948) made for an interesting comparison and contrast with the items from the "*Voodoo*" *Macbeth* (1936). On one hand, the "wardrobe plot" for the film clearly shows how its early medieval Scottish setting was a radical departure from the prior decade's setting in nineteenth-century Haiti. (The movie was largely based on a revival of the play, directed by Welles in Salt Lake City with the same cast.). Yet an oversized blueprint at the center of the case had almost exactly the same set design of a long, winding staircase as the one in the "Voodoo" *Macbeth*.

Although the timeframe of the Welles MSS excludes his screen version of *Othello*, several fascinating items relating to the film can be found among George Fanto's papers. A script excerpt with a visual key of colors and symbols (e.g., "scene to be shot silent," "big crowd," "wind machine," and so on) proves that, contrary to longstanding myth, there was in fact a screenplay for the movie. Indeed, it suggests how much forethought Welles put into the production even while constantly running out of money to make it. An item reflecting his state of mind was a handwritten page on the film's finances, which included the phrase "LIVE VERY HUMBLY."

5. THE CENTRALITY OF POLITICS AND CIVIL RIGHTS

Welles's political views have been largely obscured by his artistic accomplishments, even though his politics informed his art. A proud progressive and supporter of President Franklin D. Roosevelt, Welles used his fame and media platform to champion Popular Front causes and civil interests. It has been documented that the FBI opened a file on him at the demand of William Randolph Hearst and classified him as a threat to internal security.[11] This became a contributing factor to Welles's departure from the United States for Europe in 1947, the same year the Hollywood blacklist was formed by the House Committee on Un-American Activities (HUAC).

Case 7: Welles and Politics featured materials from *The Cradle Will Rock*, his last theatrical production for the Federal Theatre Project: a clipping pertaining to the performance ("WPA's Play within a Play"); a publicity broadside with critics' raves; and detailed illustrations of Welles's elaborate, ultimately unused set designs. A handwritten excerpt of a speech he gave while stumping for FDR was placed on display above a signed letter from Helen Keller, who had joined Welles at a political rally on the campaign trail on October 26, 1944. Although the date for a letter from Isaac Asimov praising Welles's political courage is unknown, it is likely in early 1947, following a series of Welles's most controversial commentaries that occurred as the political climate of the country started to swing right. Finally, a 1942 pamphlet with Welles's introduction to *The Sleepy Lagoon Case*, in which he joined the public defense of several Mexican Americans falsely accused of murder, offered further insight into his social activism in the 1940s.

Of the many social causes taken up by Orson Welles, he was most outspoken on the issue of civil rights (case 8). Welles put his views into practice with his Mercury Theatre adaptation of *Native Son*. Richard Wright's provocative 1940 novel about a young, impoverished black man resorting to crime in an unjust society was adapted for the stage by Wright and Paul Green, produced by Welles and John Houseman, and directed by Welles. The play debuted in March 1941 and roused the usual response to Welles: strong box office, glowing reviews, and fervent media debate. *Native Son* was Mercury's last official theatrical production and the end of the acrimonious partnership between Welles and Houseman, who never worked together again. A May 29, 1940 letter from Wright to Houseman—"Knowing what you and Welles have done in the past, I do believe that you both could do a courageous job"—concerning the rights to the adaptation was featured in the exhibition as well.[12]

The topic that generated the most correspondence in the Welles MSS—ranging from admiring and supportive to threatening and hostile—is neither "The War of the Worlds" nor *Citizen Kane* but rather an incident involving Isaac Woodard Jr., the decorated African American World War II veteran who, on February 12, 1946, was arrested and beaten blind by South Carolina police officers. The NAACP worked to gain Woodard attention in the media, and eventually Welles took notice and responded energetically. On July 28, 1946, Welles began the first of several broadcasts on his weekly political radio show, *Orson Welles Commentaries*, where he sought to bring the perpetrators to justice. (Initially Welles incorrectly identified the location as Aiken; it was Batesburg.) A growing public outcry led to an investigation by the US Justice Department and indictments of several Batesburg officers. On trial, the chief of police claimed that Woodard pulled a gun and that the beating was in self-defense. In November of that year, the all-white jury deliberated for twenty-five minutes and returned with a verdict of not guilty.

Regarding this topic, also in case 8, were a handful of the more eloquent responses to Welles's broadcasts, all dated from the month of August 1946. Private Lorenzo S. Cole wrote, "I am a negro. I am a soldier. I am an American. To you members of my race want to thank you for defending our people as Americans."[13] Secretary of the NAACP Walter White closed a telegram with the words: "It is men like you who give us faith to carry on an increasingly difficult fight against this rising tide of mob vilence [sic] which threatens not only minorities but America itself."[14] Handwritten on a small card, Ronald Sterns made a moving observation: "Mr. Welles: Thanks for a fine and courageous attempt to rectify the grievous injustice suffered by the Negro in America. It speaks well for the brain that conceived Citizen Kane that it is no less valid when the final faith in man must be upheld."[15]

Welles's preoccupation with racial issues is also represented among the items in case 5: On the Air. One of Welles' favorite writers was John Steinbeck, and at the end of the July 19, 1944, episode of *Orson Welles Almanac*, Welles read an original story by the author, "With Your Wings," about an African American pilot's return home from World War II. Thought lost for seventy years, another copy of Steinbeck's story was recently found at the University of Texas at Austin and published in the literary magazine *The Strand*. It likely was not discovered first at the Lilly because only the episode's guest (Ruth Terry) was originally listed on the collection's finding aid. Adding Steinbeck to the episode description was an unexpected example of one of the positive outcomes from preparing this exhibition—giving hidden items visibility.

6. THE VALUE OF FRAGMENTS

Another way that the archive reveals "the invisible Welles" (to use Rosenbaum's phrase) is through calling attention to the manifold forms of his compromised works.[16] So many of Welles's works were never completed that for a long time he was branded a failure for it. Now, however, in the age of the Internet, YouTube, and DVD Special Features, our culture has grown more accustomed to fragments, alternate endings, and multiple versions of the same work of art. Consequently, Welles's unfinished projects are increasingly and respectfully integrated into a comprehensive accounting of his achievements.

A few of the buried treasures on display in the exhibition were a script excerpt, photographs, and sketches from *Too Much Johnson*, Welles's aborted 1938 production adapted from William Gillette's bawdy 1894 farce. These items became particularly useful after the footage Welles filmed to accompany the stage production was discovered in the form of a sixty-six-minute nitrate work print in an abandoned warehouse in Pordonne, Italy, in 2008. The items for *Too Much Johnson* were displayed in case 9: Experiments in Mass Media, along with materials for a pair of other plays, *Around the World* and *The Unthinking Lobster*, for which Welles also shot footage incorporated into the productions.

The fragments of an unfinished project can be very extensive. The Welles MSS contains enough materials on *It's All True* to fill the entire main gallery, so it seemed appropriate to give Welles's Latin America documentary its own case (case 12: Ambassador to Brazil). Adjacent to the *Ambersons* display, the *It's All True* case had enough space (barely) for a pamphlet about Robert Flaherty's *Bonito the Bull*, a photograph of Welles filming the Carnaval in Rio, a photograph of Welles and George Fanto filming "Four Men on a Raft" in Fortaleza, and a memorial program on Jacaré (i.e., Manoel Olimpio Meira) shortly after his tragic death while filming the "Four Men on a Raft" sequence. These items offered a glimpse of the three parts Welles had at least begun shooting for his omnibus film, and a heated exchange of correspondence between Welles and RKO head George Schaefer illustrated the difficulties and desperation of both men's situation at the studio.

As mentioned above, from the beginning of his career to its end, Welles juggled multiple projects at once, often teeming with more ideas than he knew what to do with. Cases 16–17 featured items relating to films that Welles either completed (or nearly completed) but never saw released, started but never finished, or planned but never made. The first of these two cases ("Part I") featured materials from projects that Welles worked on during his early Hollywood tenure: adaptations of Joseph Conrad, the Bible, and a children's story by Antoine de Saint-Exupéry. In addition to an excerpt of the introduction from Welles's *Heart of Darkness* screenplay, there was an exchange of letters between Welles and Frederick May Eliot of the American Unitarian Association about *The Life of Christ,* a never-realized dream project similar in spirit to his previous updates of classic texts (Haiti in the "Voodoo" *Macbeth,* fascist Europe in *Julius Caesar,* Grover's Mill in "The War of the Worlds"). Welles's plan to transport the Christ tale from first-century Judea to the nineteenth-century American West, while leaving the words of the Gospels unchanged, received tentative encouragement (if also a few caveats) from Eliot and other religious leaders, but the project was ultimately shelved. Either from lack of interest or cooperation from Walt Disney, Welles's proposed live-action/animation collaboration on *The Little Prince* met a similar fate, but the subject matter offered yet another example of Welles's imaginative versatility.

Even after Welles returned to Hollywood circa 1969, he remained the prototypical independent filmmaker, inspiring other artists who toiled in studio productions to finance their personal projects. Rosenbaum estimated that Welles was working on at least twelve separate projects in the few years prior to his death in 1985. "It has become increasingly clear that the legacy [Welles] left behind ... is immeasurably larger and richer, and more full of potential surprises, than any of us had reason to expect," he wrote—words that have been validated in the years since.[17]

Welles's late-period projects were chronicled in the second "Unreleased, Unfinished, or Unmade" case ("Part II"). A letter from Welles to Peter Bodganovich, dated September 28, 1969, indicated the former's difficulties with two simultaneous projects, *Don Quixote* and *Dead Reckoning* (eventually titled *The Deep*), an original screenplay of *The Dreamers* and posthumously published screenplays *The Big Brass Ring* and *The Cradle Will Rock* provided examples of his burst of creativity in the early 1980s immediately prior to his death.

Due to the highly publicized announcement of an agreement reached to complete *The Other Side of the Wind,*[18] materials in the Bogdanovich MSS concerning this film continue to be of interest to researchers. Included in the exhibit was a photo of Welles seated on set with his back to the camera, while several members of the cast and crew gravitate around him, and an "editor's cut" continuity dated June 29, 2007, which featured a lengthy list of scenes in an Excel spreadsheet.

One of the most unique items belonged to Kenneth Tynan, the powerful and controversial theater critic for *The London Observer,* whose personal diaries are housed at the Lilly Library. Tynan idolized Orson Welles, and in this handwritten 1975 journal entry he relates a conversation with John Huston about playing the lead in *The Other Side of the Wind*:

> Shooting, as always with Orson, was spread over several years, with sudden and protracted suspensions of activity whenever the money ran out. John . . . didn't hear from Orson for a year or more, and assumed the project was cancelled. One day Orson summoned him to Arizona, where he explained that the picture was completely finished except for Huston's part which was the lead. Orson had managed to "shoot round" the Huston character so that nothing remained but to cut in solo shots of John himself. "And so," as John put it, "I can boast that have starred in a movie without meeting anyone else in the cast."[19]

Although there is plenty of evidence that Huston is exaggerating, his entertaining anecdote confirms Welles's unorthodox methods in the filming of *The Other Side of the Wind* described in accounts such as Josh Karp's *Orson Welles's Last Movie: The Making of* The Other Side of the Wind.[20]

❋ ❋ ❋

When Richard Wilson informed Orson Welles of the official sale of his papers to the Lilly Library, Welles replied, in a short, undated letter (presumably 1978) not in the Lilly's collection, but at the University of Michigan, "Now it's in the hands of the cineastes, God help us all."[21] By "cineastes" Welles presumably meant "academics," a frequent target of his disdain. Yet it is academics who have played a leading role in keeping Welles's name alive, in preserving his materials to ensure their longevity, in pushing back vigorously against the "failure thesis" and outright falsehoods such as the claim that "Welles didn't write a word of *Citizen Kane.*" Unlike the collections of private citizens, the Welles Manuscripts at the Lilly Library are accessible to all.

Rosenbaum concludes his piece on ideological challenges by noting that "For generations to come, I suspect, Welles will remain the great example of the talented filmmaker whose work and practices deconstruct what academics . . . are fond of calling 'the cinematic apparatus.'" Rosenbaum hastened to add that he believed Welles did not achieve this deconstruction by way of conscious objective, "but more precisely because his sense of being an artist as well as an entertainer was frequently tied to throwing monkey wrenches into our expectations—something that the best art and entertainment often do."[22]

More than thirty years after his death, Welles continues to surprise. It took a streaming service, Netflix, to free *The Other Side of the Wind* from a four-decade imbroglio and begin readying Welles's footage for release.[23] It took a home video distribution company, Criterion, to restore and release *Chimes at Midnight* (to great acclaim) in 2016 and *Othello* in 2017. As recipients of this ongoing inheritance, we can find context for the remarkable body of work Welles bequeathed in the rich archive he left behind. The inherent challenges in presenting Orson Welles are worth the rewarding payoffs, as when a visitor to the Lilly, after spending a considerable amount of time touring the exhibition, came over to me afterward and said, "I didn't realize everything he did." This may well be the response of even experienced Welles watchers as more of Welles's creative work comes to light.

CRAIG SIMPSON is the Lilly Library Manuscripts Archivist. He curated the Lilly's exhibition, *100 Years of Orson Welles: Master of Stage, Sound, and Screen.*

NOTES

1. Jonathan Rosenbaum, *Discovering Orson Welles* (Berkeley: University of California Press, 2007), 3.

2. Jessica Lacher-Feldman, *Exhibits in Archives and Special Collections Libraries* (Society of American Archivists, 2013), 2.

3. Rosenbaum, *Discovering Orson Welles*; James Naremore, *The Magic World of Orson Welles*, Centennial Anniversary Edition (Urbana: University of Illinois Press, 2015); Joseph McBride, *What Ever Happened to Orson Welles: A Portrait of an Independent Career* (Lexington: University Press of Kentucky, 2006); Charles Higham, *Orson Welles: The Rise and Fall of an American Genius* (New York: St. Martin's Press, 1985); David Thomson, *Rosebud: The Story of Orson Welles* (New York: Alfred A. Knopf, 1996).

4. Rosenbaum, "Orson Welles as Ideological Challenge," in *Discovering Orson Welles*, 269–88.

5. Naremore, *The Magic World of Orson Welles*, 2.

6. Maurice Bernstein to Orson Welles, 21 May 1930, box 1, Welles MSS, Lilly Library, Indiana University.

7. Orson Welles, "Martian Broadcast (Talk)." Undated, box 163, Bogdanovich MSS, Lilly Library, Indiana University.

8. Arthur William Brown to Orson Welles, August 19, 1941, box 3, Welles MSS, Lilly Library, Indiana University.

9. Rosenbaum, "Orson Welles as Ideological Challenge," 275–76.

10. Michael Anderegg, *Orson Welles, Shakespeare, and Popular Culture* (New York: Columbia University Press, 1999), 58.

11. Naremore, *The Magic World of Orson Welles*, 7.

12. Richard Wright to John Houseman, May 29, 1940, box 1, Welles MSS, Lilly Library, Indiana University.

13. Pvt. Lorenzo S. Cole to Orson Welles, August 25, 1946, box 3, Welles MSS, Lilly Library, Indiana University.

14. Walter White, August 19, 1946, box 3, Welles MSS, Lilly Library, Indiana University.

15. Ronald L. Sterns, August 27, 1946, box 3, Welles MSS, Lilly Library, Indiana University.

16. Rosenbaum, "Orson Welles as Ideological Challenge," 280–83.

17. Rosenbaum, afterword to Orson Welles, *The Big Brass Ring: An Original Screenplay*, with Oja Kodar (Santa Barbara, CA: Santa Teresa Press, 1987), 138.

18. Doreen Carvajal, "Orson Welles's Last Film May Finally Be Released," *New York Times*, October 28, 2014, accessed July 24, 2016, http://www.nytimes.com/2014/10/29/movies/hollywood-ending-near-for-orson-welles-last-film.html?_r=0.

19. Kenneth Tynan, Journal of Kenneth Tynan, no. 15, April 23, 1975, box 1, Kenneth Tynan, MSS, Lilly Library, Indiana University.

20. Josh Karp, *Orson Welles's Last Movie: The Making of* The Other Side of the Wind (New York: St. Martin's Press, 2015).

21. Orson Welles to Richard Wilson, undated [1978?], box 6, Richard Wilson-Orson Welles Papers, University of Michigan Special Collections Library.

22. Rosenbaum, "Orson Welles as Ideological Challenge," 287.

23. "Netflix to restore and release unfinished Welles film." *The Guardian*, March 14, 2017, accessed July 20, 2017, https://www.theguardian.com/film/2017/mar/14/netflix-restore-orson-welles-film.

INDEX

Page numbers in italics refer to images.

100 Years of Orson Welles: Master of Stage, Sound, and Screen, 6, 201

A Bell for Adano, 124
Abracadabra, 166
Adams, Samuel Hopkins, 125
Ade, George, 116
Adventures of Philip Marlowe, The, 46
Ailey, Alvin, 20
Albuquerque, Chico, 93, 102
Algiers, 21
Altman, Rick, 153
"American" (script), 62
American Broadcasting Company (ABC), 46, 132, 142, 143
American Home, The, 119
Anderson, Eddie "Rochester," 119
anti-fascism, 128
Antoine, Dominique, 146, 217
Aranha, Oswaldo, 91
Armstrong, Louis, 81, 96
Around the World (play), ix, 3, 5, 56, 134, 151–170, *163*, 217
Around the World in 80 Days (novel), 125, 132, 153
Around the World with Orson Welles, 187, 192, 193

Asadata African Opera and Dramatic Company, 21. *See also* Shogola Oloba
Asimov, Isaac, 214
Aslan, Grégoire, 182
Assen, Abdul, 5, 12, 14–16, 18–21, 22, 23, 26, 27, 29
Associated-Rediffusion, 187
Atkinson, Brooks, 18
auteur, 6, 8, 11, 12, 18, 37, 82, 83, 204

Bakhtin, Mikhail, 83
Barnouw, Erik, 39, 43
Barrie Craig, Confidential Investigator, 46
Barrier, Edgar, 59
Barroso, Ary, 97
Barrymore, John, 55, 115, 126
Battle for Survival, 144, 145
Baxter, Anne, 64
Bazin, André, 150–152
Becker, Jacques, 177, 189
Benny, Jack, 119
Bernstein, Maurice, 210
Beware of the Greeks, 184
Big Brass Ring, The, 9, 218
Biroc, Joseph, 95
Birth of a Nation, The, 65, 70–72
Black Boy, 119, 124
blacklist, ix, 214
Black Magic, 180

Black Museum, 180

Blake, Nicholas, 52

Blood and Sand, 65

Bogdanovich, Peter, 52–55, 57, 59–66, 68, 69, 71, 72, 151, 205, 218

Bolter, Jay David, 41

Booth, Edwin, 126

Bourdieu, Pierre, 37

Bowser, Eileen, 63

Bradley Collection, David, 56

Brault, Michel, 104

Brecher, Ludovic, 178. *See also* Dolivet, Louis

Brecht, Bertolt, ix, 168

Brook, Peter, 180

Brown, Arthur William, 211

Bugler of Battery B, The, 64

Burroughs, Eric, 14

Burroughs, Norris, 17

Cabinet of Dr. Caligari, The, 55

Caboré, Geraldo, 93

Callow, Simon, 18, 112, 125, 178

Candomblé, 96

Cantor, Marla, 142

Cantril, Hadley, 34

Capra, Frank, 57, 116, 123

Carnaval (festival), 84–88, 90–91, 92, 93–102, 103, 217. *See also* Carnival

"Carnaval" (part of *It's All True*), 81–87, 91, 92, 97, 98, 100, 102, 104

Carné, Marcel, 196

Carnegie Hall, 16, 19

Carnival, 117. *See also* Carnaval

Carter, Jack, 23, 27, 28

Cervantes Films, 181, 192, 195

Chaney, Lon, 65

Chaplin, Charlie, 54, 60, 66, 67, 157

Chicago Times, 117

Chicago Tribune, 118, 167

Chimes at Midnight, 2, 105, 196, 205, 220

Cinédia Studio, 86, 91, 92, 102

Citizen Kane, vii, viii, 2–4, 9, 47, 52, 53, 55, 59–62, 69, 81, 88, 90, 153, 161, 202, 205, 206, 208, 215, 216, 219

civil rights, 23, 28, 132, 133, 208, 214, 215

Clair, René, 60

Clark, VéVé, 17

Cocteau, Jean, 151

Cognet, Christophe, 176

Colomina Boti, Alberto, 182

Columbia Broadcasting System (CBS), 34, 36, 42, 44–46, 180, 189

Columbia Workshop, 34, 41, 44, 45

Confidential Report, 177, 190, 192–196. See also *Mr. Arkadin*

Conquering Power, The, 69

Conrad, Joseph, 52, 217

Copland, Aaron, 213

Copperfield, David, 166

Corwin, Norman, 44, 45

Cotten, Joseph, 59, 72

Cow-Boy Girl, The, 64

Cradle Will Rock, The (play), 9, 168, 209, 214

Cradle Will Rock, The (screenplay), 218

Dafora, Asadata, 5, 11, 12, 13, 14–21, 23–29

Daily Worker, The, 70

Dallas Morning News, 23

Dance Heritage Collection, 27

Danton's Death, 67

Death Mills, 135

Death Valley Days, 44

Deep, The, 3, 218

Del Rio, Dolores, 206

De Moraes, Vinicius, 92, 93, 104

Denning, Michael, 121, 133

Departamento de Imprensa e Propaganda (DIP), 86–88, 90, 95, 101

De Souza Prata, Sebastião "Grande Othelo," 97. *See also* Grande Othelo

Dickens, Charles, 114

Dietrich, Marlene, 167

Discovering Orson Welles, 203
Disney, Walt, 88, 91, 97, 218
Doctor Faustus, 27, 209
Dolivet, Louis, 4, 176–198, 177. *See also*
    Brecher, Ludovic
Don Quixote, 187, 218
Double Indemnity, 122
Dragnet, 46
Dreamers, The, 218
Duarte, Anselmo, 91
Dunbar, Paul, 117
Duro Alonso de Celada, José Luis, 182
Duvivier, Julien, 197
Dwan, Allan, 61

Edison, Thomas, 53, 64
Edwards, Hilton, 105
Eisenstein, Sergei, 115, 122, 169
Ellington, Duke, 28
epic theater, 168
Essanay, 64, 66, 157
Everybody's Shakespeare, viii, 24. *See*
    also Mercury Shakespeare

Fairbanks, Douglas, 55
fake news, 34, 35, 39, 41, 47
Fanto, George, 102, 105, 205, 214, 217
fascism, viii, 9, 10, 113, 115, 116, 118, 124,
    128, 135–137
Feder, Abe, 23
Federal Theatre Project, 11, 207, 208, 214
Fellini, Federico, 197
F for Fake, 9, 105, 146
Fields, W. C., 55, 67, 179
Filming Othello, 105
film noir, 94, 208
Filmorsa, 2, 176–200
First Person Singular, 34, 36
Flaherty, Robert, 66, 217
Fleming, Victor, 57
Flicker Flashbacks, 56
Flon, Suzanne, 185
Focus, 131, 138, 140, 145

Follow the Boys, 167
Fontes, Lourival, 86
Ford, Francis, 64
Ford, John, 67, 65, 123
Ford, John Anson, 141
Foster, Norman, 2, 87, 112, 115
Four Horsemen of the Apocalypse, The, 65
"Four Men on a Raft," 81, 84, 217
Fowler, Gene, 126, 179
Francis, Arlene, 59, 64
Franklin, Benjamin, 115, 214
Freeburg, Victor Oscar, 69
Frontier Gentleman, 46

Gershwin, George, 25
Ghost at Circle X Camp, 64
Gilbert and Sullivan, 23
Gillett, Roland, 187
Gillette, William, 217
Godard, Jean-Luc, 127
Golden Jubilee, 53, 70
Goldin, Horace, 166, 167
Gold Rush, The, 66
Goldwyn, Samuel, 124
Gonzaga, Adhemar, 86
Goodman, Ezra, 69
Good Neighbor Policy, 83, 86, 87, 95, 99,
    105, 144
Gorelik, Mordecai, 168
Gosling, John, 34
Goya, 184
Grande Othelo, 84, 86, 91, 93, 97, 102,
    104. *See also* Sebastião "Grande
    Othelo" De Souza Prata
Grand Illusion, 68
Graver, Gary, 18, 54, 55
Gray Film, 176, 194
Great Flamarion, The, 68
Great Gabbo, The, 68
Greed, 68
Green, Paul, 215
Green Goddess, The, 66, 152
Griffith, D. W., 53, 61, 65, 68–72

Groux, Gilles, 104
Grusin, Richard, 41
Guitry, Sacha, 181
Gwynn, Nell, 115

Hale's Tours, 158
Hammond, Percy, 14–17, 21, 23, 25, 27, 28
Hardy, Oliver, 67
Hathaway, Henry, 180
Hayworth, Rita, 205, 209, 210
Hearst, William Randolph, viii, 60, 117,
    121, 214
Heartbreak House, 209
Heart of Darkness (film/screenplay), 20,
    27, 217
Heart of Darkness (novel), 52
Heart of Darkness (radio show), 27
Hearts of Age, 55
Heifetz, Jascha, 114
Hello Americans, 27
Her Husband's Wife, 64
Hersey, John, 124
Heyer, Paul, 36
Hill, Roger, viii, 100
Himber, Richard, 166
Hispano Film, 181
Hitchcock, Alfred, vii
Hjort, Mette, 82, 103
Hold Up of the Rocky Mountain Express,
    The, 158
Hollywood, vii, 52–54, 57, 59–62, 65,
    69–71, 91, 93, 102, 116, 120, 122–124,
    128, 136, 180, 184, 186, 206, 212, 213,
    214, 217, 218
Hollywood Cavalcade, 54
Holt, Jack, 64
Holt, Tim, 64
Hoover, J. Edgar, viii
Houseman, John, 14, 18, 21, 39, 212,
    213, 215
House Un-American Activities Com-
    mittee, 139
Huston, John, 69, 123, 181, 205, 219

illustrated song, 154
Ince, Thomas, 60
Ingram, Rex, 65, 68, 69
Intolerance, 55, 70, 71
"invisible Welles," 111, 216
Iron Horse, The, 65
Irving, Henry, 125
It's All True, 105
Ivan the Terrible, 122
Ives, Beatrice, 210

Jacaré, 91, 95, 102, 217. See also Meira,
    Manoel "Jacaré" Olimpio
Jacobs, Lewis, 70
Jacob's Pillow, 28
Jameson, House, 45
"Jangadeiros," 81, 84, 86, 91, 95, 99, 102,
    103, 104, 105
J. Arthur Rank, 193
Jesse James, the Missouri Outlaw, 64
Johnny Dollar, Yours Truly, 46
Joint Anti-Fascist Refugee Committee,
    139
Jonson, Ben, 191
Jouhaux, Léon, 178
Journey into Fear, 87, 208
Joyce, James, 114
Julius Caesar, viii, 9, 23, 24, 137, 151, 168,
    206, 209, 212, 213, 218

Kafka, Franz, 24
Kaiser, Georg, 168
kaleidosonic, 38
Karp, Josh, 219
Karson, Nat, 23
Keaton, Buster, 54, 55, 167
Keller, Helen, 214
Kelley, B., 157
Keystone Cops, 66, 67, 157
Killiam, Paul, 55
kinetoscope, 53
King, Henry, 180
King Lear, 5, 180, 192

Kitt, Eartha, 28
Koch, Howard, 34–36, 39, 40
Kodar, Oja, 18
Koszarski, Richard, 68
Krohn, Bill, 56, 81
Kykunkor, 12, 13, 14, 16, 19, 21, 22, 24, 25

Lacher-Feldman, Jessica, 202
La Dolce Vita, 197
Lady from Shanghai, The, 47, 105, 152, 208
lantern slide, 154
Lattuada, Alberto, 197
Laura, 122
Laurel, Stan, 67
Lee, Canada, 27, 28
Leigh, Janet, vii
Lerner, Irving, 157
Lévi-Strauss, Claude, 101
Lewis, Jerry, 67
Life of Christ, The, 218
Lights Out, 45
Lippmann, Walter, 118
Lives of Harry Lime, The, 180
Living Newspaper, 115
Lizzani, Carlo, 197
Lloyd, Harold, 67, 141
López Heredia, Irene, 183
Luce, Claire Boothe, 118
Luce, Henry, 118
Lucidi, Renzo, 183, 184, 186, 187, 192
Lyons, Leonard, 113, 124

Macbeth (film), 150–152, 208, 213
Macbeth (play), ix, 3, 6, 9, 11–33, 202, 206, 209, 212–214, 218
MacLeish, Archibald, 41, 45
Magic Show, The, 67, 154, 166
Magic Trick, The, 16, 155, 165, 166
Magnificent Ambersons, The, 52, 62–64, 72, 81, 87, 134, 204, 206, 208, 211
M. and A. Alexander, 193
Mankiewicz, Herman, 18
Manning, Susan, 25

March of Time, The, 34, 41, 53, 88
Margetson, Arthur, 156
Margolis, Henry, 188–192
Martínez Gil, Jesús "Chucho," 98
Martínez Olcoz, Angel, 182
Martins, Herivelto, 86, 91, 93, 97, 98, 100
Masquerade, 98, 180, 181
Mauldin, Bill, 127
Maxwell, Elsa, 112, 114
Mayer, Louis B., 68
McBride, Joseph, 1
McCarten, John, 128
McCormick, Tobert, 117, 118
McLuhan, Marshall, 121
Meira, Manoel "Jacaré" Olimpio, 91, 217. *See also* Jacaré
Meisel, Myron, 81
Méliès, George, 64, 157
Meltzer, Robert, 86, 91, 95, 98
Merchant of Venice, viii, 5
Mercury Productions, 4, 35, 45, 134, 153, 206
Mercury Shakespeare, 24. See also *Everybody's Shakespeare*
Mercury Text Records, viii
Mercury Theatre, 24, 34–37, 40, 41, 43, 45–47, 86, 87, 88, 102, 204, 206, 207, 208, 209, 212, 215
Mercury Theatre on the Air, 34, 206
Mercury Wonder Show, 167
Mexican Melodrama, 206
Milestone, Lewis, 57
Miller, Arthur, 131, 138, 140
Miranda, Carmen, 91, 99
Mis-Sent Letter, The, 64
Mix, Tom, 44
Moby Dick (film), 181
Moby Dick—Rehearsed (on stage), 188
Moby Dick—Rehearsed (planned TV show), 189, 191, 194
modernist primitivism, 24
Monicelli, Mario, 197
Mon Oncle, 196

Moorehead, Agnes, 45, 46
Moreira da Silva, Francisca, 102
Morel, Edmar, 86
Morton, William, 183
Movies March On!, 53
Mr. Arkadin, ix, 3, 176–178, 180, 181,
   183–190, 197. See also *Confidential
   Report*
Mutual Broadcasting System, 34
"My Friend Bonito," 81, 84, 87, 97, 99, 102

Names on the Land, 125
Nanook of the North, 66
Napoléon, 181
National Association for the Advance-
   ment of Colored People (NAACP),
   136, 215, 216
Native Son, 27, 28, 206, 215
Naylor, Genevieve, 86, 91
Nazi Concentration Camps, 134
NBC (National Broadcasting Com-
   pany), 42, 44–46, 88, 189
Needham, Maureen, 25
Neely, Matthew M., 140
Negri, Pola, 54
Netflix, 220
"New Actor, The," 206
New Deal, 105
New Yorker, 128, 129, 212
New York Post, 5, 111–130, 132
New York Times, 18, 25, 36
Nicolson, Virginia, 53, 209
Noah, 184, 187, 194
Nolan, Jeanette, 208

Oboler, Arch, 44–46
Office of Inter-American Affairs
   (OIAA), 86–88, 90, 91, 97, 101
Office of War Information, 157
Olivier, Laurence, 151
Operation Cinderella, 184
Orozco, José, 127
Orphans of the Storm, 70

Orson Welles Almanac, 216
Orson Welles Commentaries, 215
Orson Welles' Sketch Book, 28, 189
Orson Welles' World of Tomorrow, 184
Ortiz, Fernando, 83
Othello, 105, 181, 189, 205, 214, 220
Other Side of the Wind, The, ix, 9, 69, 105,
   197, 205, 218–220

Paris by Night, 182, 184
Patterson, Eleanor, 117
Paxinou, Katina, 185, 186
Pereira dos Santos, Nelson, 104
Perry, Edward, 29
Picasso, Pablo, 115
Pictorial Beauty on the Screen, 69
Piscator, Erwin, 168, 169
Popular Front, viii, 124, 168, 214
Porgy and Bess, 25
Porter, Cole, 132, 154
Praça Onze, 94, 96–101, 103
Primus, Pearl, 16, 20
Prince of Foxes, 180
Psycho, vii

"Race Hate Must Be Outlawed," 137
Ramsaye, Terry, 53
Rankin, John, 134, 139
Ratoff, Gregory, 180
Rebecca, vii
Redgrave, Michael, 182
Reed, Carol, 162, 180
Reisman, Phil, 86
Return to Glennascaul, 105
Ribeiro, Pery, 93
Rivelles, Amparo, 183
Rivera, Diego, 127
RKO Pictures, 4, 52, 54, 56, 61, 80, 81,
   85–88, 90, 93, 95, 97, 101–103, 134, 206,
   211, 217
RKO Radio Studio, 86
Roach, Hal, 53
Robinson, Edward G., 134

Rocha, Glauber, 104
Rolle, Esther, 16, 20
Roosevelt, Franklin Delano, 9, 16, 113,
    116, 118, 214
Rosenwald, William, 143, 144

Salt, Barry, 63, 213
Saltzman, Harry, 189, 190
Saunders, Lloyd F., 141
Schaefer, George, 54, 217
Schubert, Franz, 100
Scott, Randolph, 18, 192
Selander, Lesley, 193
Sennett, Mack, 54, 66, 157
Sganzerla, Rogerio, 101
Shadow, The, 34, 38, 202
Shadow of a Doubt, vii
Shakespeare, William, viii, 11, 12,
    23–25, 29, 88, 114, 125, 207–209, 212,
    213, 213
Shaw, George Bernard, 23
Shogola Oloba, 12, 16, 19–21, 25, 26.
    See also Asadata African Opera and
    Dramatic
Shores, Lynn, 81, 90
Shubert, Lee, 99
Side by Side, 168
Silence est d'or, 60
silent film, ix, 54, 55, 59, 63, 68, 153
Silent Years, The, 54, 55, 65, 70, 71
Sinai, Nathan, 141
Sinatra, Frank, 116
Siqueiros, David, 127
Smiler with the Knife, The, 52
Society of American Magicians, 167
Soler, Domingo, 102
Steinbeck, John, 216
Stern, Seymour, 56, 112
Stevens, George, 123, 134
Stewart, George R., 125
Stewart, Paul, 39
"Story of Jazz, The," 96
Straight, Beatrice, 178

Stranger, The, vii, 45, 105, 123, 124, 132,
    134–137, 145, 208
Suspense, 45, 46

Tall Man Riding, 192
Tamiroff, Akim, 182
Tanks, 144
Tarkington, Booth, 72, 211
Tati, Jacques, 196
Temple, Shirley, 121
Terrain Vague, 196
Terry, Alice, 69
Texas Centennial Celebration, 23
Third Man, The, 180
This is Cinerama, 158
This is Orson Welles, 52, 55, 59, 60,
    69, 151
Thompson, Dorothy, 114, 205
Thomson, Virgil, 23, 203
Time (magazine), 128
Todd, Michael, 151
Todd School, viii, 55, 209, 210
Toland, Gregg, 4
Tonight!, 166
Too Much Johnson, 56, 57, 59, 66, 67, 84,
    152, 153, 157, 160, 167, 217
Touch of Evil, vii, 2, 202, 205, 208
"Trangama-Fanga," 27
Trial, The, 24
Trimble, J. W., 131
Trip Through the Black Hills, 158
Trosper, Kathryn, 61
Trouble in the Glen, 181
Tumbleweeds, 66
Tynan, Kenneth, 205, 218, 219

United Jewish Appeal, 143–145
United Nations, 118, 178
Unthinking Lobster, The, 66, 153, 217

Vacances en novembre, 189
Valentino, Rudolph, 55, 69
Van Dyke, W. S., 57

Van Eyck, Peter, 182
Van Voorhis, Westbrook, 53, 54
Vargas, Getúlio, 86, 90, 98, 101
Vásquez, Jesús, 87, 102
vaudeville, 66, 152, 154
Ventura, Ray, 98
Verma, Neil, 38, 46
Verne, Jules, 125, 132, 153, 154
Vertigo, vii
Vidor, King, 57, 69
Vitagraph, 157
vodou, 14, 21, 25–27
voice-over, ix, 35, 40–44, 48, 56, 133, 143, 145
Volpone, 191
Von Stroheim, Erich, 68, 69
voodoo, ix, 3, 14–17, 19–21, 23, 25–27, 202, 206, 209, 212–214, 218

Wallace, Edgar, 116, 125
Waltz, Gwendolyn, 66
Warner Bros., 190, 193, 195

"War of the Worlds," vii, 4, 5, 9, 34–51, 202, 206, 207, 210, 215, 218
Webster, Margaret, 115, 125
Weissberger, L. Arnold, 205
Wells, H. G., 38, 40
Wertenbaker, Lael, 193
When Strangers Marry, 122
White God, The, 27
Whitney, John Hay, 86, 87
Wilcox, Herbert, 181
Wild, Harry, 95, 158
Wilson, Richard, 81, 95, 134, 135, 204, 219
Wood, John S., 139, 211
Woodard, Isaac, Jr., 5, 9, 28, 136, 137, 145, 215
Woollcott, Alexander, 125
Wright, Richard, 119, 124, 206, 215
Wyler, William, 151
Wylie, Max, 42, 43

Zinnemann, Fred, 104
Zunguru, 19, 27

CPSIA information can be obtained
at www.ICGtesting.com
Printed in the USA
LVOW13s0039070318
568944LV00013B/70/P